The Photographers' Gallery
5 Great Newport Street
London WC2H 7HY

Telephone 0171 831 1772
Fax 0171 836 9704
E-mail info@photonet.org.uk

First published in 1997 by The Photographers' Gallery in association with the Nederlands Foto Instituut, Rotterdam and the Netherlands Design Institute, Amsterdam.

The Photographers' Gallery would like to acknowledge the generous financial support of the Arts Council of England, the Nederlands Foto Instituut, Rotterdam and the Netherlands Design Institute, Amsterdam.

Design North

Typography
Neue Helvetica 45 Light/46 Light Italic

Printed and produced in Great Britain by the Colour House

British Library Cataloguing in Publication Data
A catalogue record for this book is available from the British Library.

ISBN 0 907879 50 0

Funded by THE ARTS COUNCIL OF ENGLAND

The editors and The Photographers' Gallery would like to thank the authors and publishers for permission to reproduce the following works: Paul Andreu, © 1991 Flammarion, Paris / Fondation Cartier pour l'art contemporain, Paris; Marc Auge, 'Prologue' from *Non-places: Introduction to an Anthropology of Supermodernity*, (Verso, London 1995) reprinted by permission of the publishers; JG Ballard, 'The Ultimate Departure Lounge', © the author. Reprinted by permission of the author. First published in *Blueprint*, September 1997; Douglas Coupland, 'Hubs', © 1995-1997 Wired Digital Inc. Reprinted by permission. All rights reserved; FT Marinetti, 'Futurist Manifesto of Aeral Architecture', reprinted by permission of Alenia Aerospazio / Finmeccanica; Martha Rosler, 'In the Place of the Public: Observations of a Frequent Flyer', reprinted by permission of the author; Robert Smithson, 'Towards the Development of an Air Terminal Site', reprinted by permission of Nancy Holt and the Estate of Robert Smithson; John Thackara, 'Lost in Space: A Traveller's Tale', reprinted by permission of the author.

We would also like to thank the following individuals and organisations for their assistance and support on this project: Janet Abrams; Accademia Italiana; Thomas Adlercreutz; Airlife Publishing Ltd; EG Boardman at AMEC–Tarmac Joint Venture; Amsterdam Airport Schiphol, Art coordinator; Sasha Lubetkin, the Architecture Centre, Bristol; Atlas Translations; Helen Cadwallader, BAA Art Project Coordinator; Sue Hankin, BAA Corporate Affairs; JG Ballard; Hannah Benthem, Benthem Crouwel; BFI; Marcus Field, *Blueprint*; Martin Boyce; Photographic Library, The British Library; Chris Burden; Graham Ellard and Stephen Johnstone; Karen Eslea; European Academy for the Arts, London; Film and Video Umbrella; Peter Fischli and David Weiss; Pip Hurd and Amy Grant, Flammarion; Fondation Cartier pour l'art contemporain, Paris; Foster Asia (Hong Kong Ltd); Friends of the Earth (Manchester branch); Stephen Gill; Rodney Hill, Jay Gorney Modern Art; Nicolas Grimshaw & Partners; Nancy Holt; Marc Jancou; KPN; Lisson Gallery; London Arts Board; London Film and Video Development Agency; Lufthansa; Magnum Photos; Chris Marker; Elizabeth D Mazza, Strategic Moves; Victoria Miro Gallery; Pam Quick, MIT Press; Frank Morel; Netherlands Design Institute; Koos Kroon, Netherlands Photo Archive; Sean Perkins, Simon Browning and Paul Austin at North; Sally Williams, Public Art Development Trust; Qantas; Fiona Raby; Martha Rosler; Gabriella Sancisi; Michiel Schwarz; Robbie Shaw; Guy Cheston, Sky Sites Ltd; Deborah Smith; Monika Sprüth Gallery; John Thackara; Trans World Airlines Inc; The University of California Press; Lucy Heller, Verso; Virgin Atlantic Airways Ltd; Nicolai Wallner; Warner Brothers; Elyse Goldberg, John Weber Gallery; Wired Digital Inc; Zone Books.

Airport

Foreword

The initial impetus for *Airport* — this publication and the exhibition of the same name — came from Steven Bode at Film and Video Umbrella and myself in 1995. We had previously collaborated in 1991 on *Photo Video: Photography in the Age of the Computer*, again involving both publication and exhibition. The aim of *Photo Video* was to bridge the gap that we perceived existed between photography and the developments taking place with video and computer technology. During the early 1990s very little crossover existed between these different areas in British museums and galleries. This has changed markedly in recent years.

We both wanted to continue our initial dialogue, bringing together our own interests and concerns regarding the shifting boundaries between different technological forms of visual communication. At that time, there was and is a growing interest in all things digital, often accompanied by a utopian vision of technological change and a fetishism related to the formal qualities of computer technology. We started looking for a way which did not follow the same path.

We were aware that some contemporary artists using photography, video and the computer had started to produce work on the airport (of course, the computer also plays a central role in both the design and control of information in the airport and thus indicates the further dimension of technology defining social space). It soon became apparent that the airport was to be our next project.

By 1996 Jeremy Millar had joined The Photographers' Gallery and soon started working with Steven and myself on the project. Jeremy brought his own considerable knowledge of contemporary art to the project; with his increasing involvement I took the back seat on the project, Jeremy taking the front seat on behalf of The Photographers' Gallery. The resulting exhibition and in particular this publication is much richer because of his involvement.

Airport could not have happened without the goodwill and assistance from many individuals and organisations. The support we received from the public funding sector has been critical in making this project happen.

In particular I would like to thank the Arts Council of England, London Arts Board and London Film and Video Development Agency. I would also like to acknowledge gratefully the support from the Netherlands Design Institute and the Nederlands Foto Instituut towards this publication.

Fortunately we have been successful in finding partners in the corporate sector. I would like to thank BAA plc and Skysites Ltd for their imaginative support of *Airport*. Janette Scott deserves praise for the role she played in securing these two sponsors.

The archives of the Dutch photographer Frits Rotgans are held at the Netherlands Photo Archives in Rotterdam; we are very grateful to the Archives for making the work of Rotgans accessible and assisting with the production of photographic prints.

We were very fortunate that all the artists, photographers, writers and architects we approached agreed to participate in this project. We thank them all for their commitment and assistance. The designers North did more than design this book. They became part of the team in the realisation of the publication. At different stages in the project both The Architecture Foundation and the Architectural Association have played important roles.

Steven Bode has always been in the front seat on the project. I would like personally to acknowledge his dedication and support over three years.

Paul Wombell, Director
The Photographers' Gallery, London

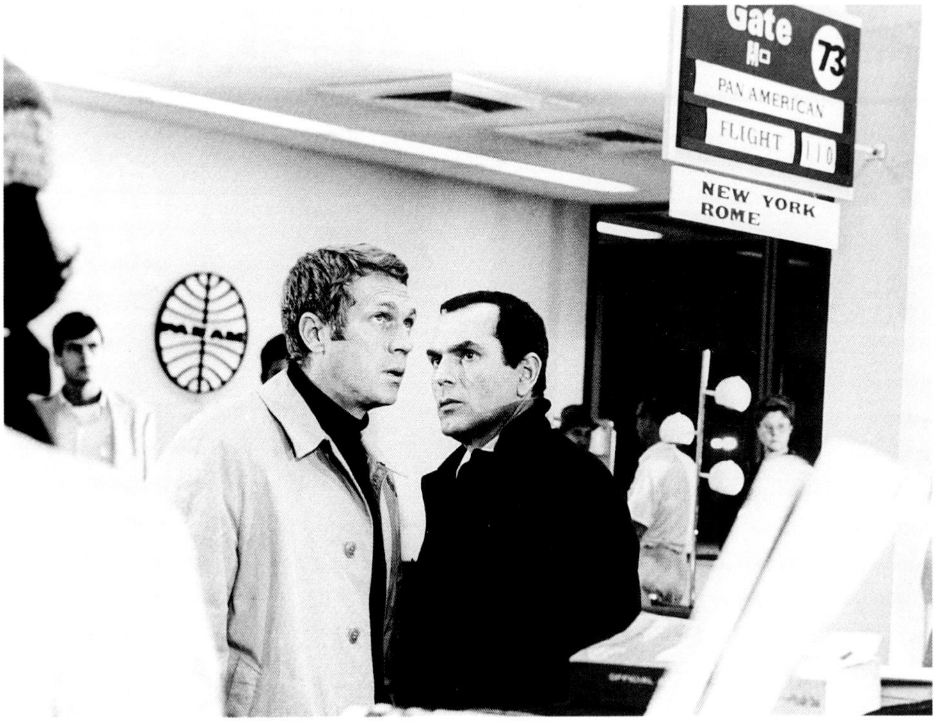
Gate
73
PAN AMERICAN
FLIGHT
110
NEW YORK
ROME

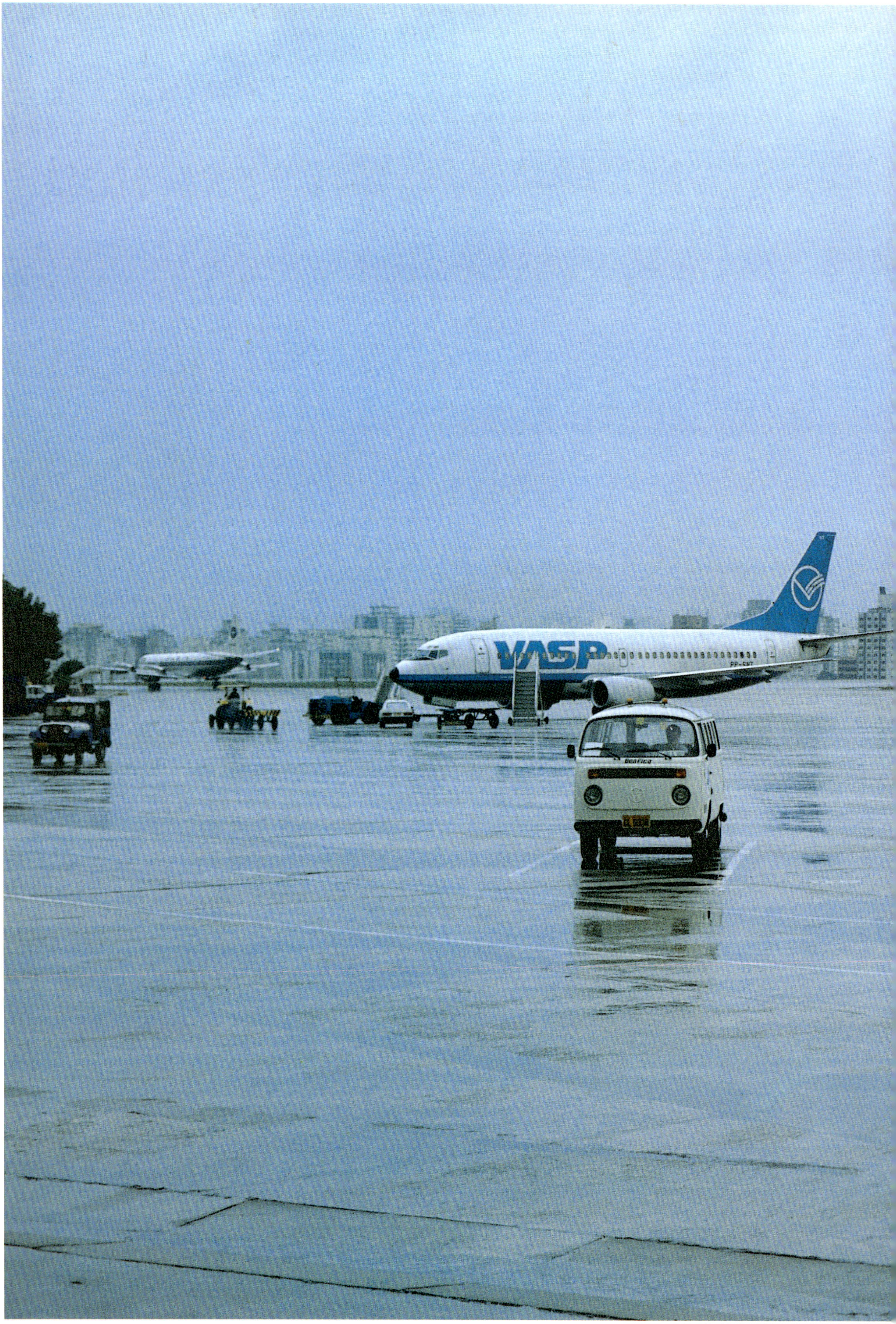
VASP

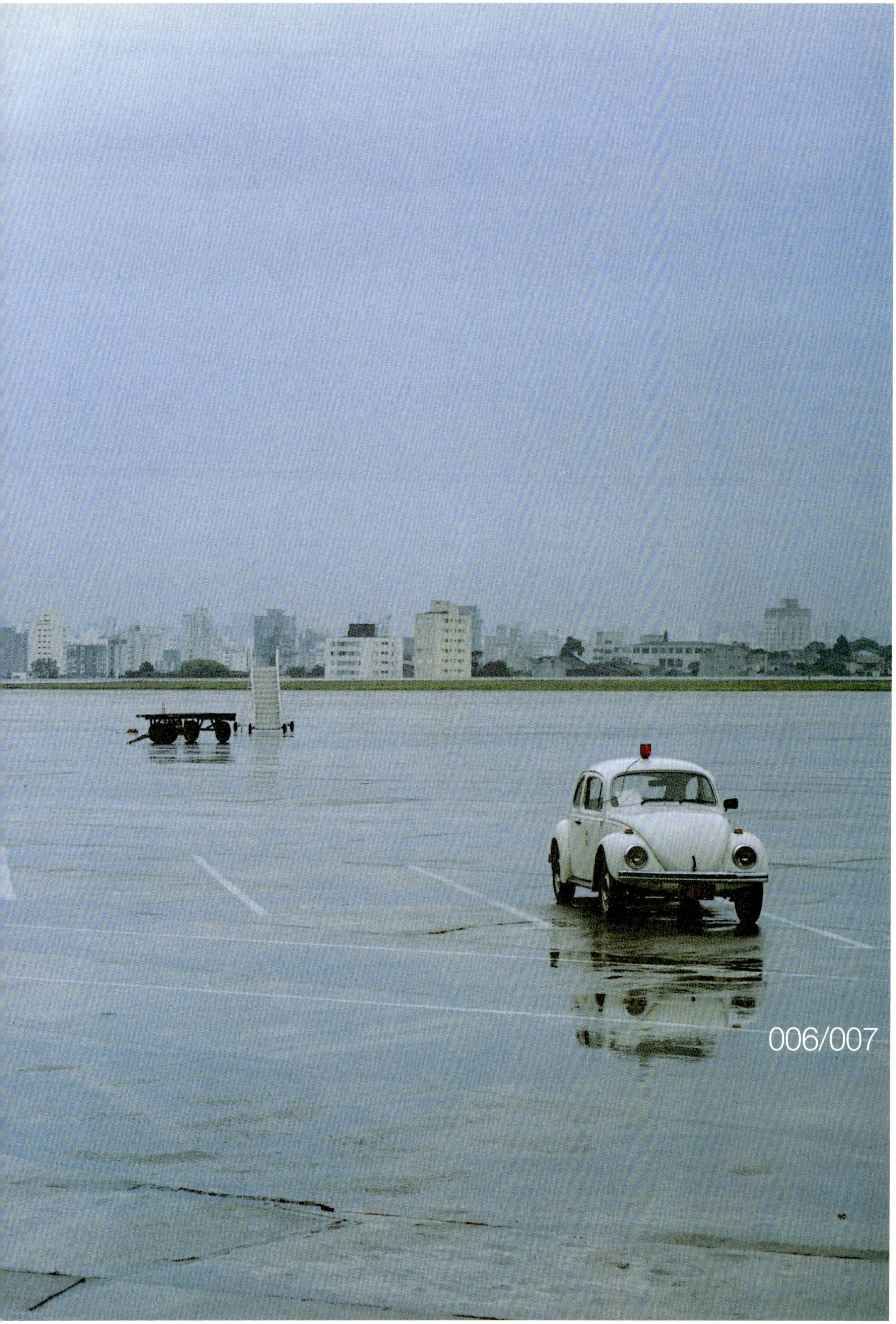

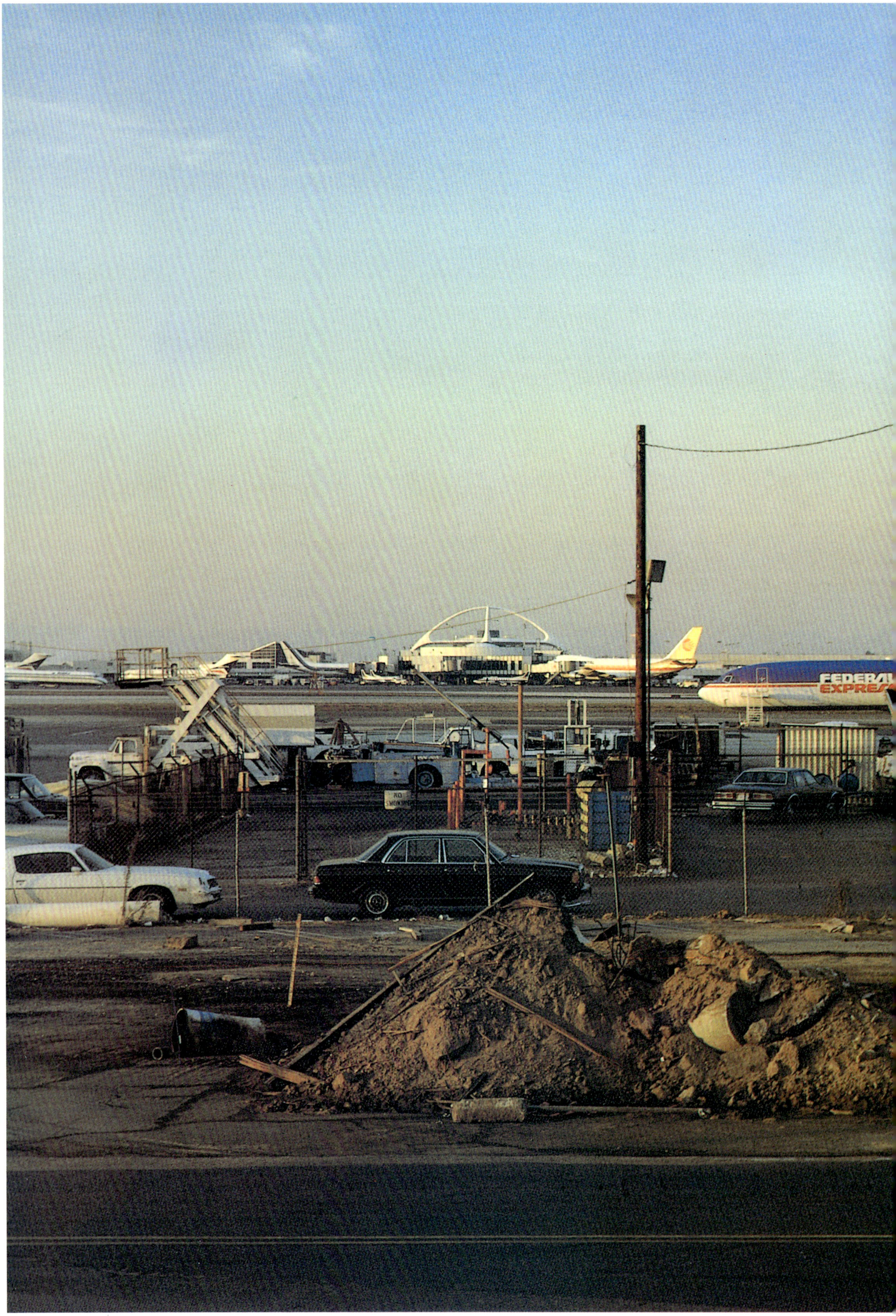

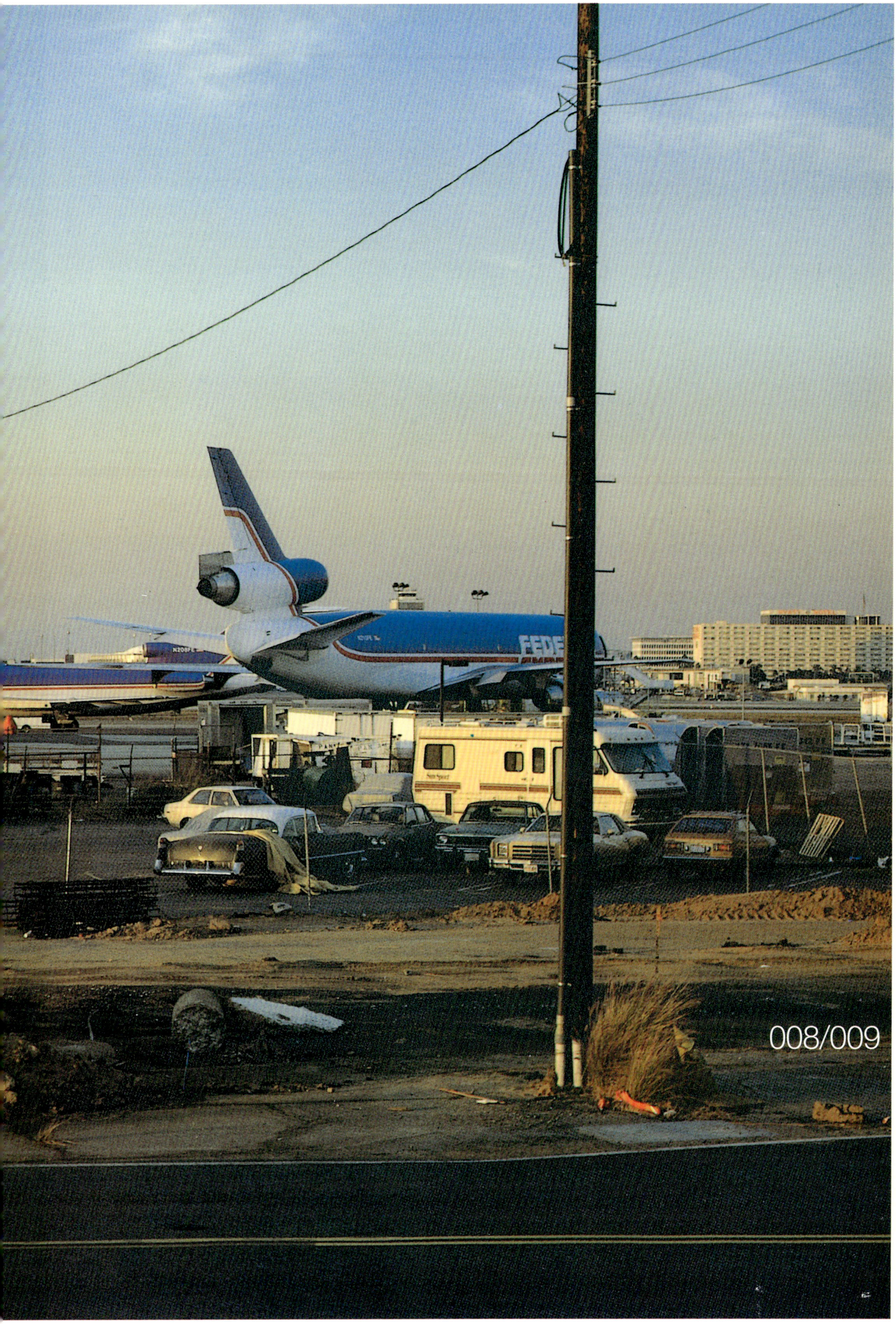
FEDE

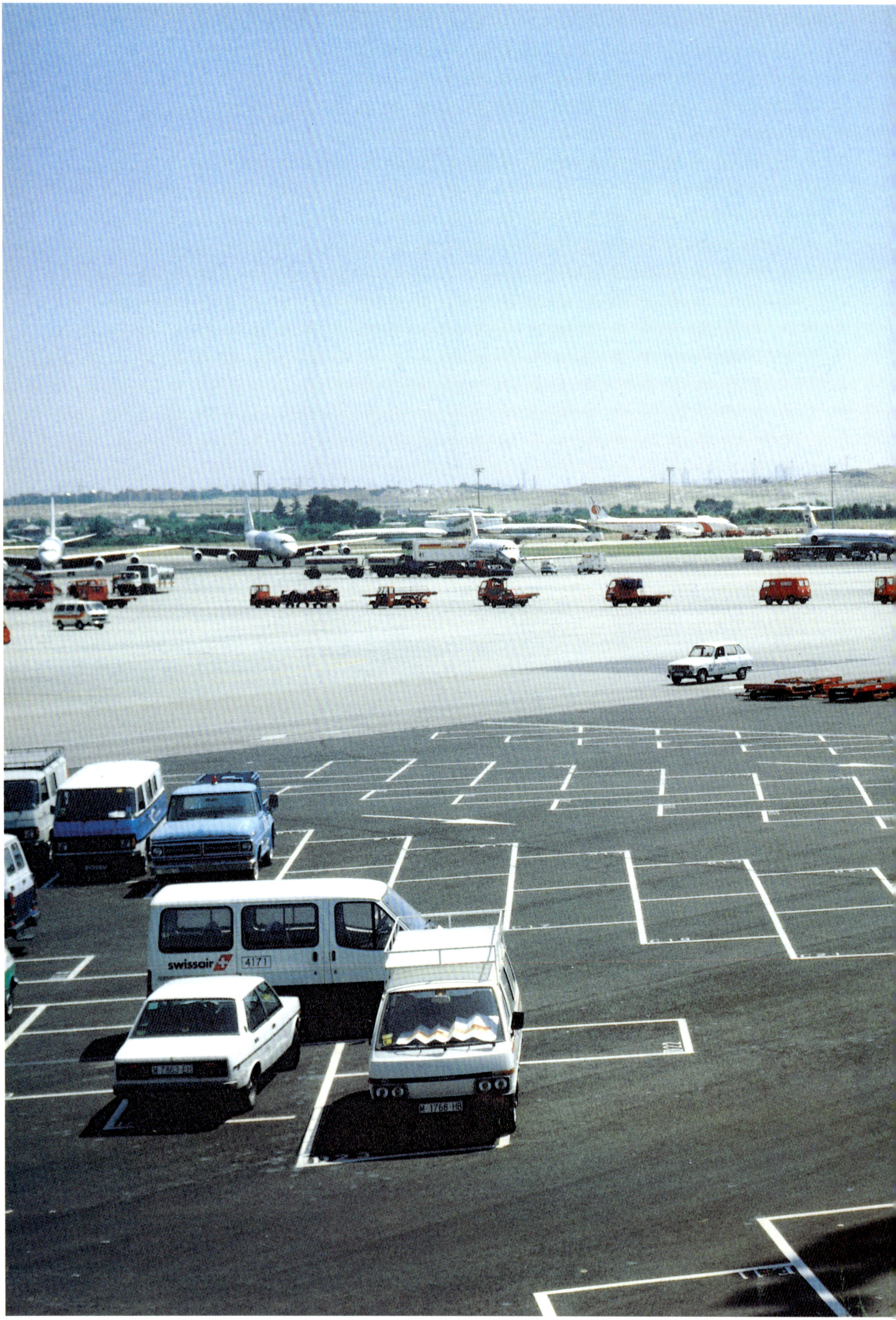
swissair
4171

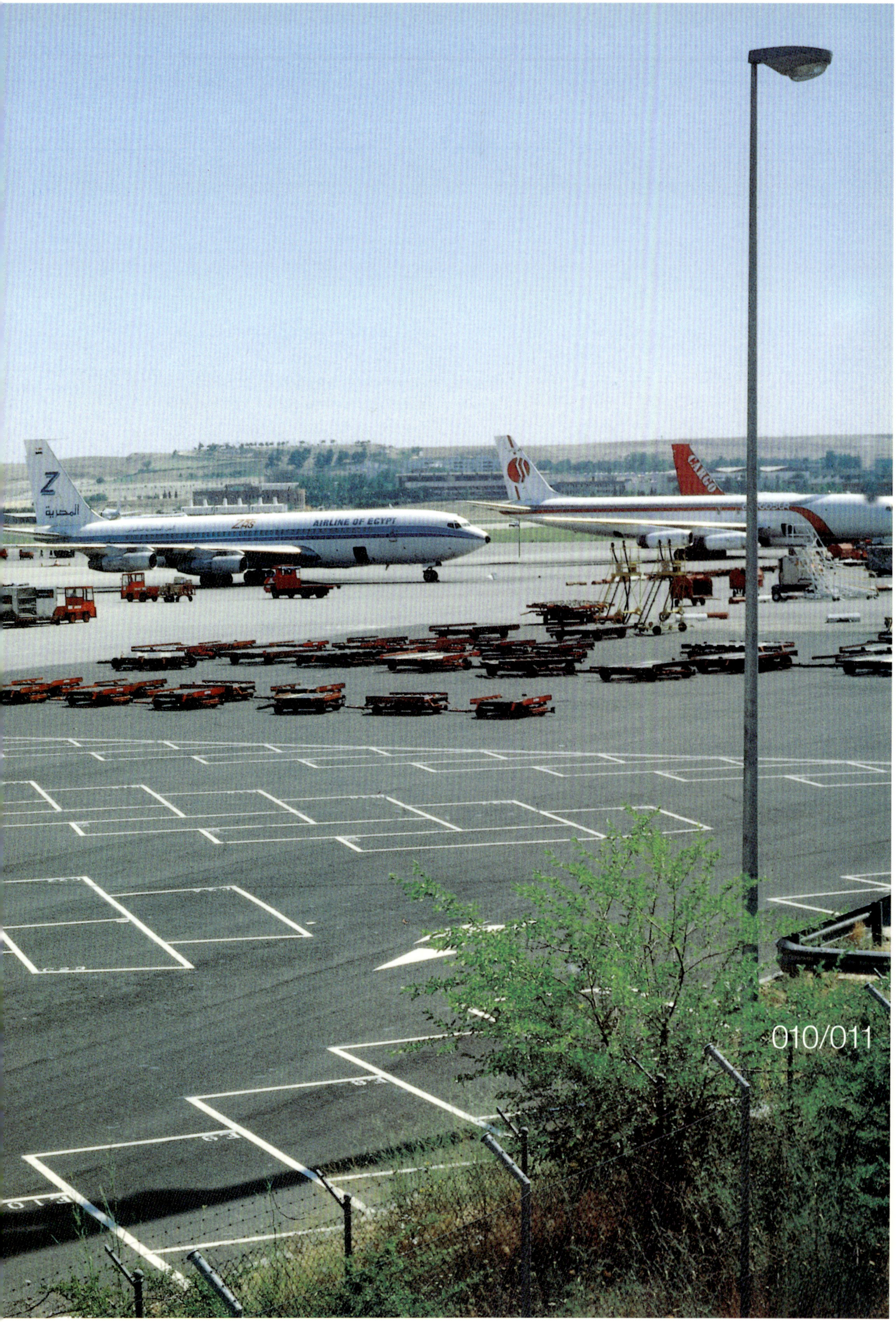
Z
المصرية
ZAS
AIRLINE OF EGYPT
CARGO

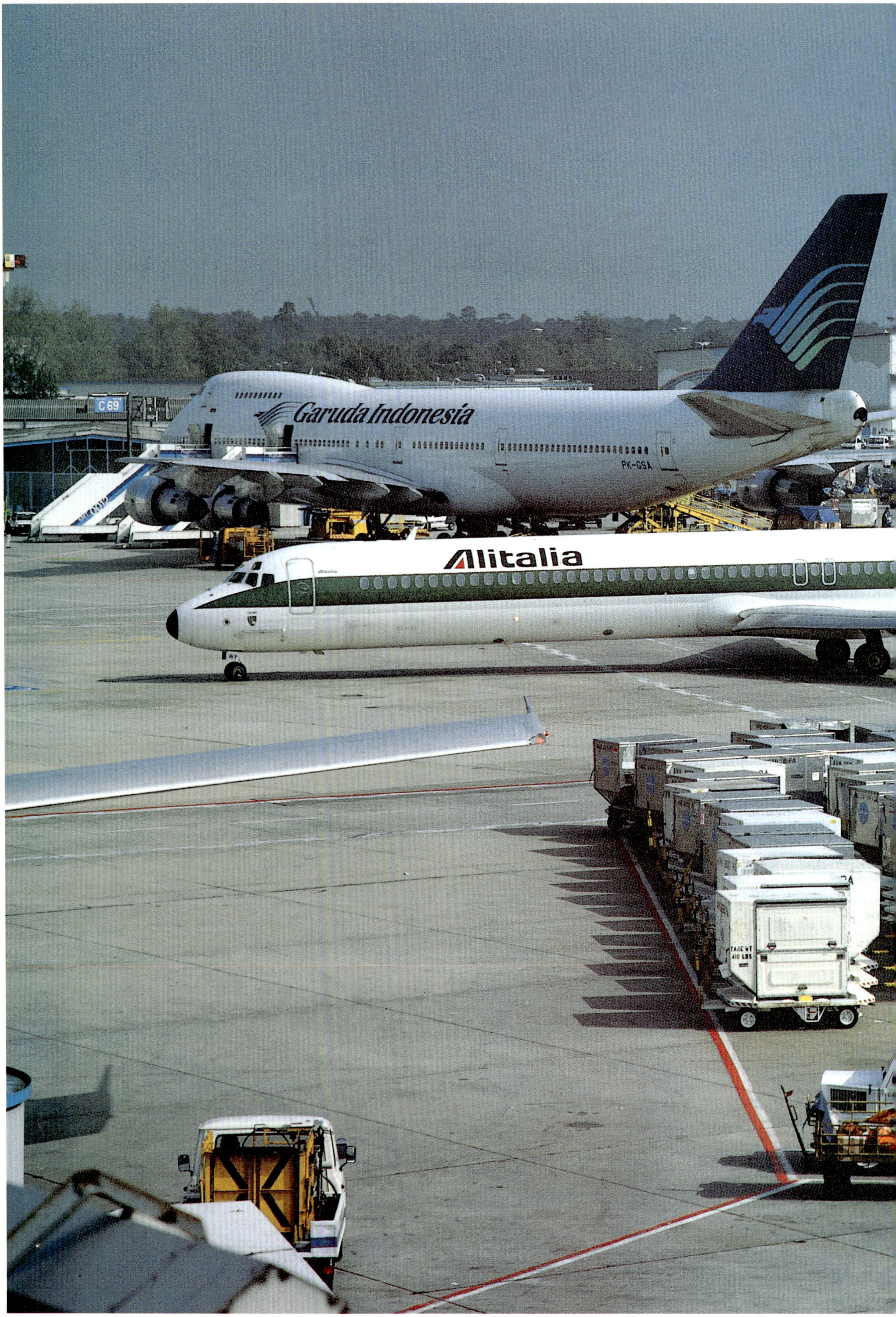

C 69
Garuda Indonesia
PK-GSA
Alitalia

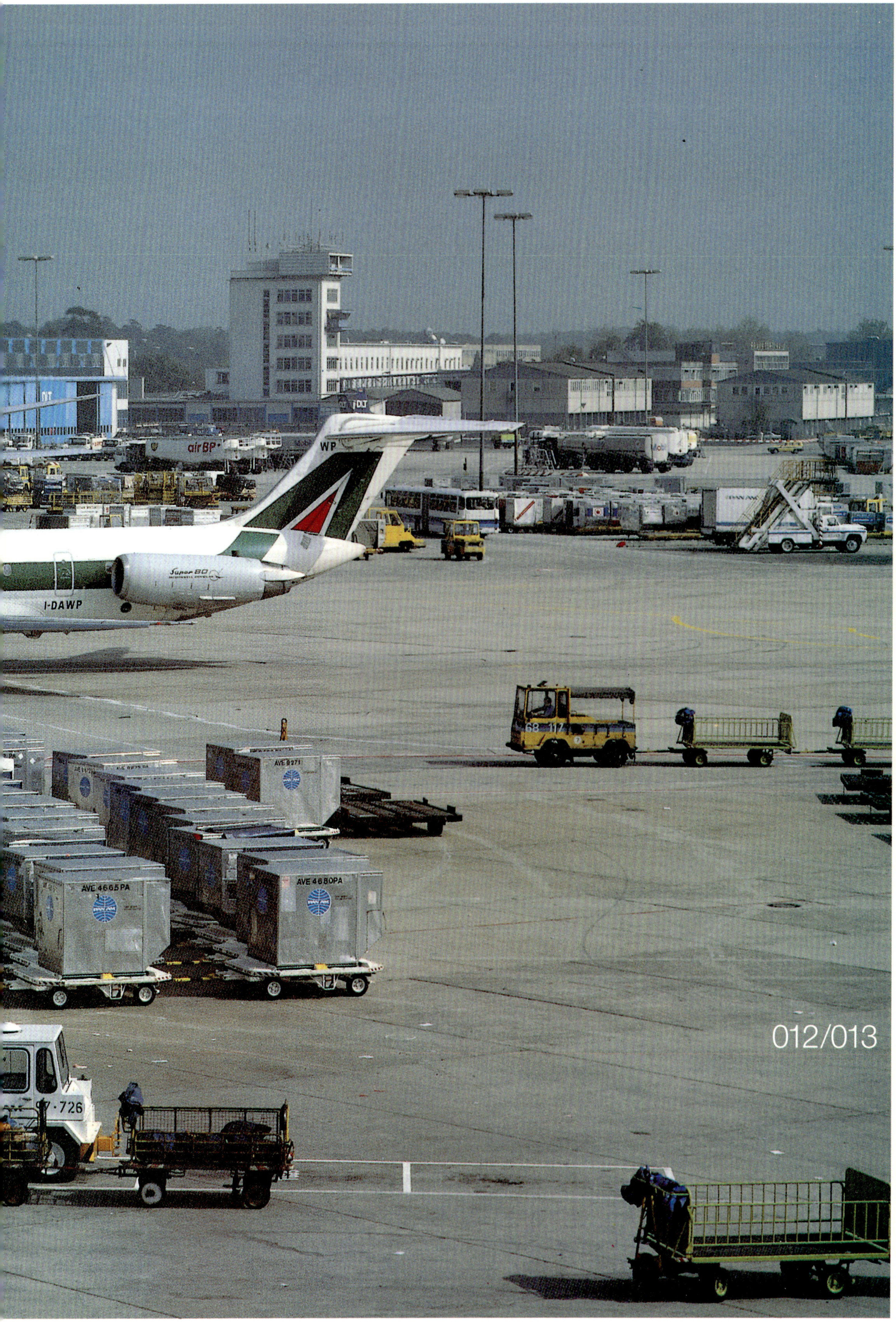
airBP
I-DAWP
AVE 4665PA
AVE 4680PA

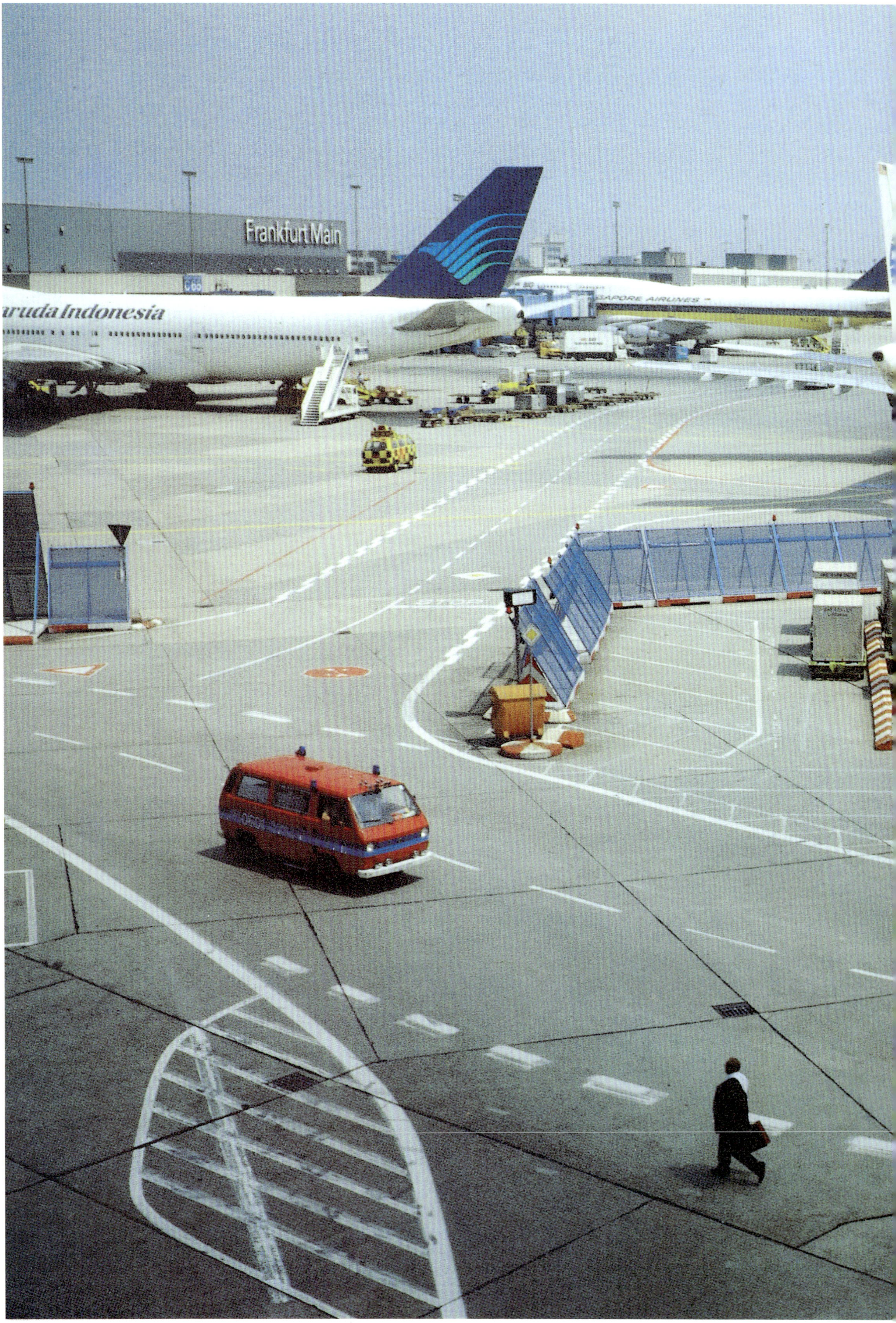
Frankfurt Main
aruda Indonesia

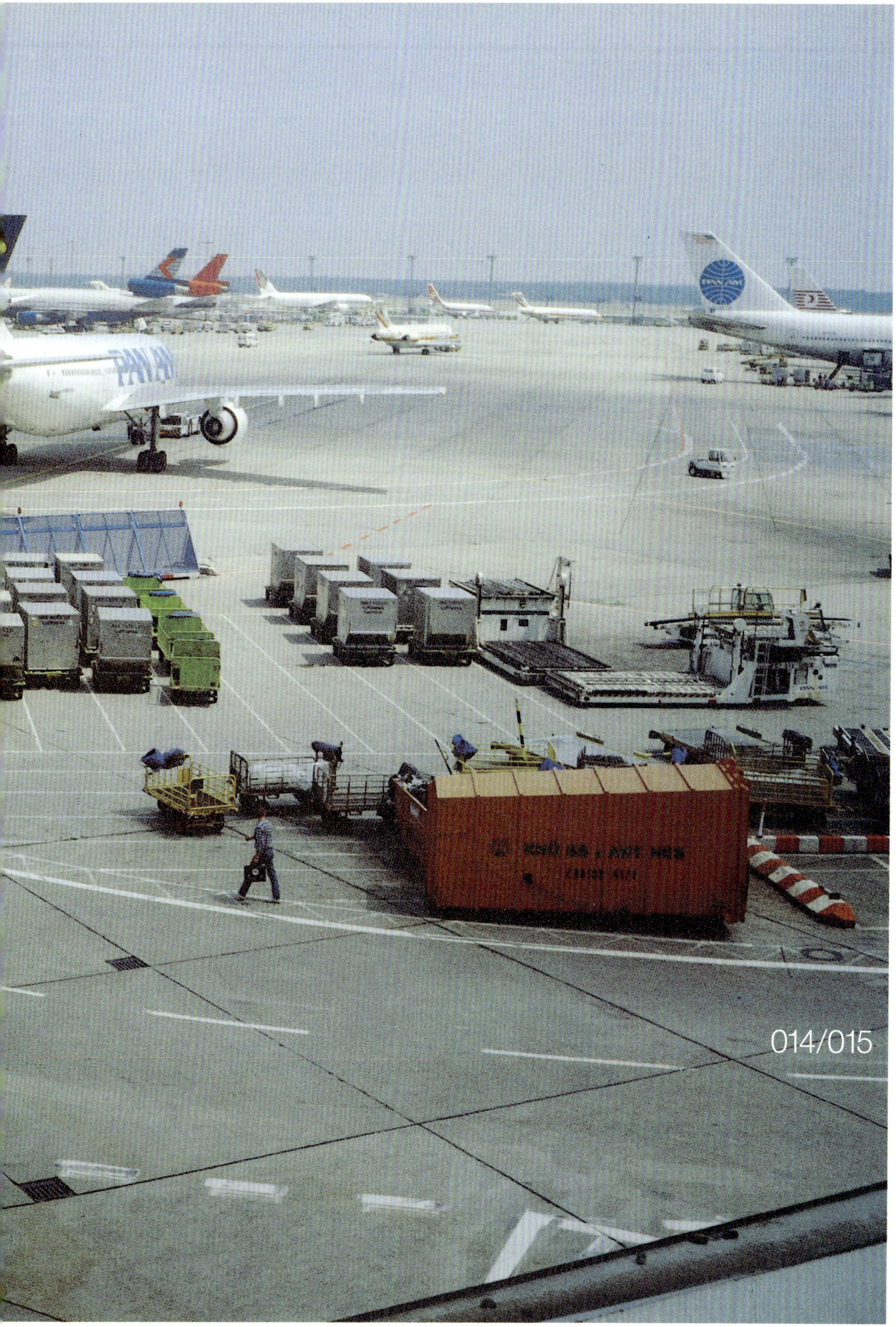
PAN AM

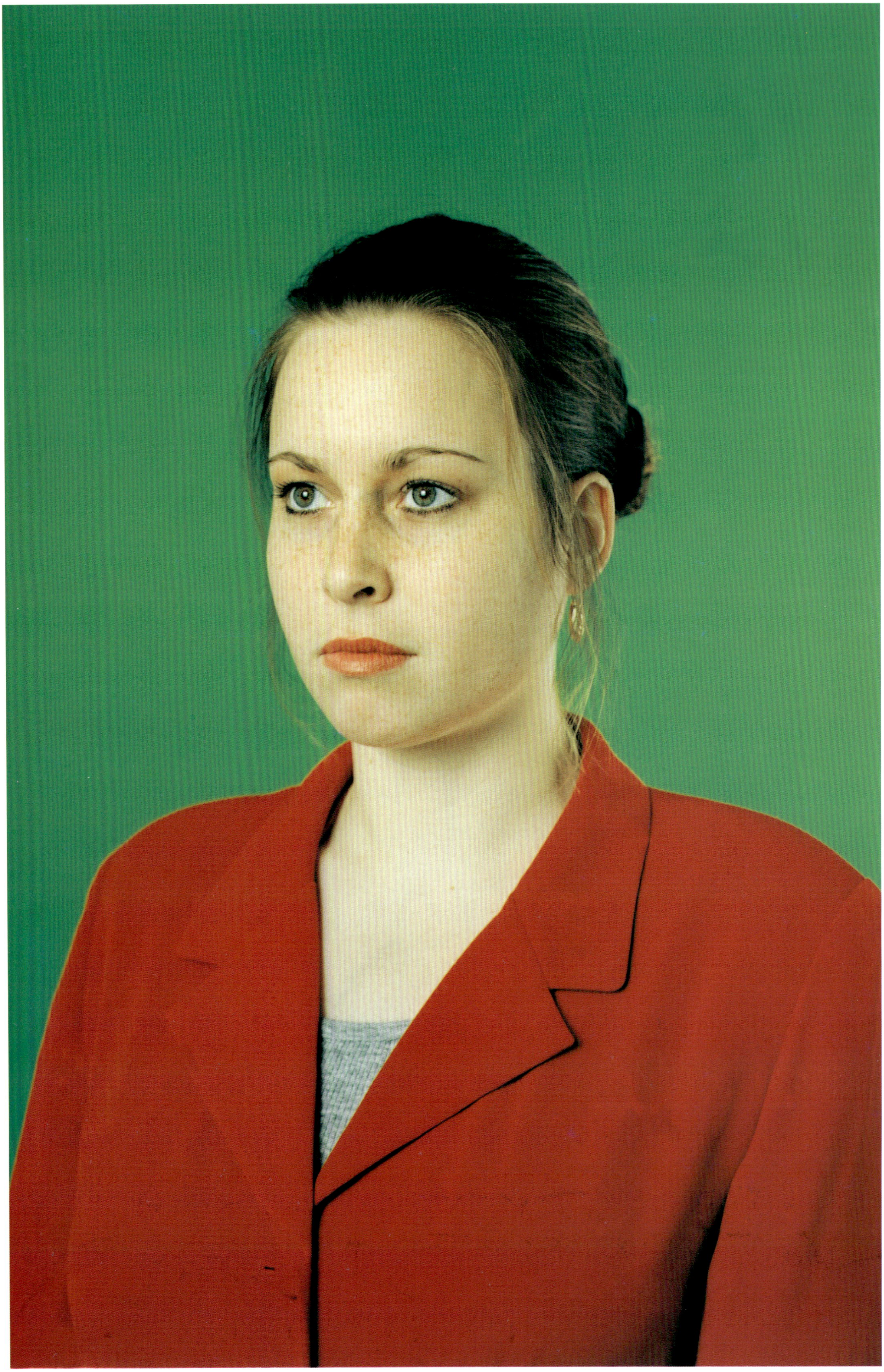

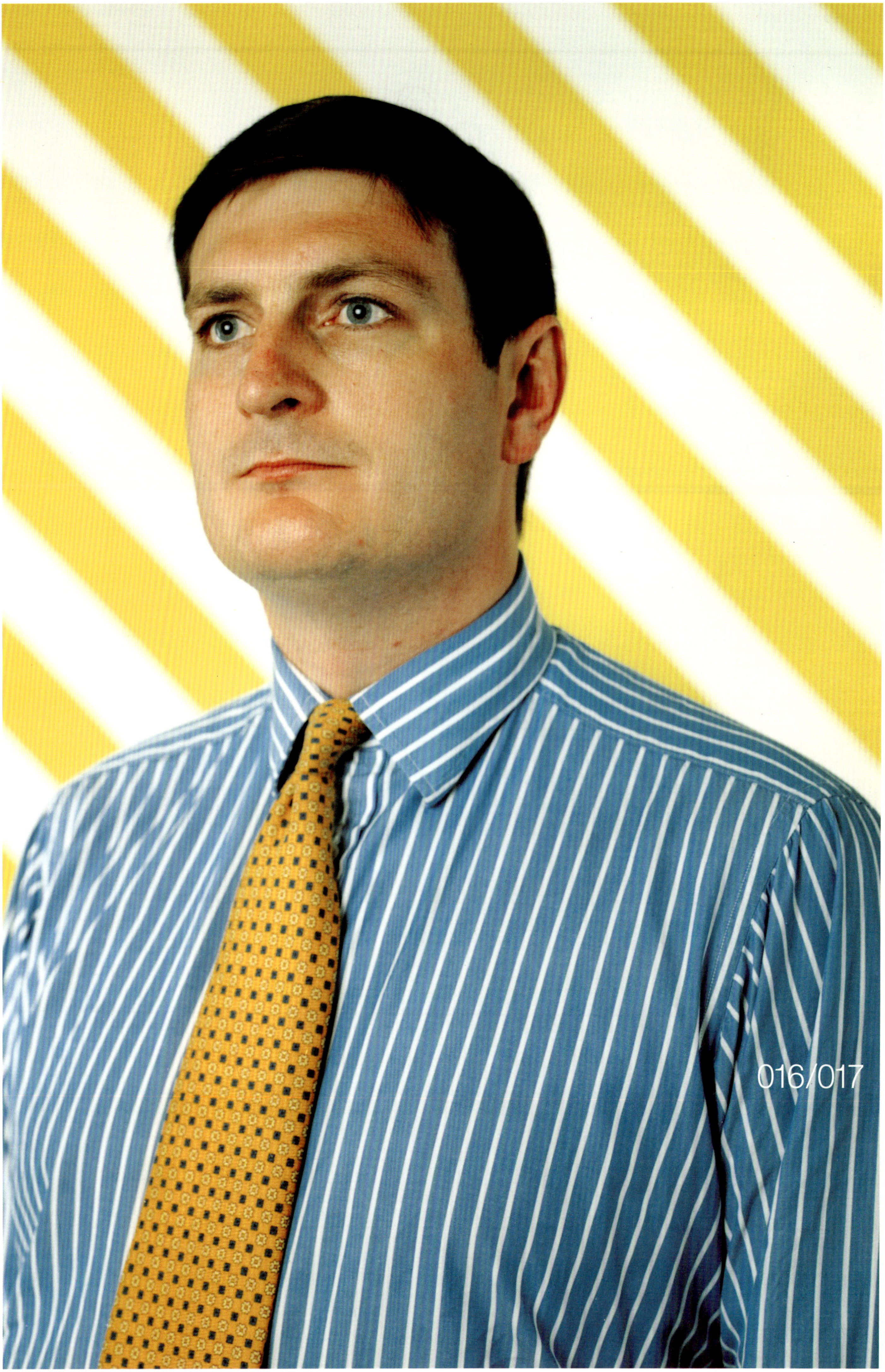

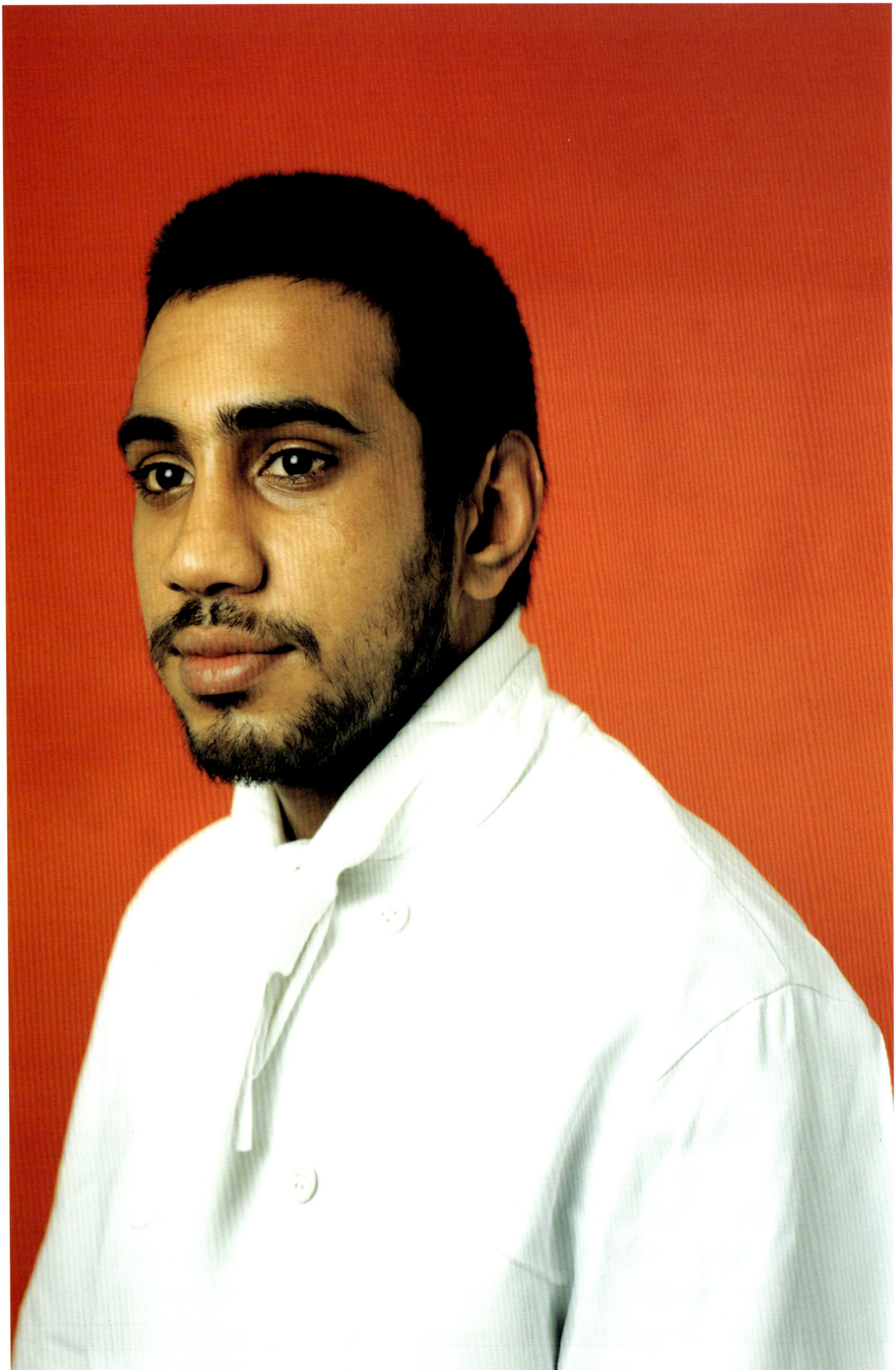

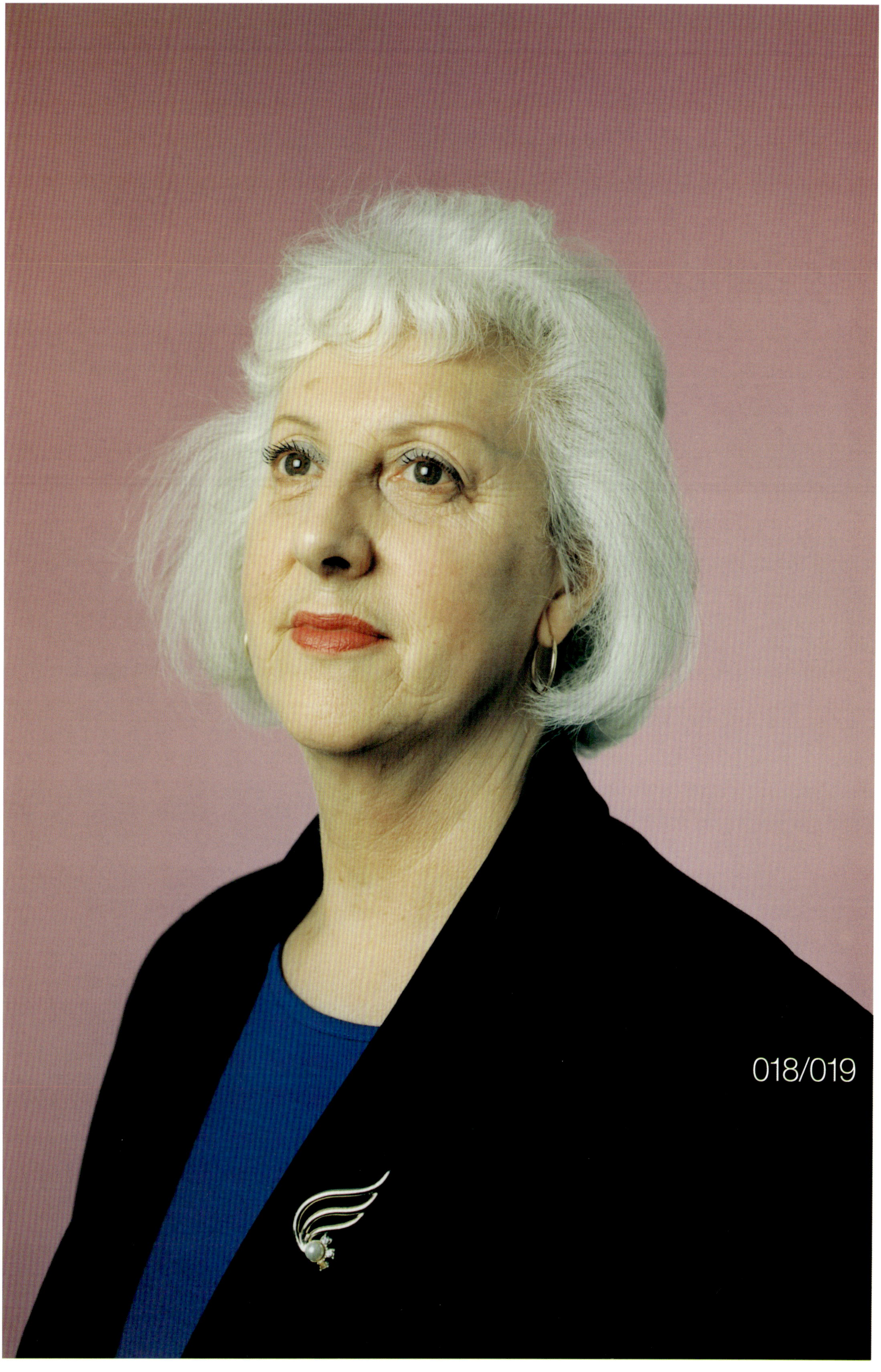

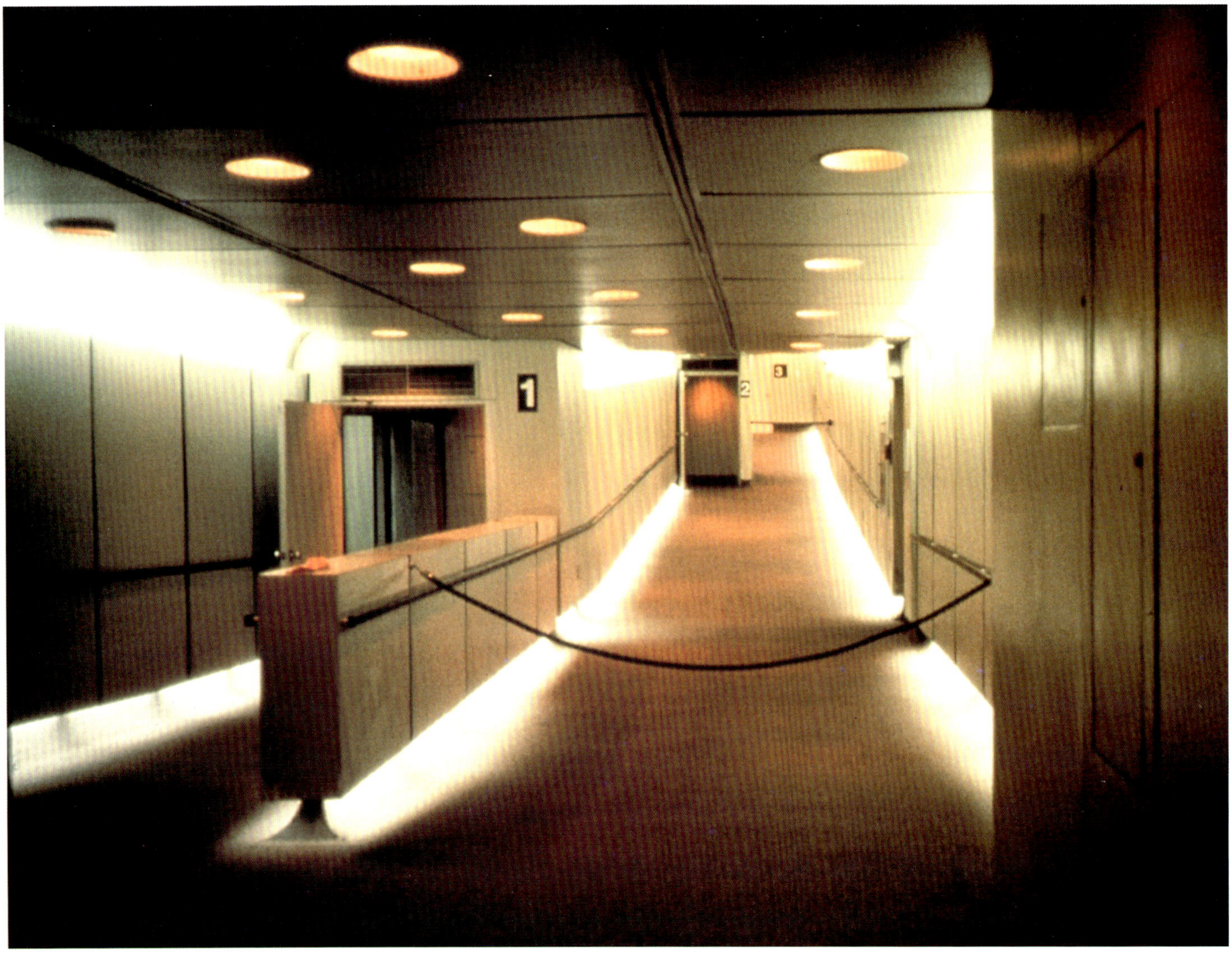
1

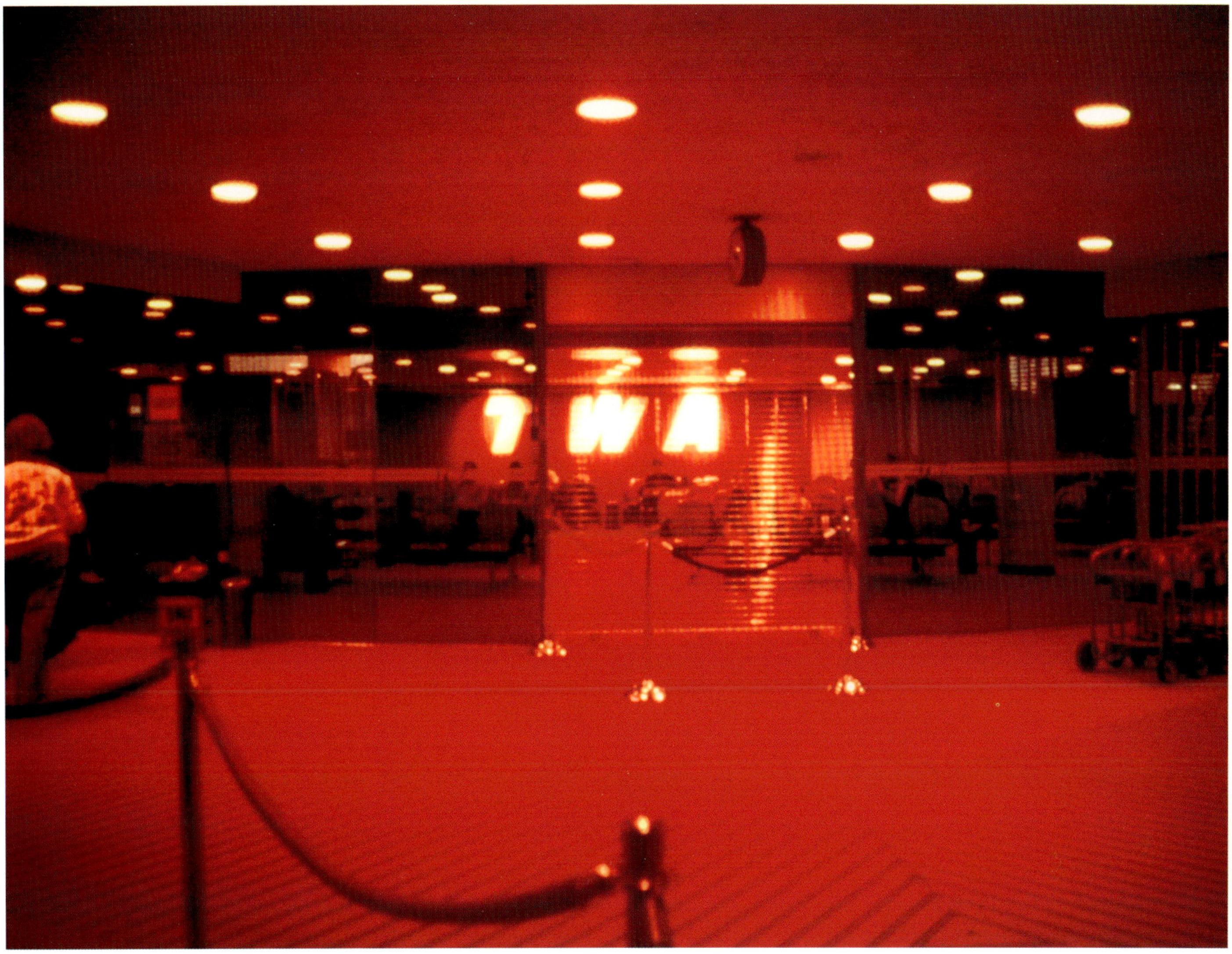
TWA

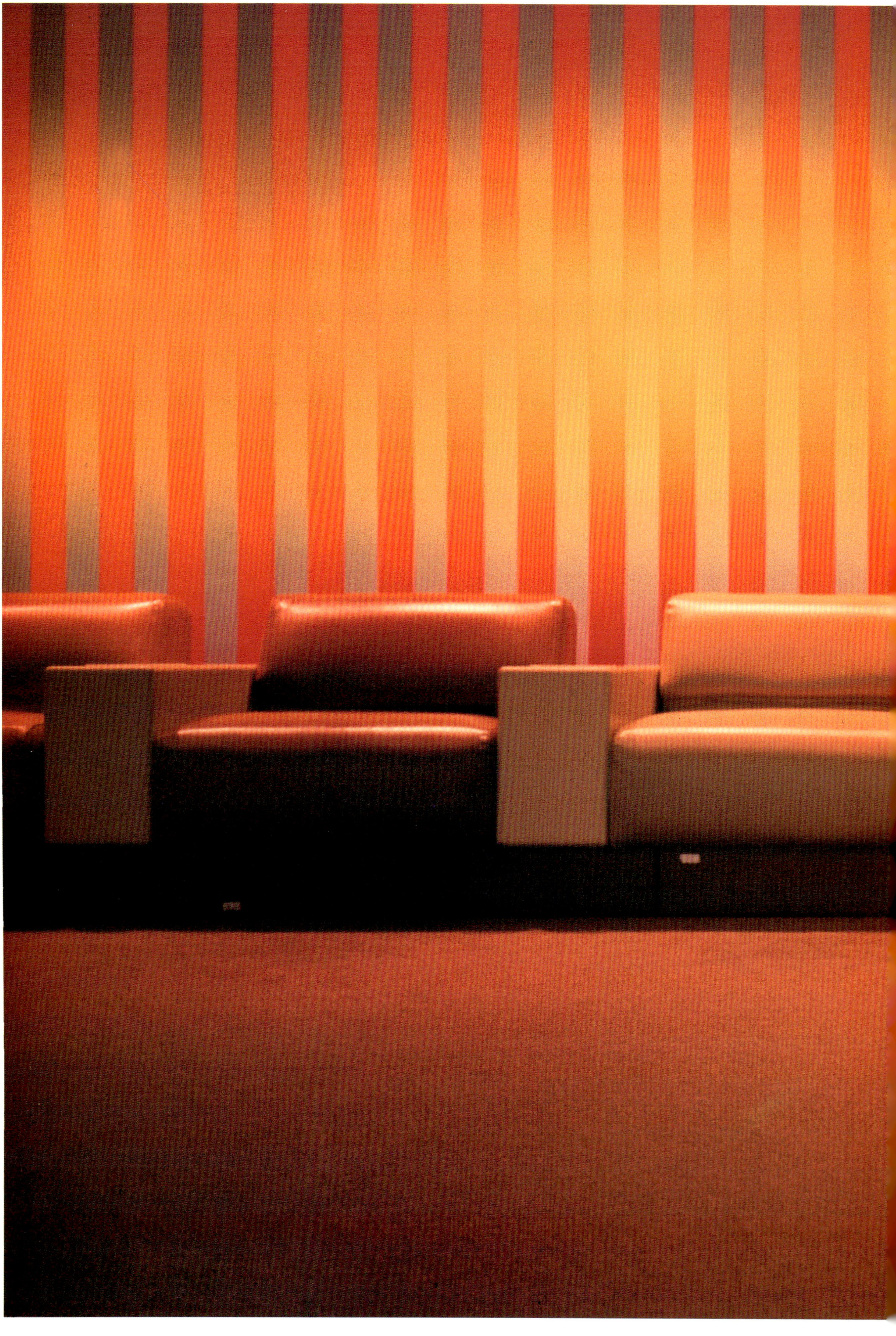

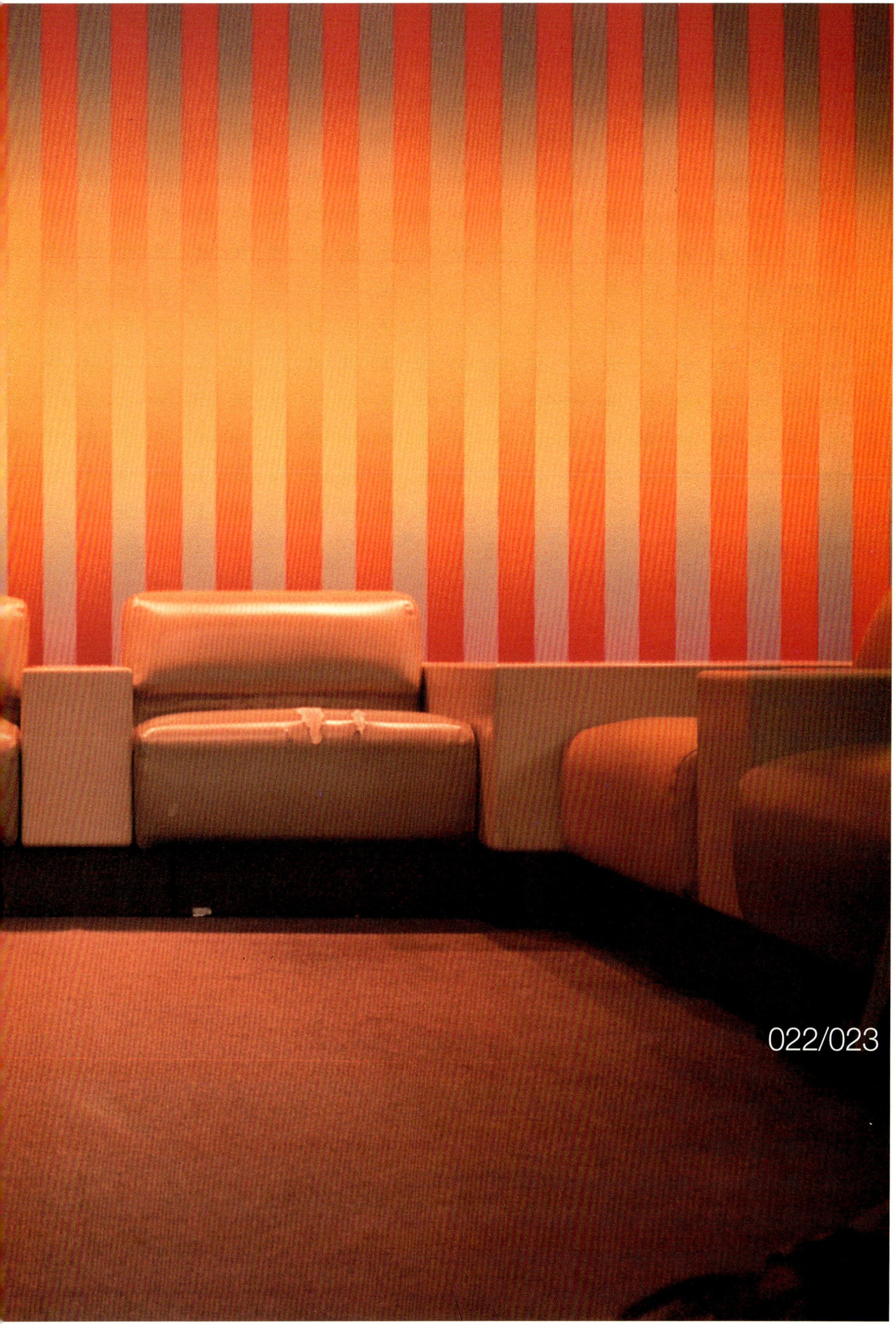

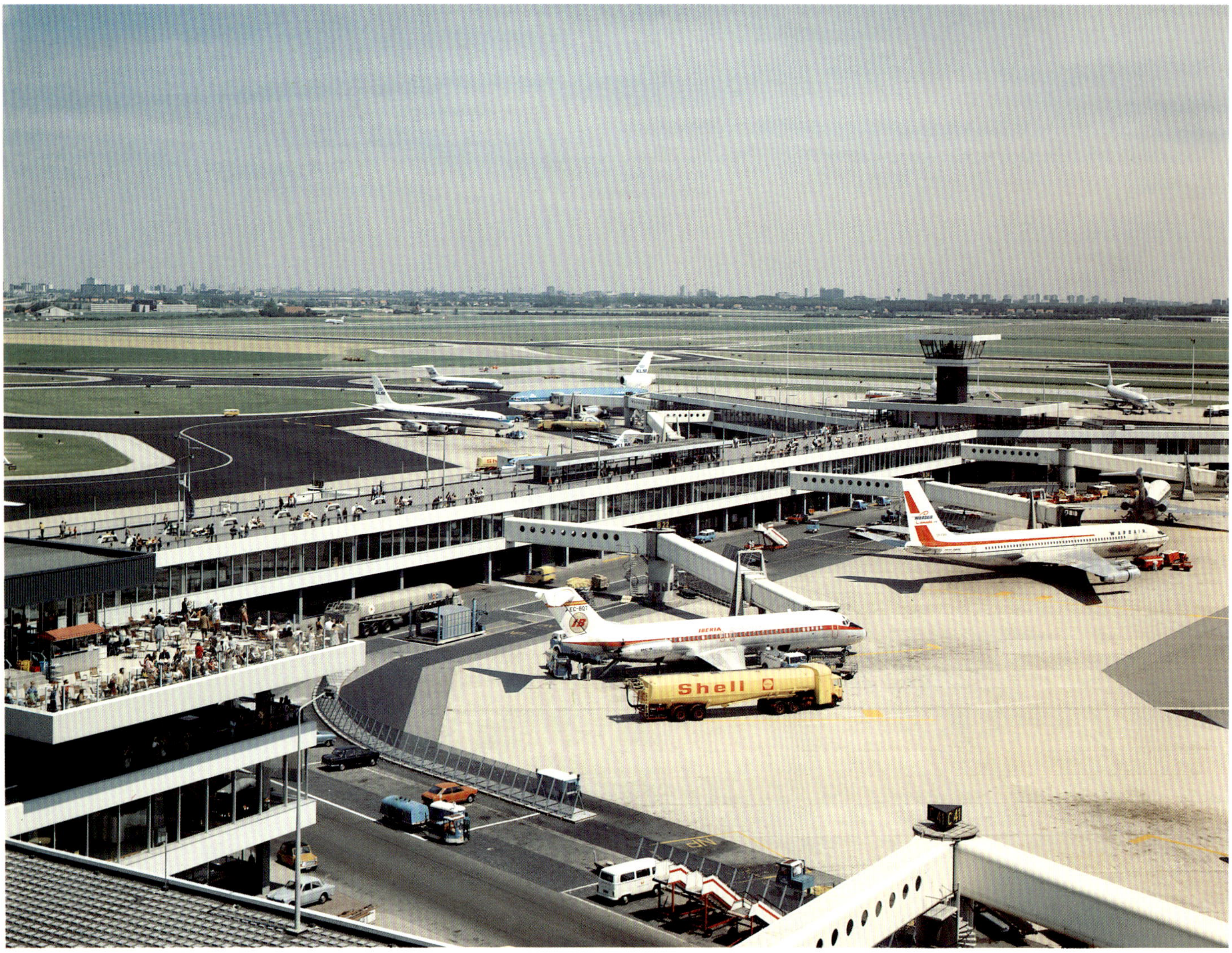
Shell
C41

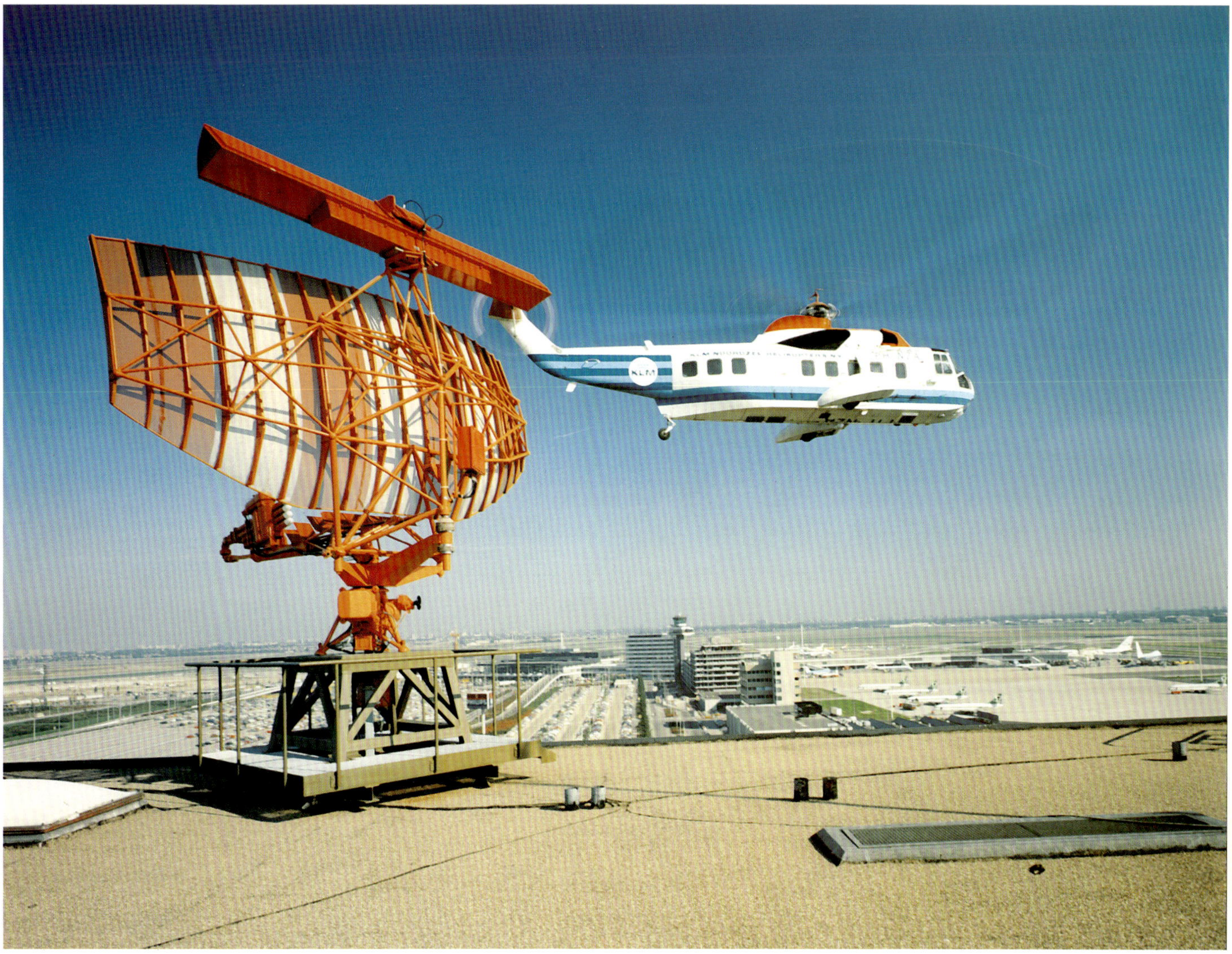

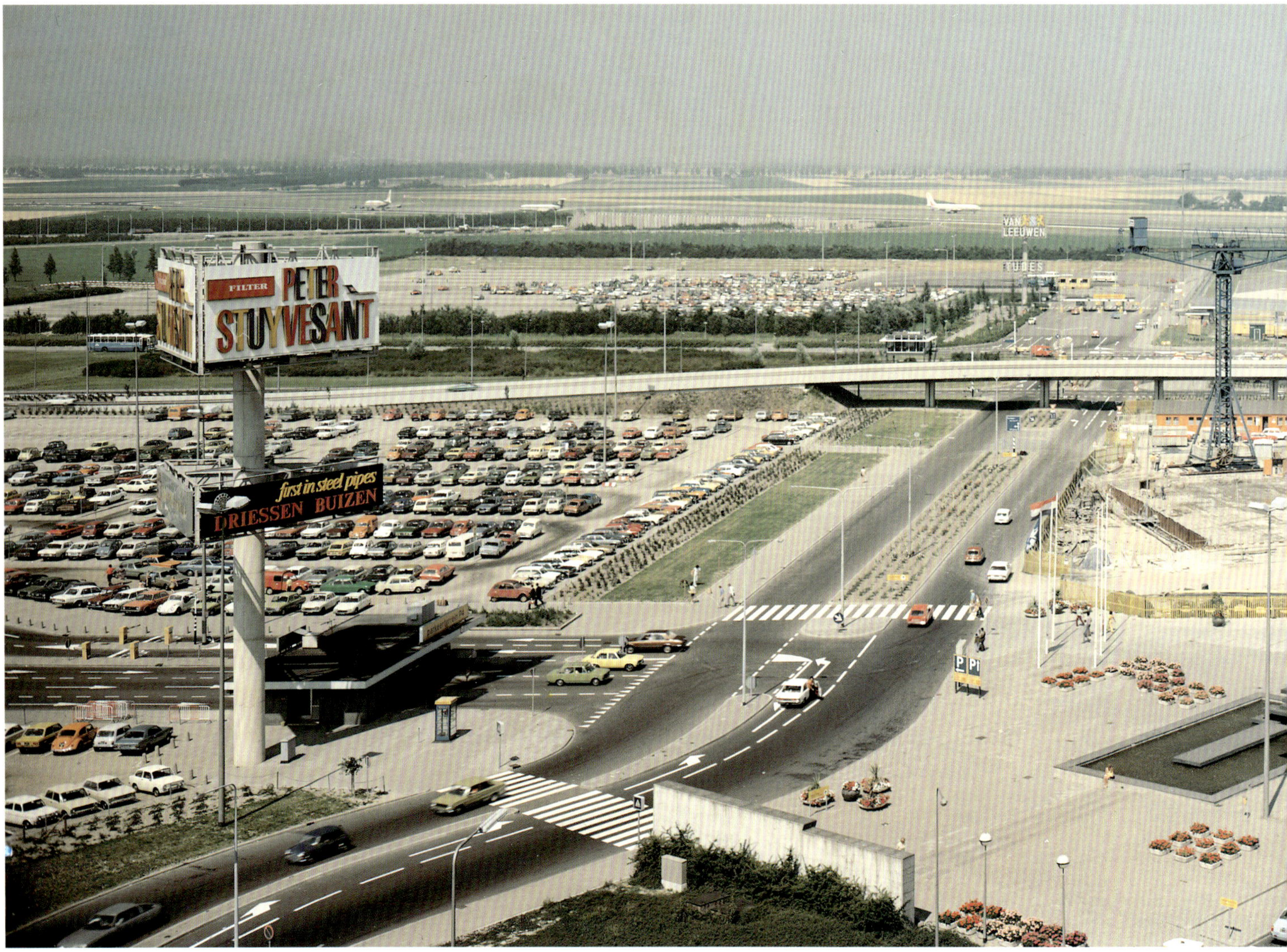
FILTER
PETER
STUYVESANT
first in steel pipes
DRIESSEN BUIZEN
VAN LEEUWEN
TUBES

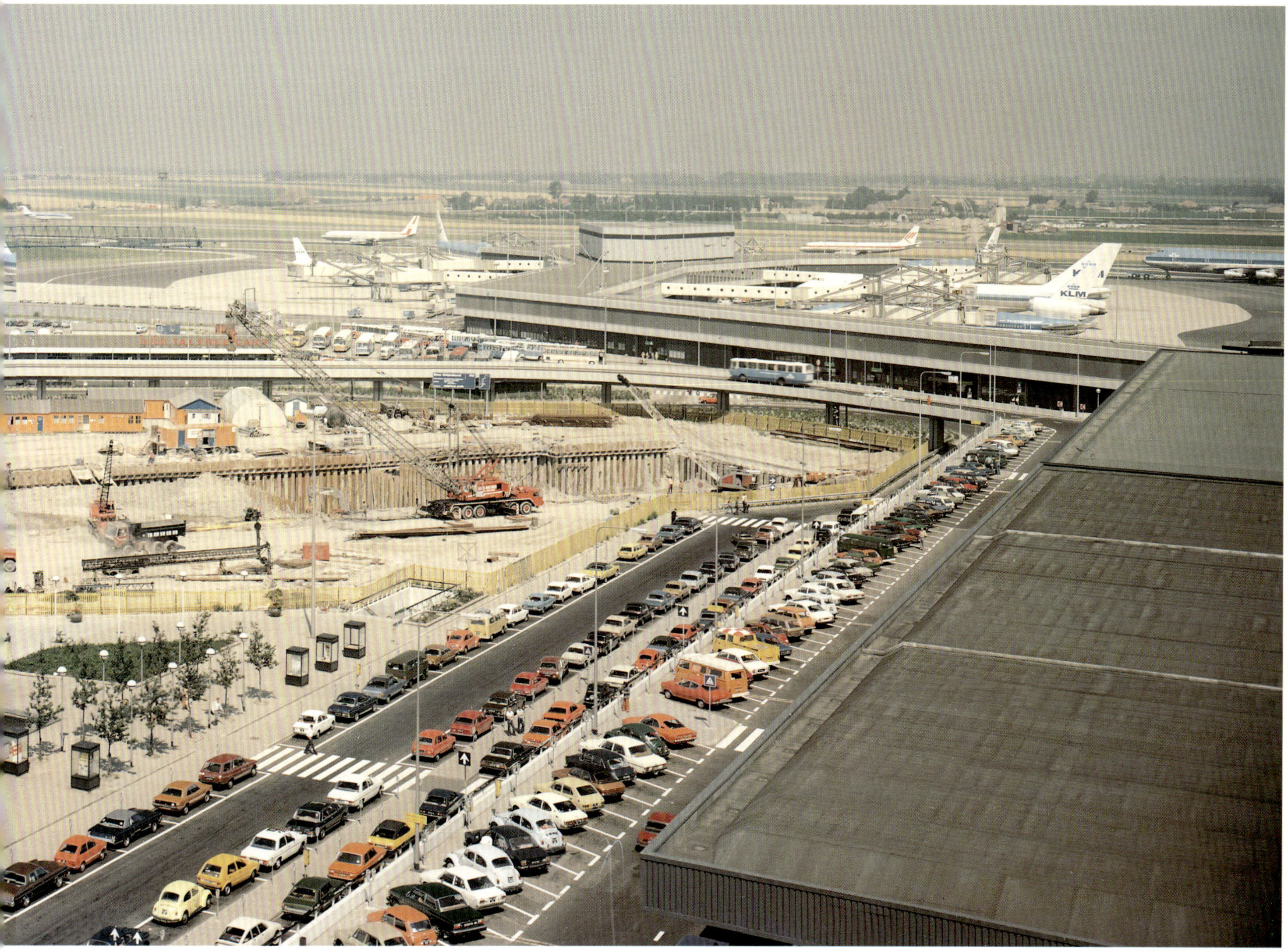
KLM

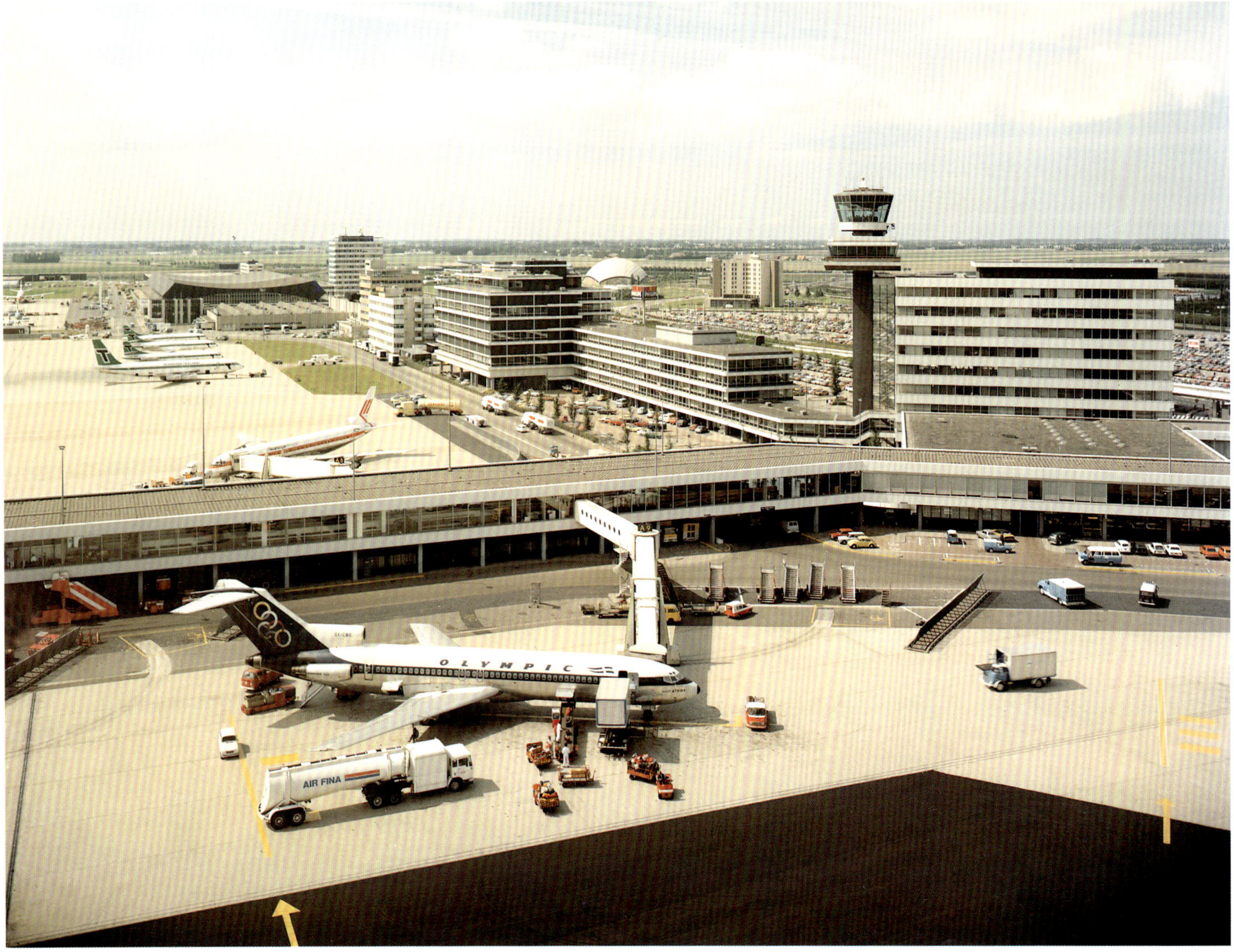
OLYMPIC
AIR FINA

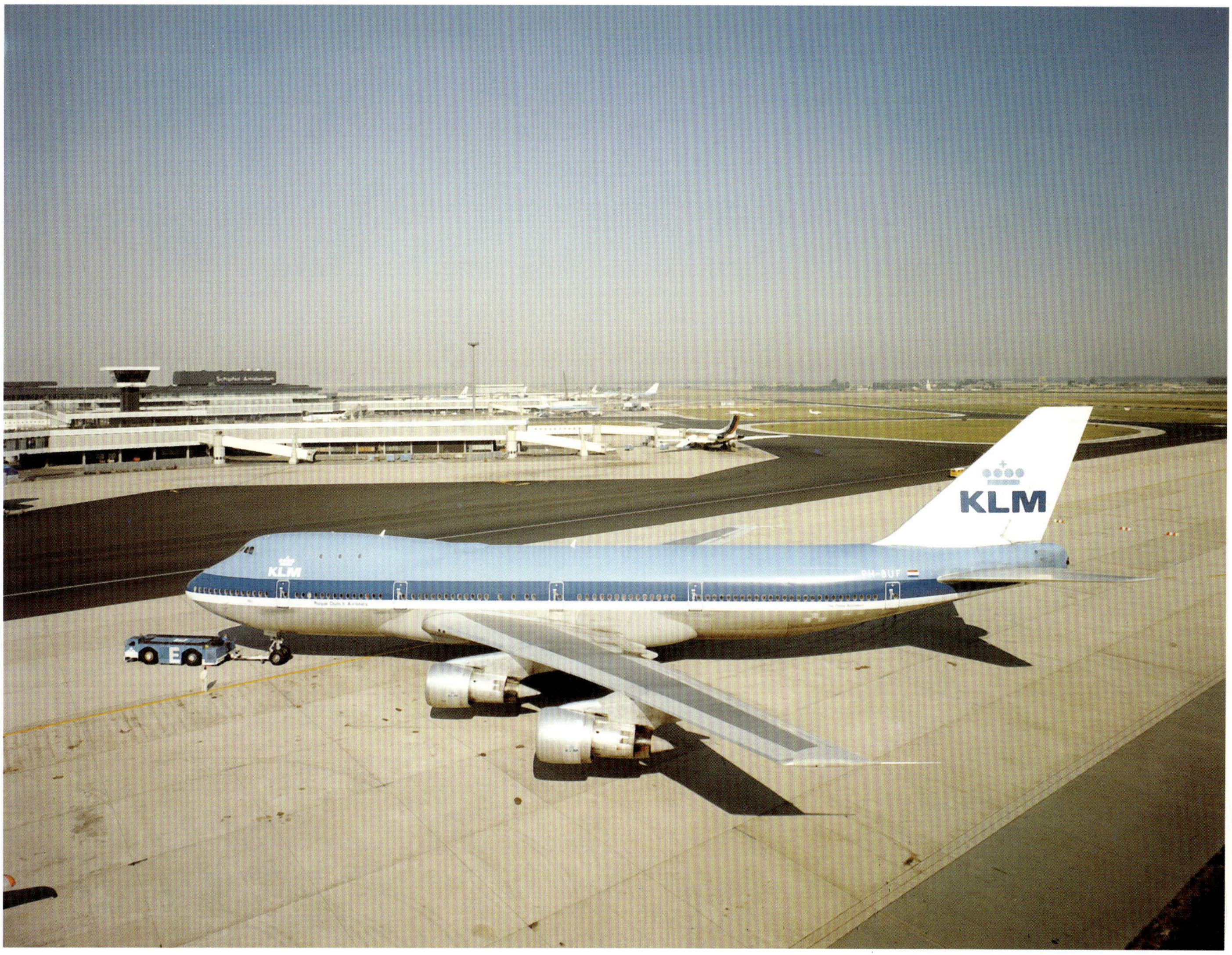

028/029

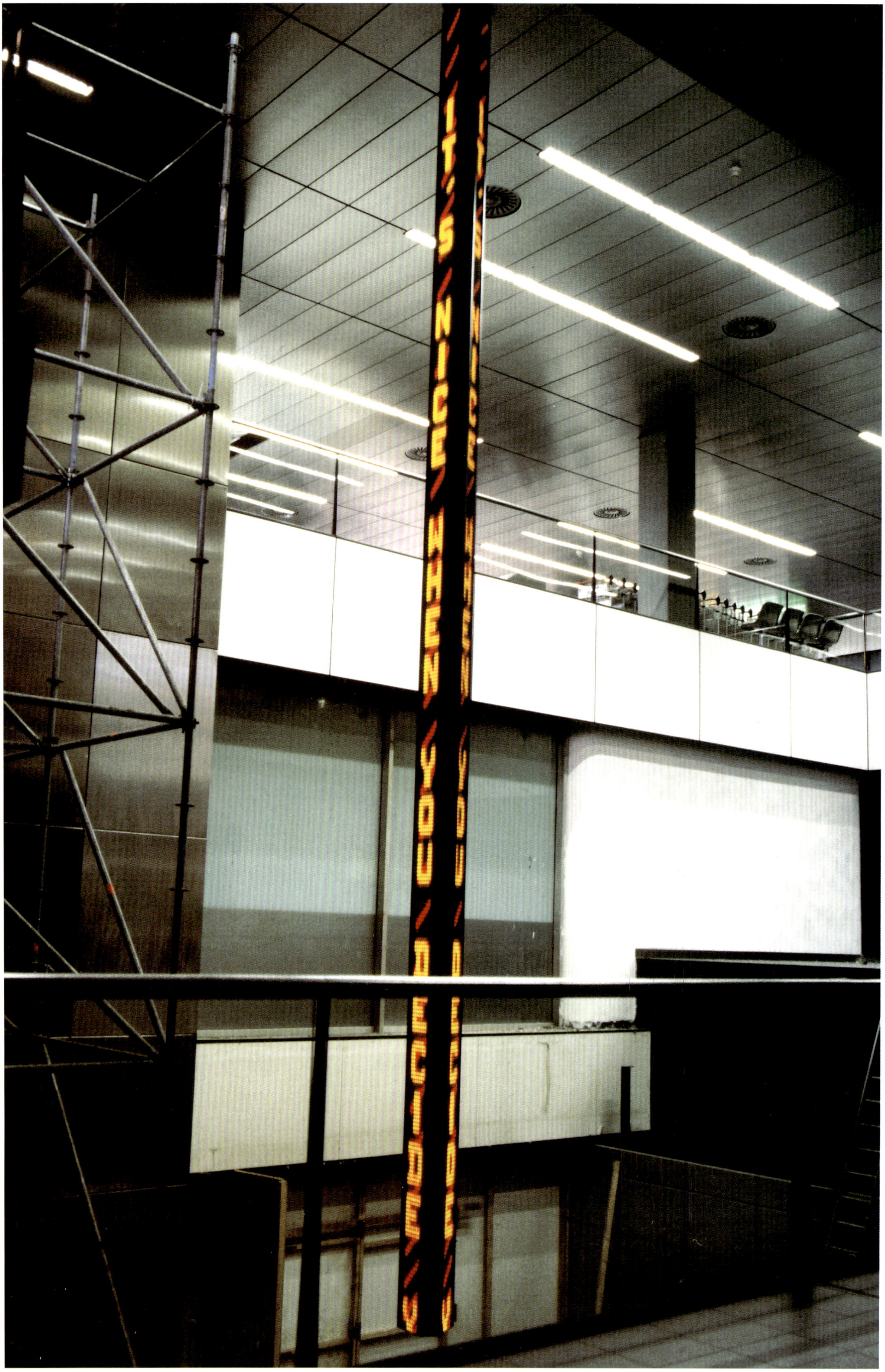
IT'S NICE WHEN YOU DECIDE

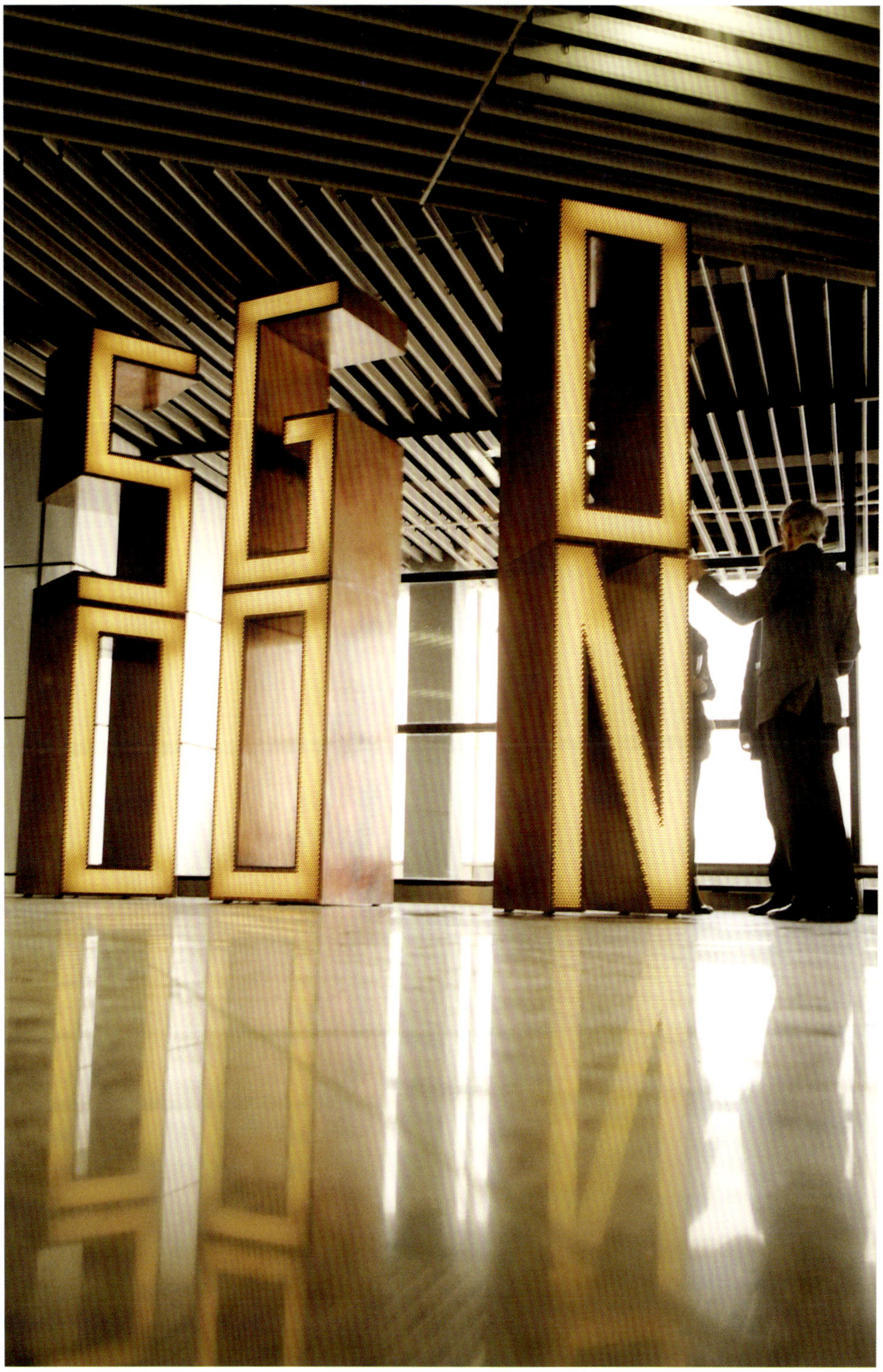

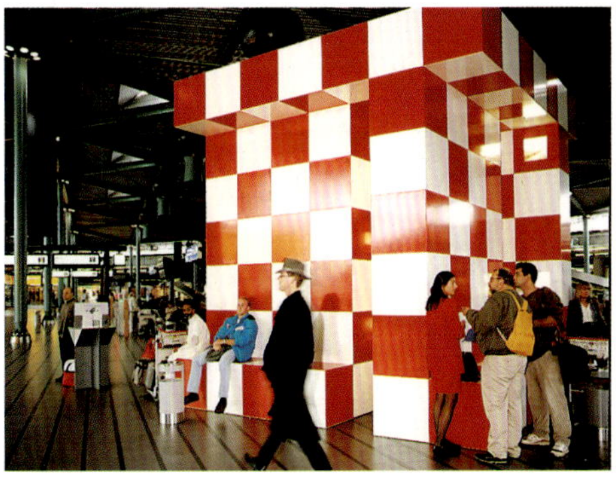

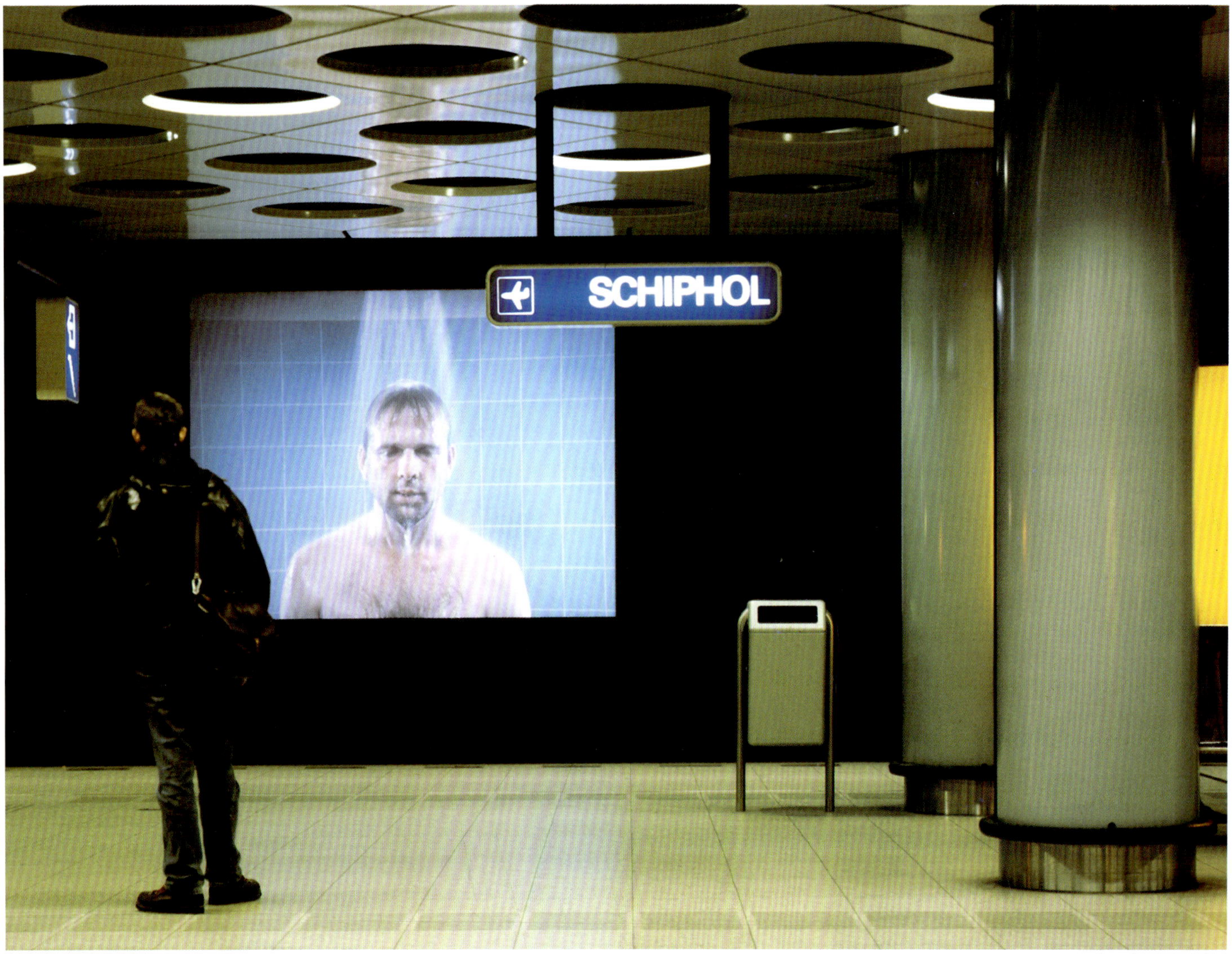
SCHIPHOL

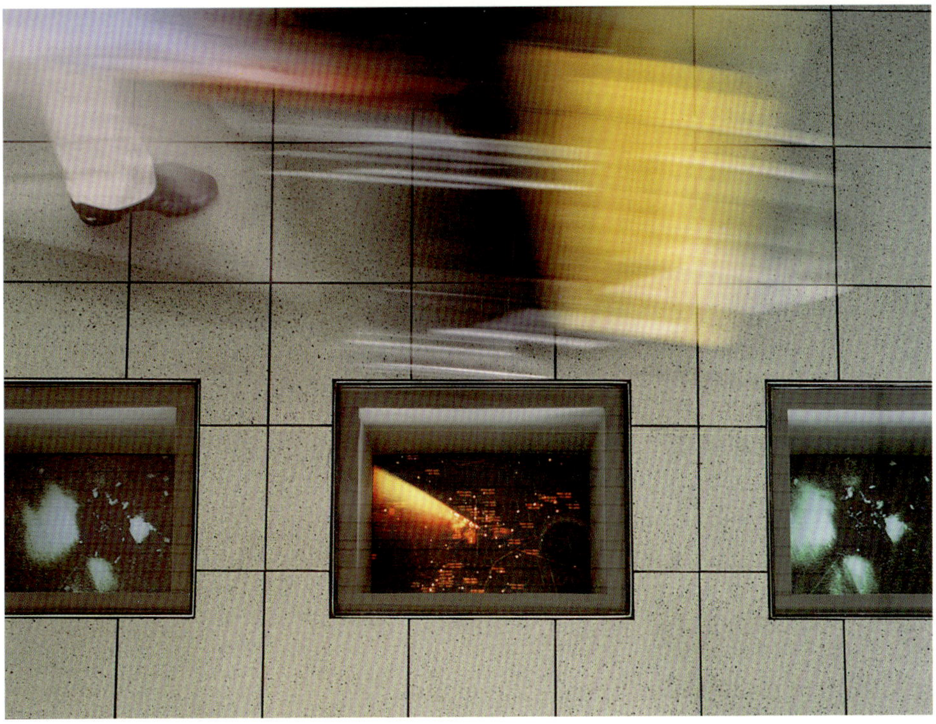

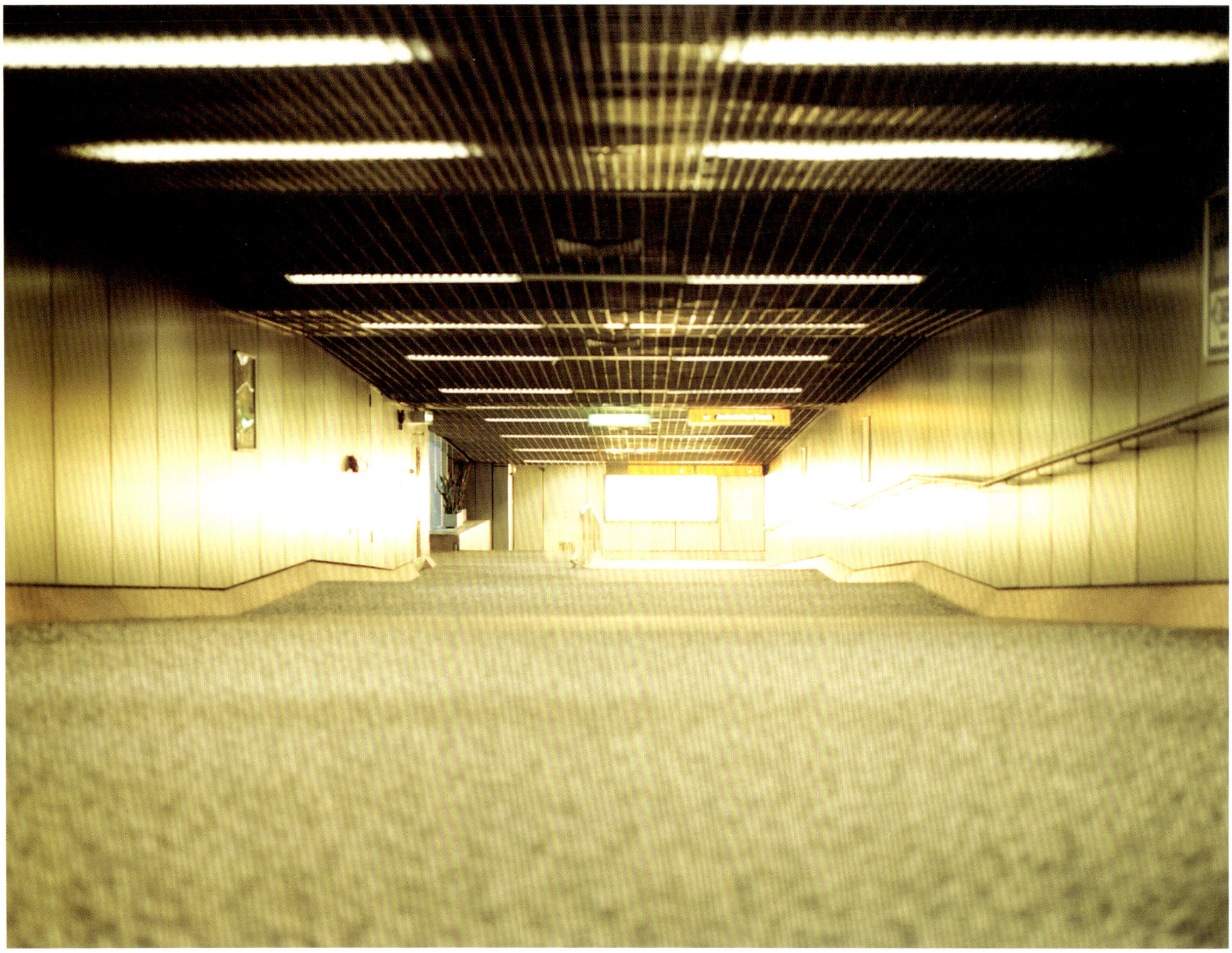

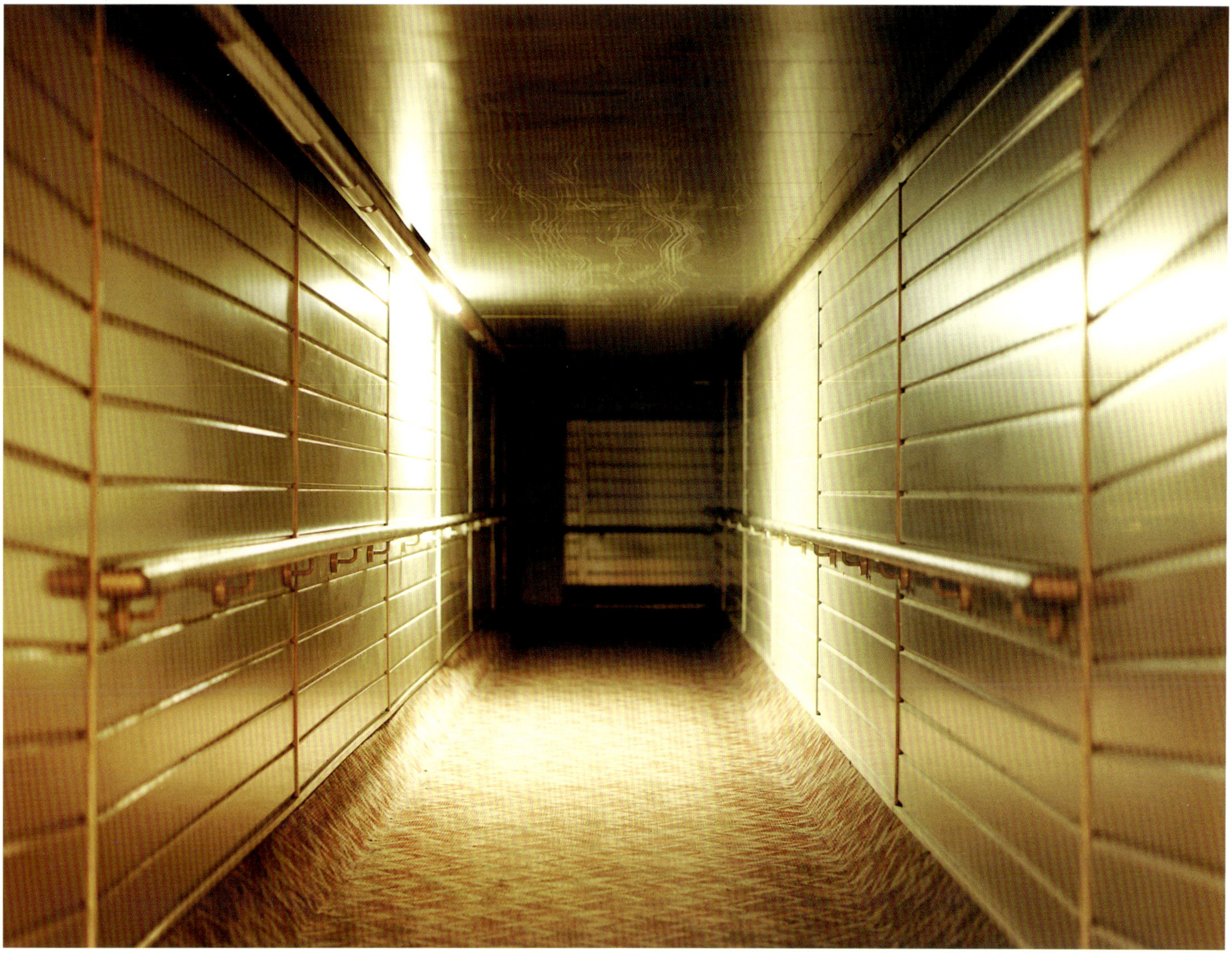

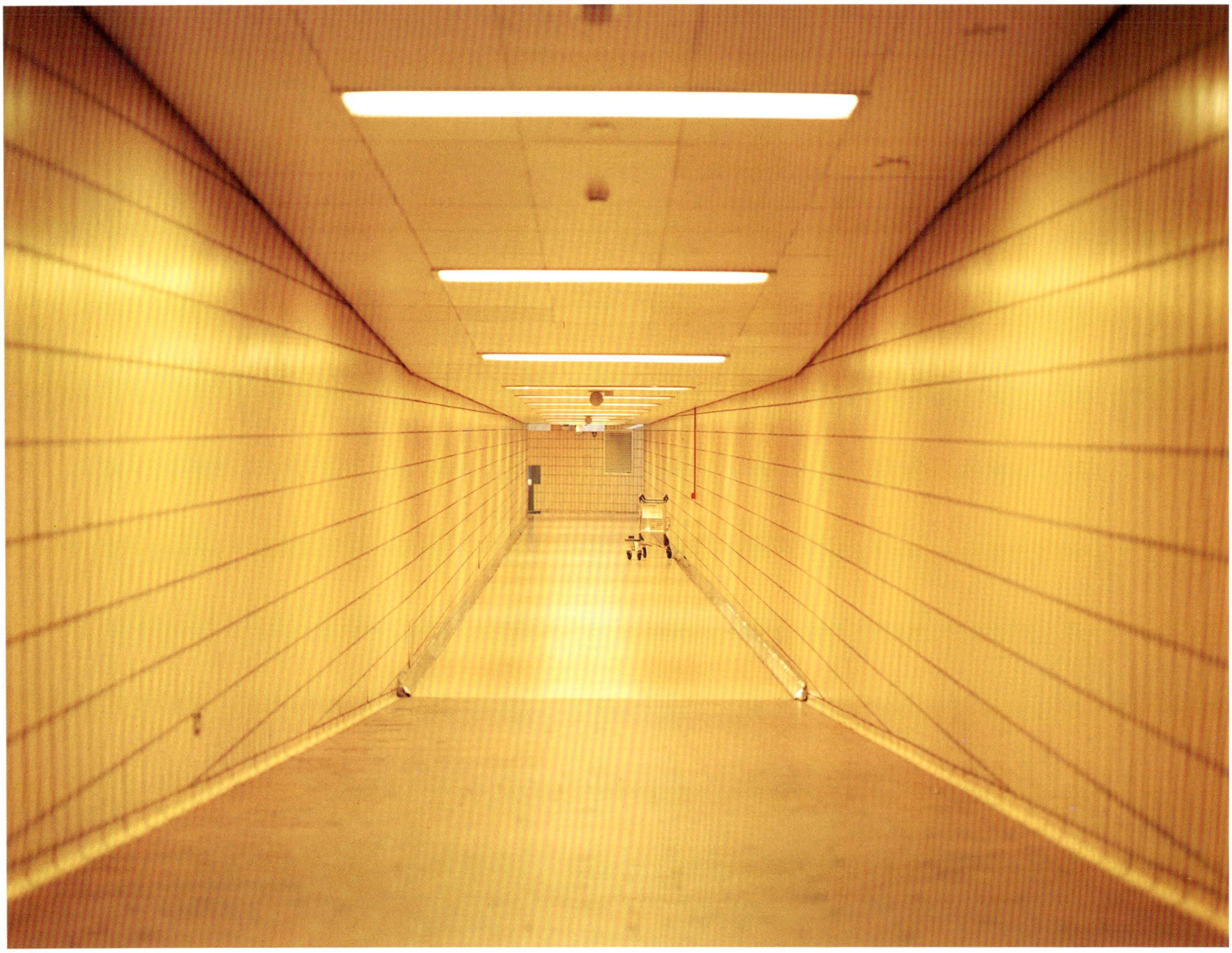

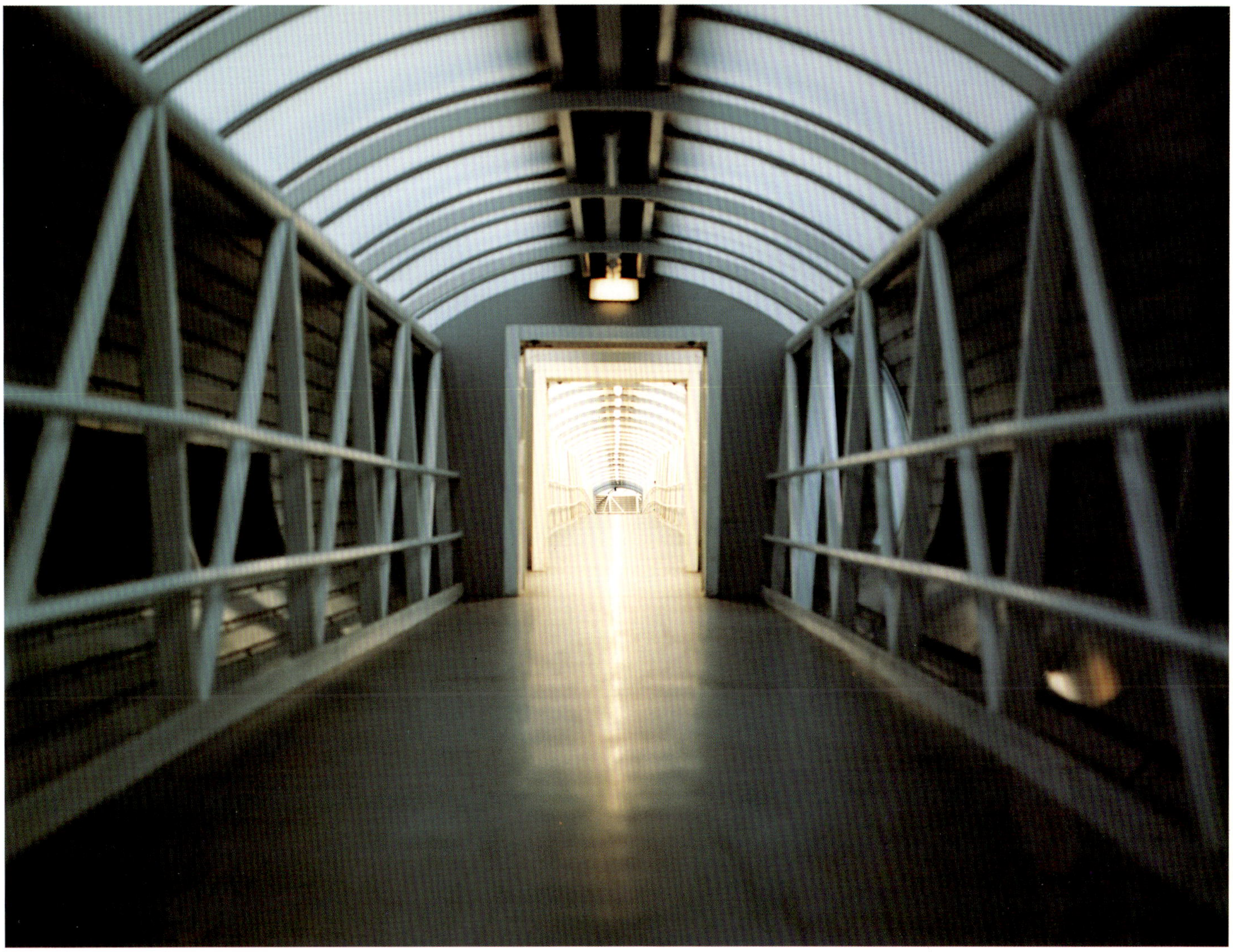

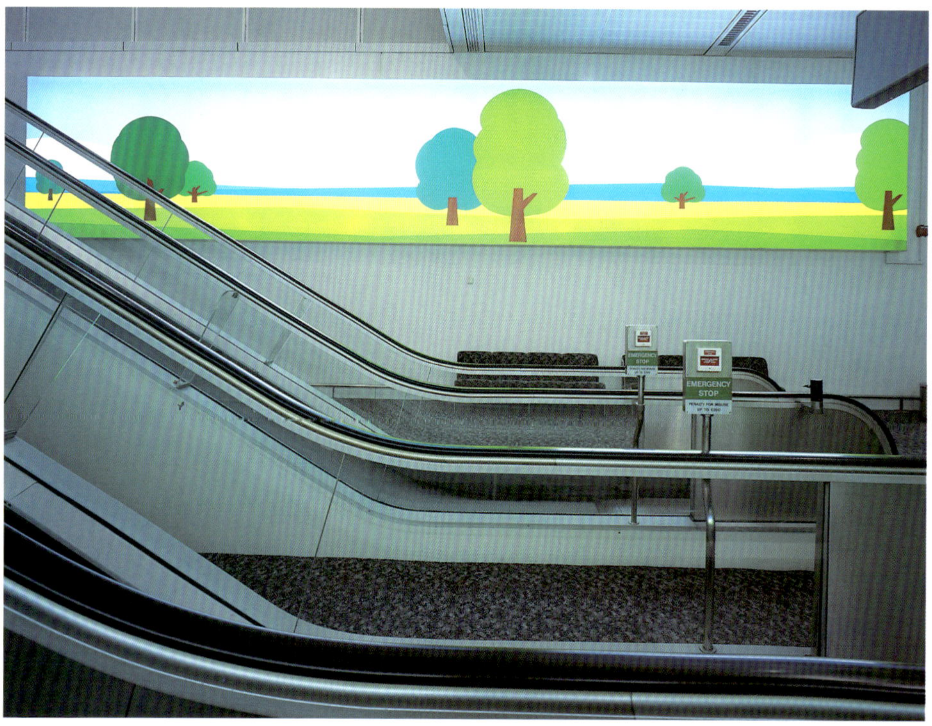
EMERGENCY
STOP

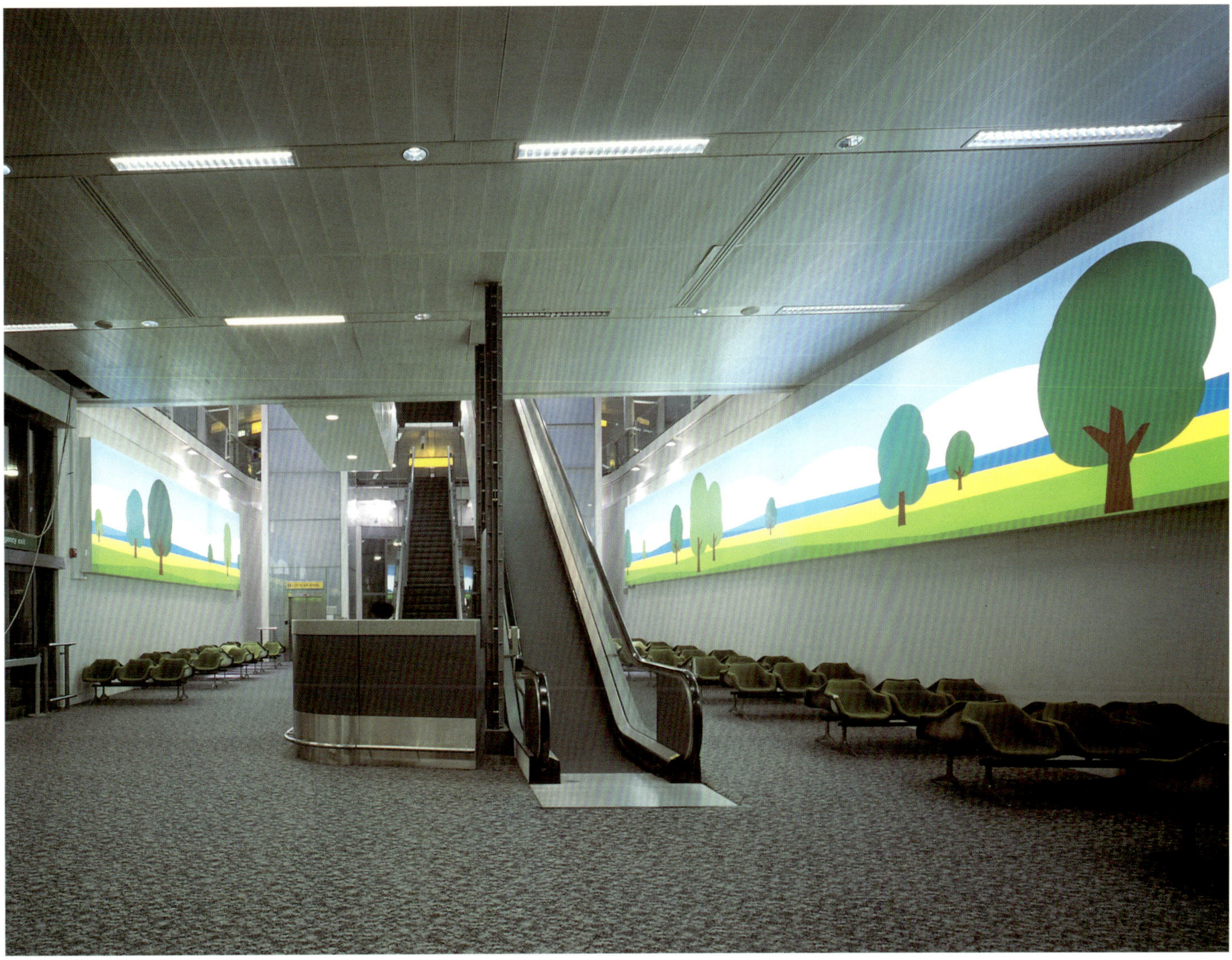

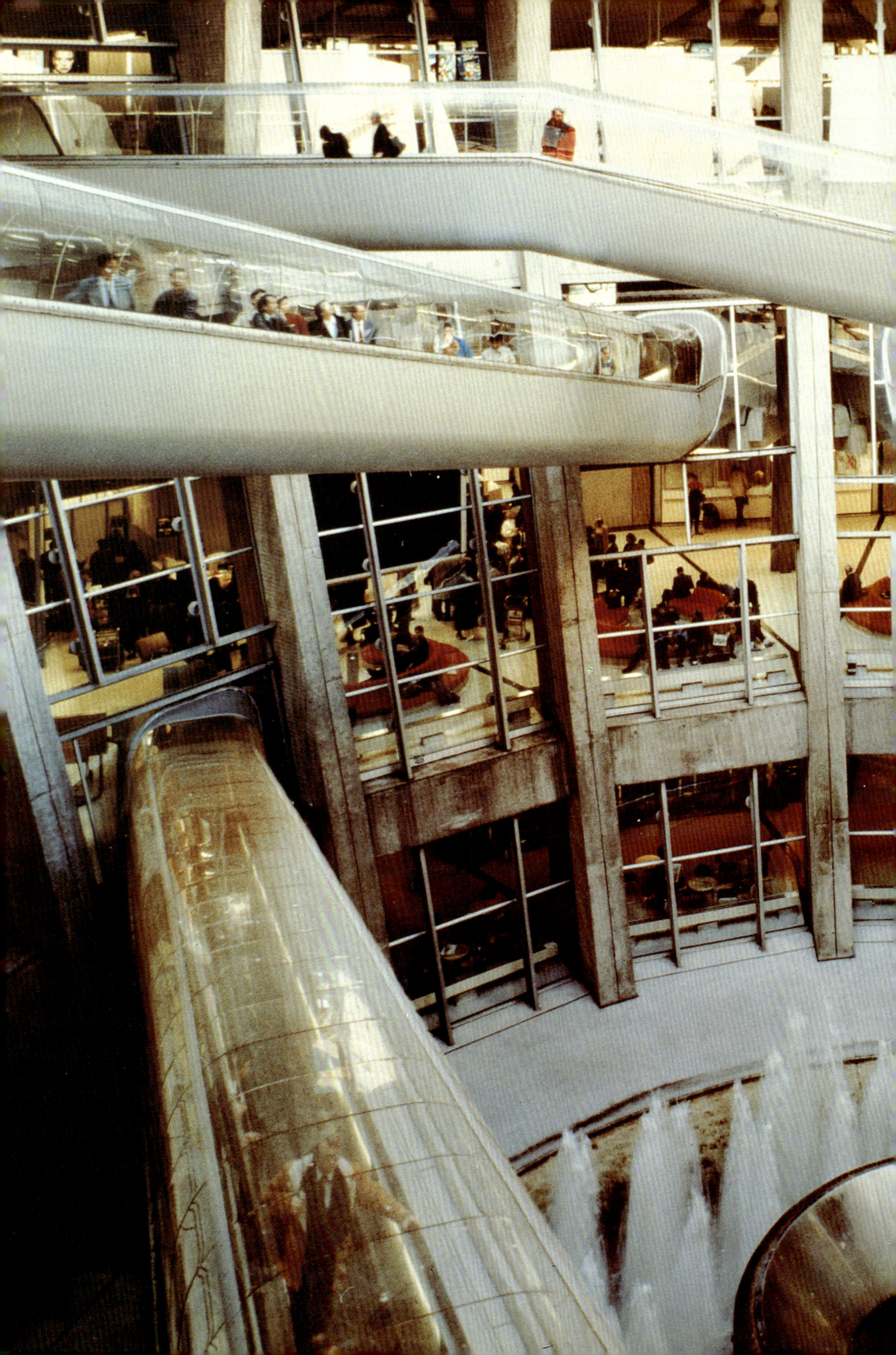

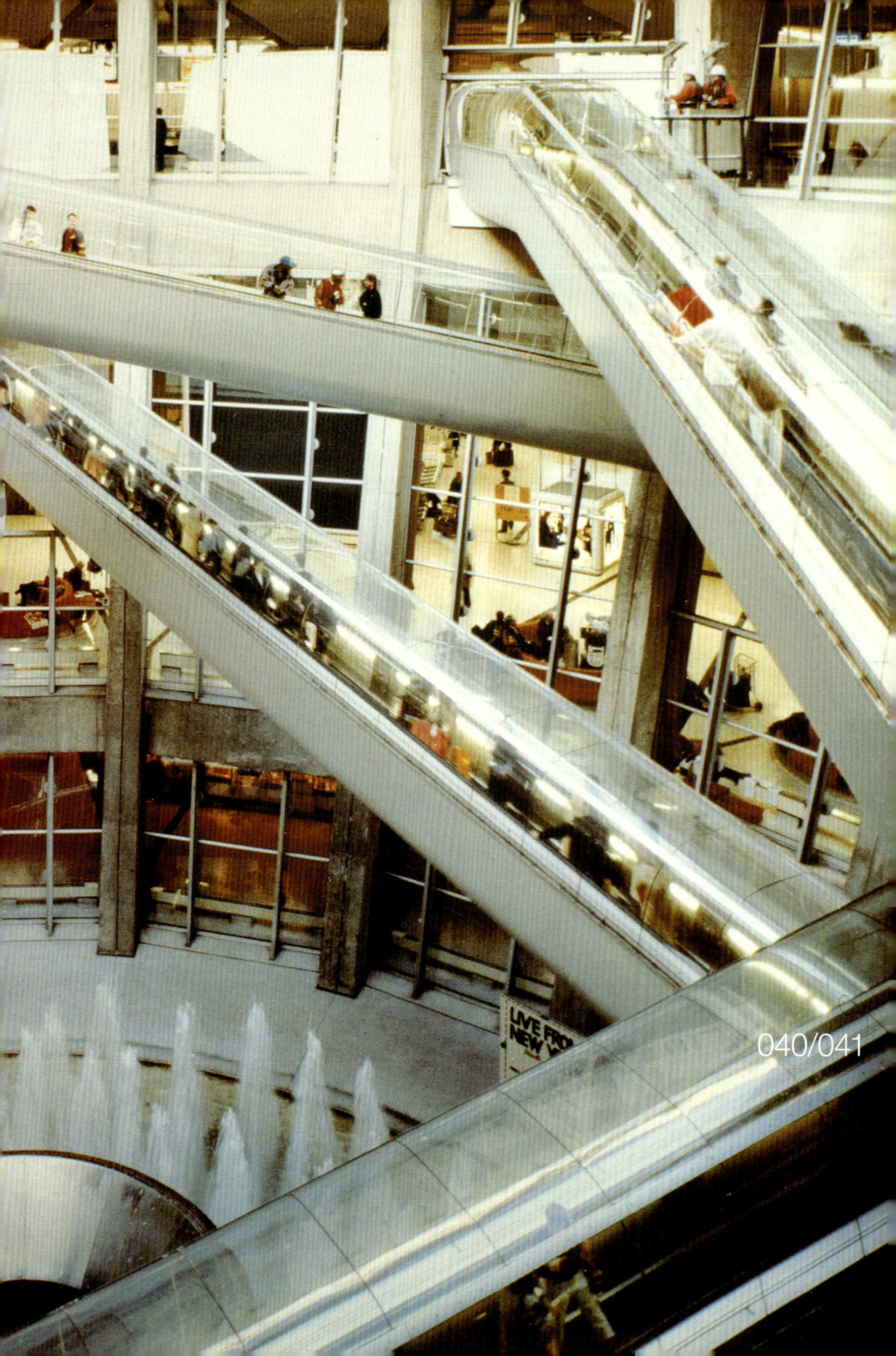

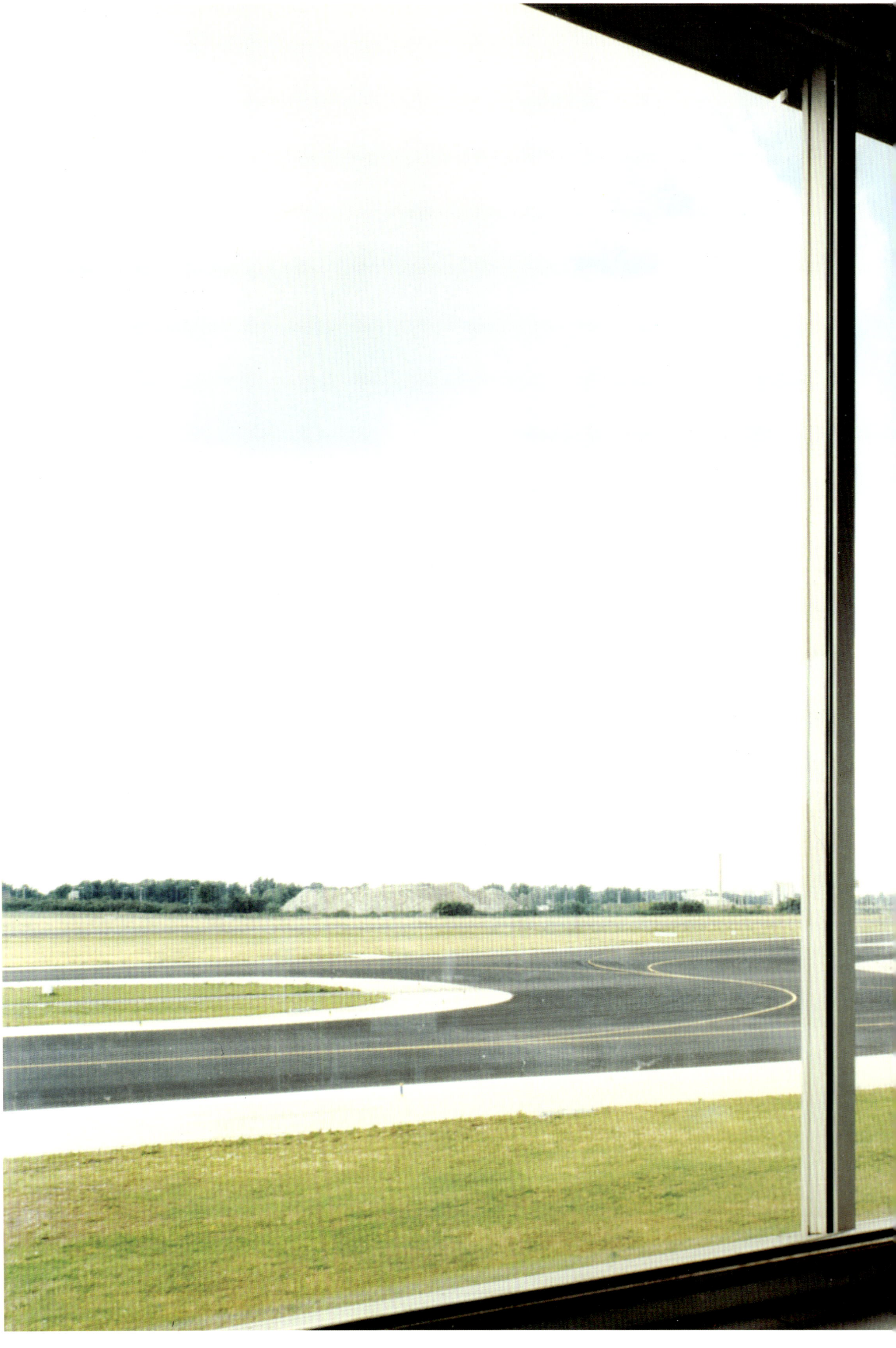

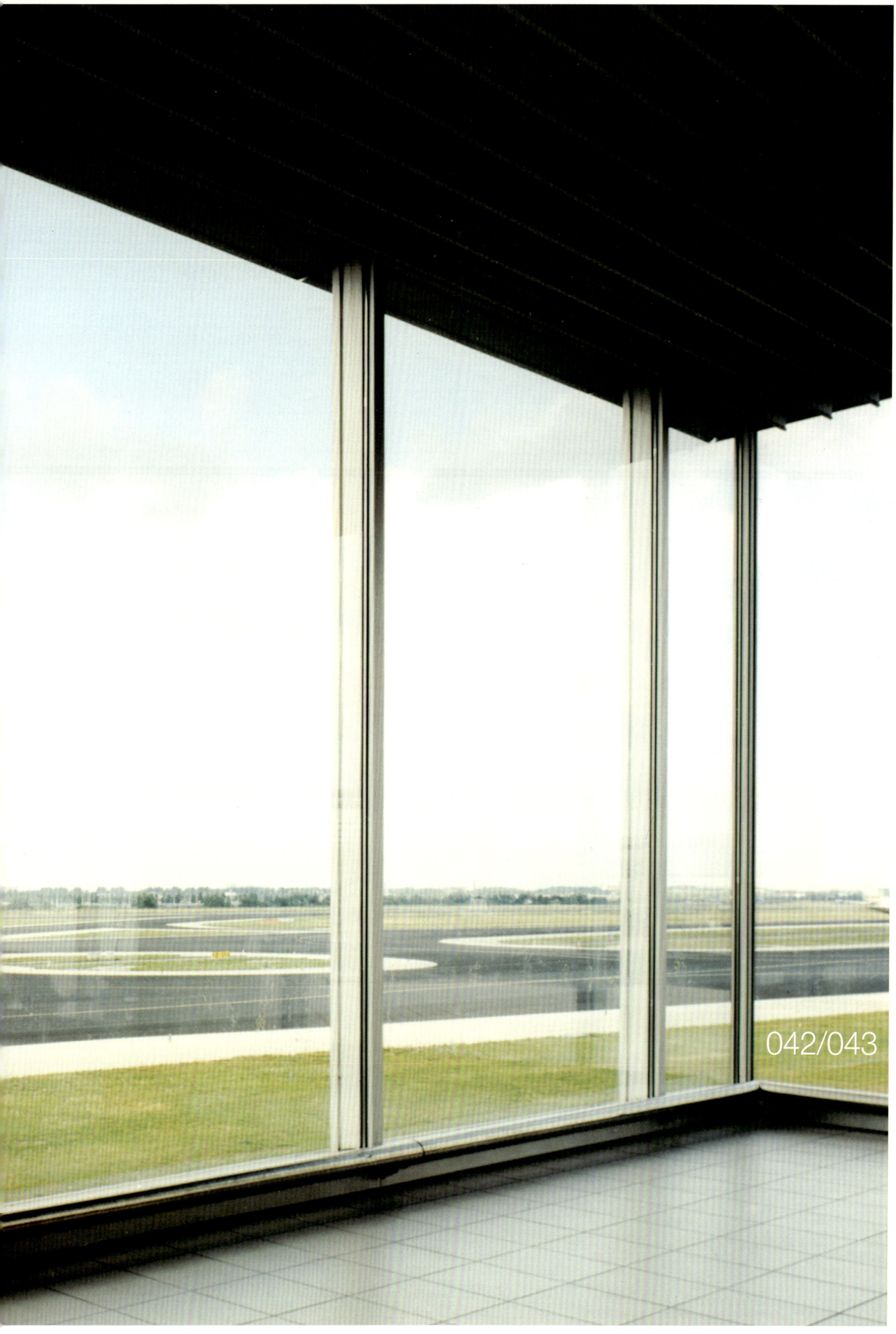

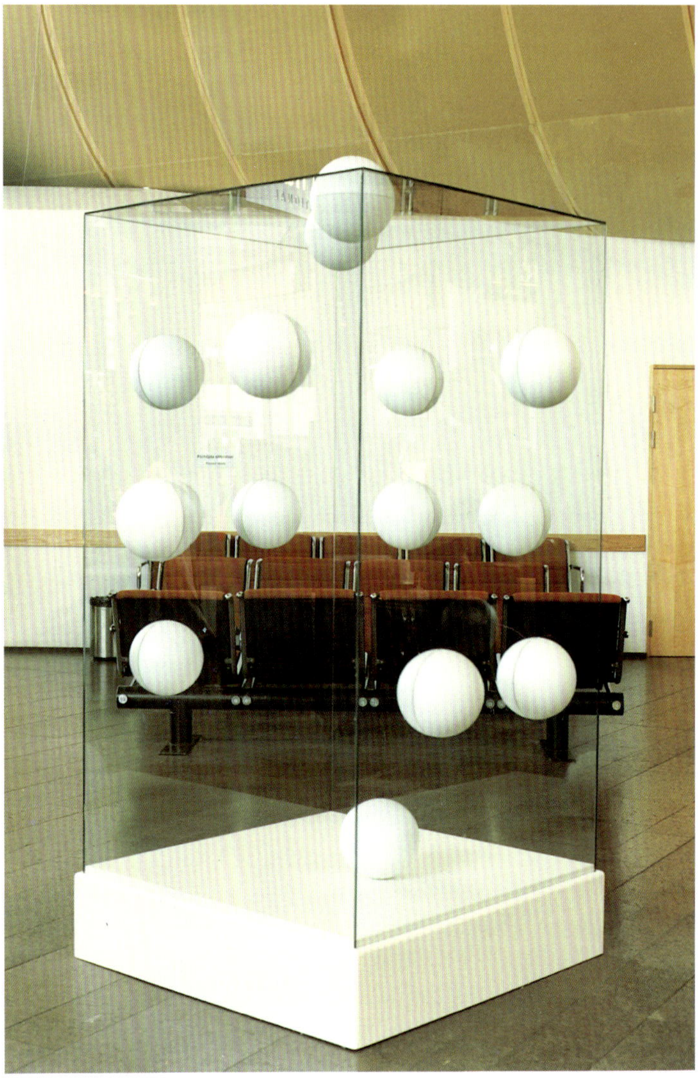

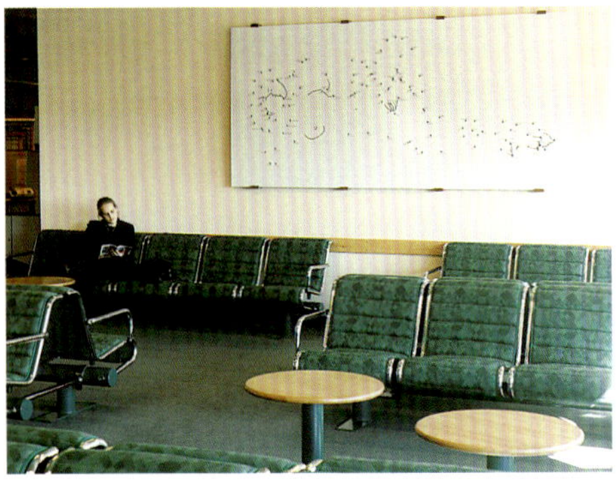

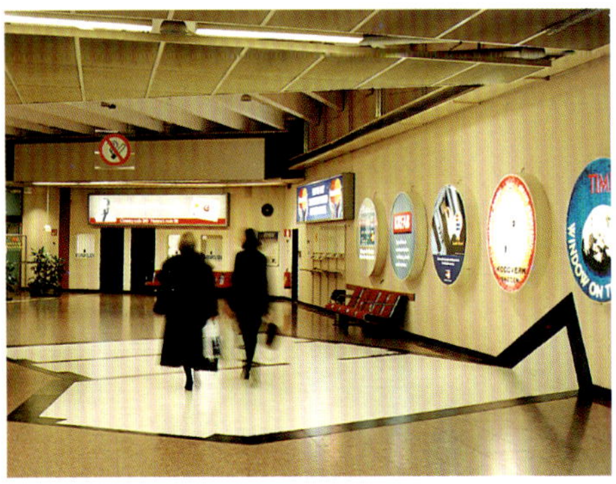

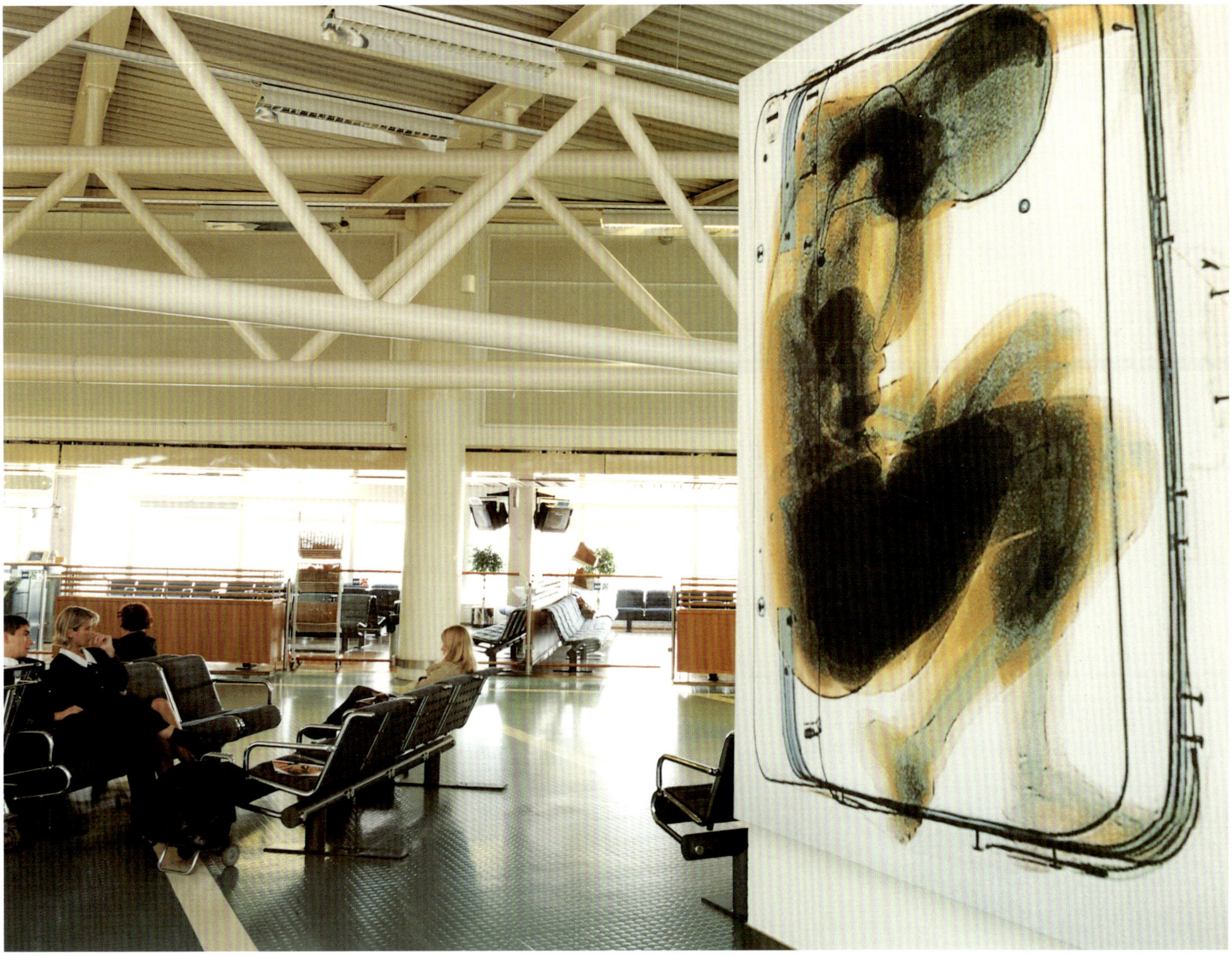

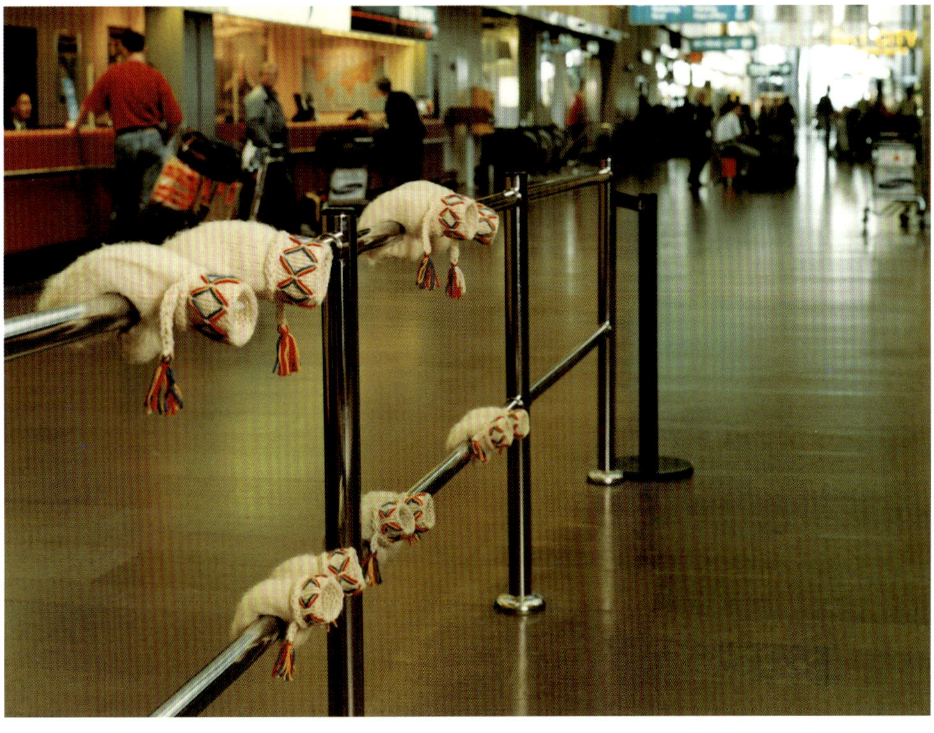

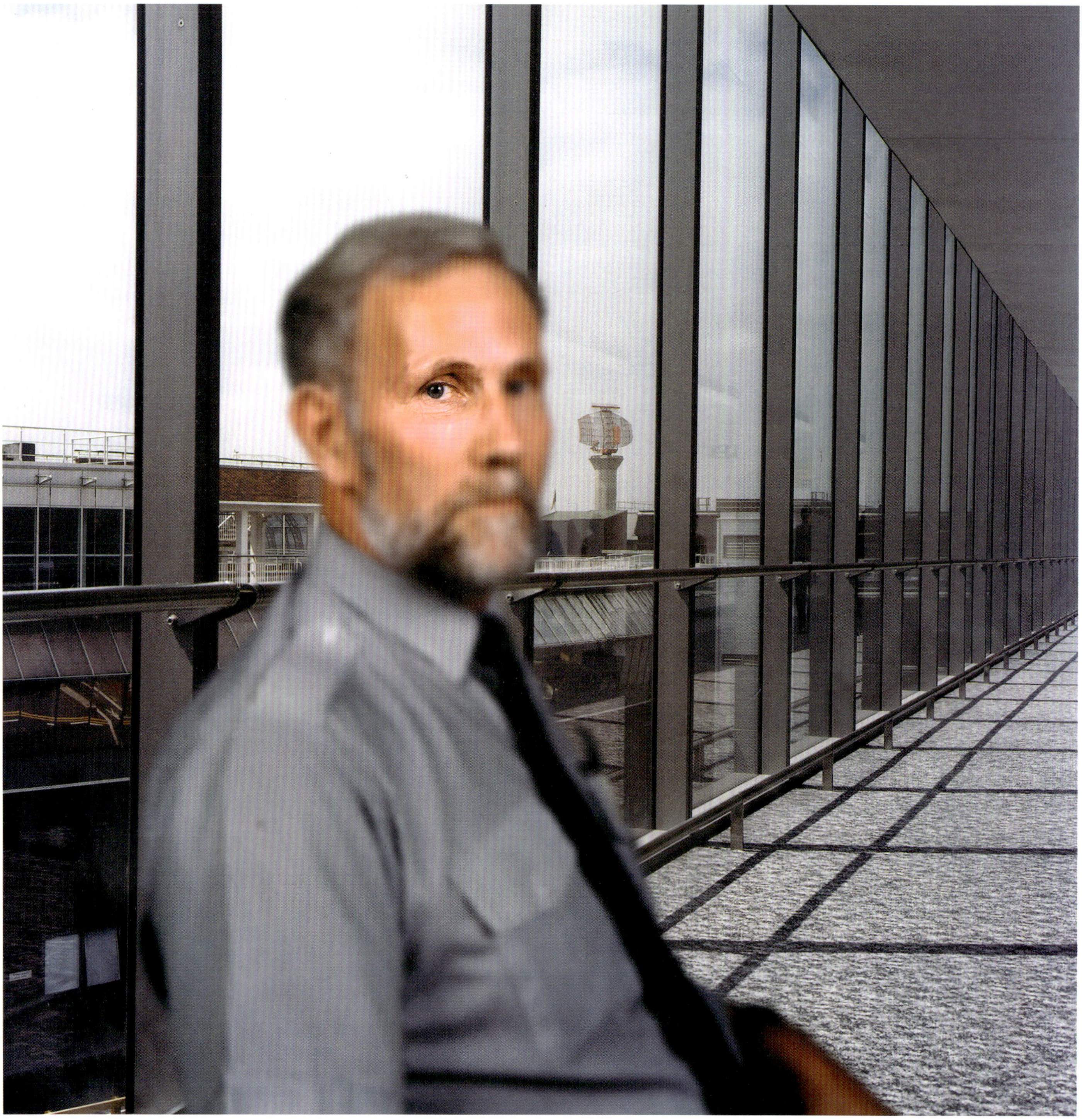

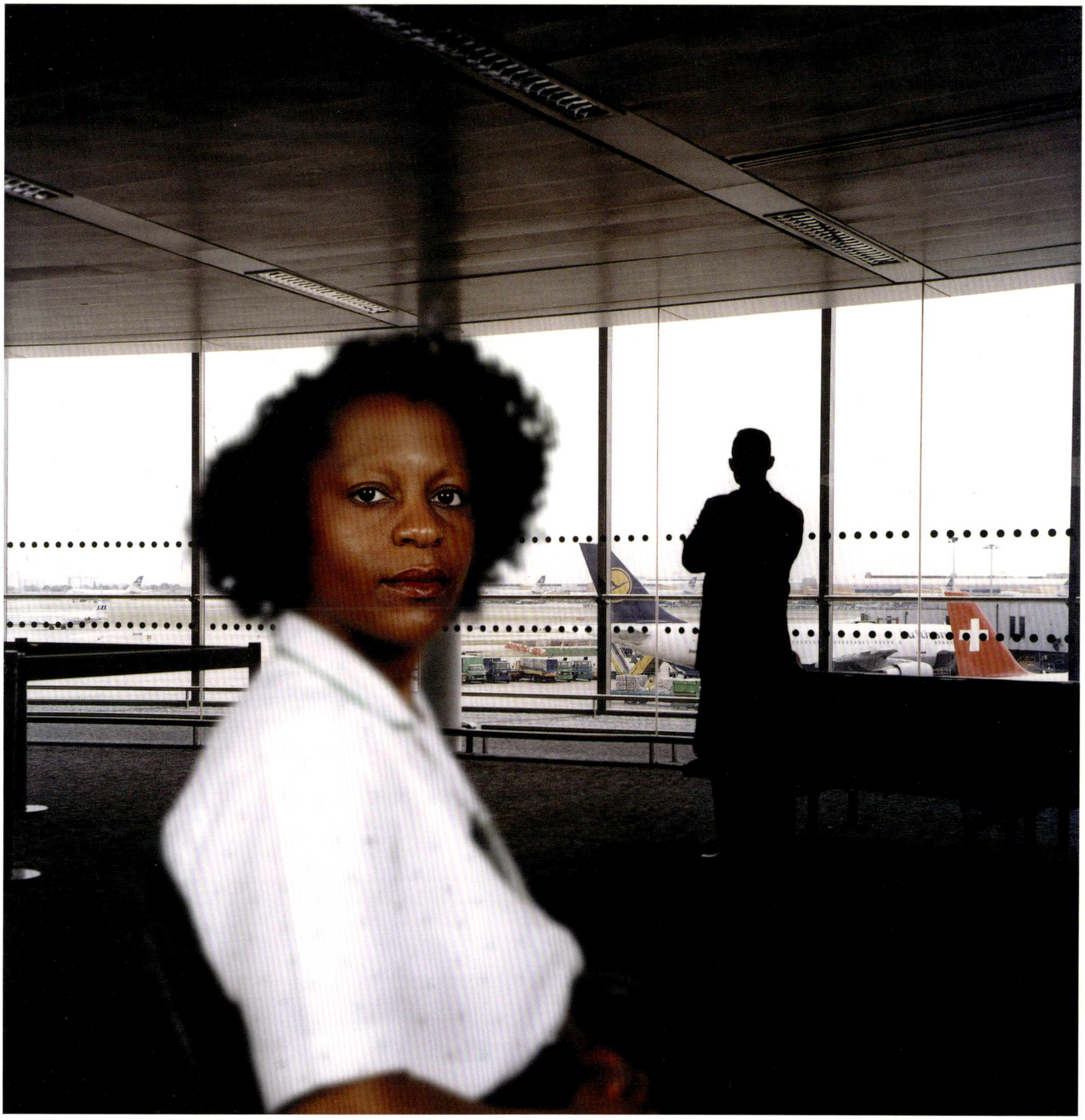

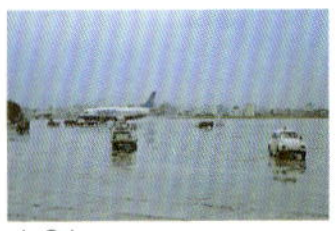
1.01
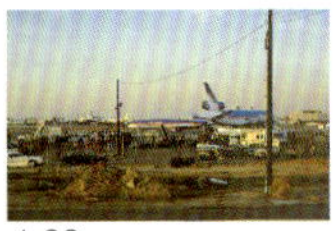
1.02
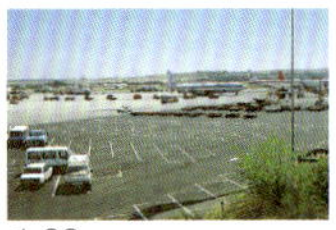
1.03
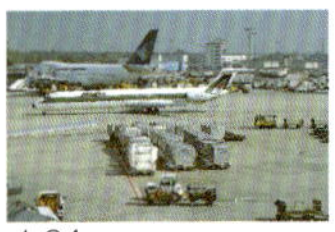
1.04
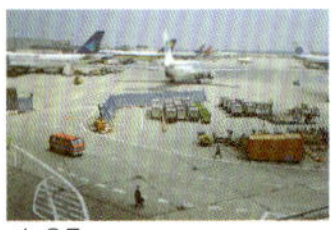
1.05
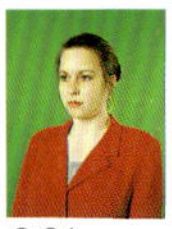
2.01
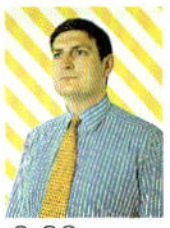
2.02
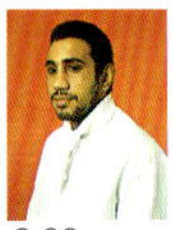
2.03
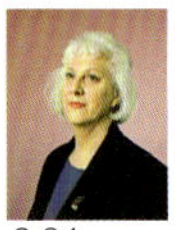
2.04
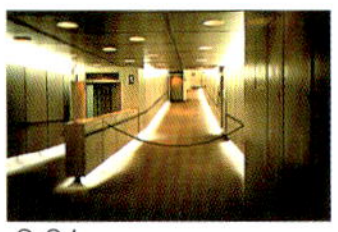
3.01
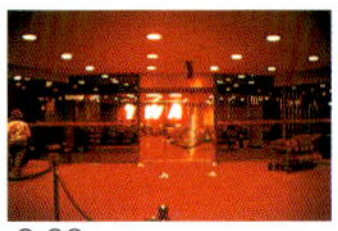
3.02
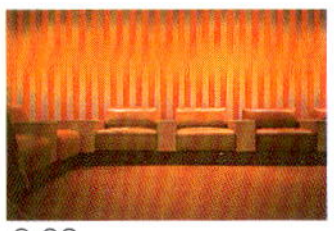
3.03
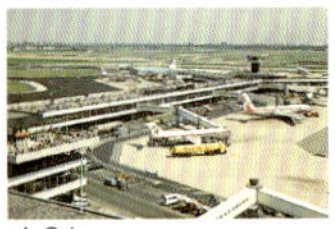
4.01
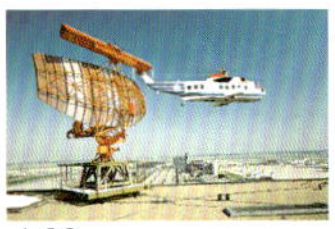
4.02
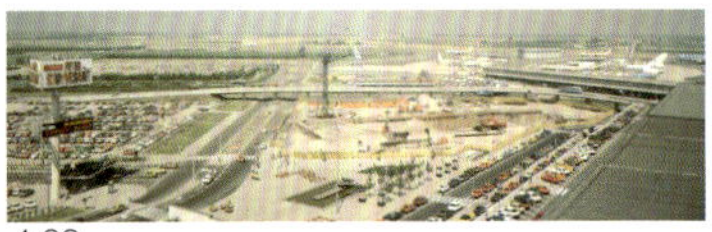
4.03
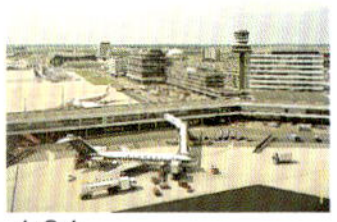
4.04
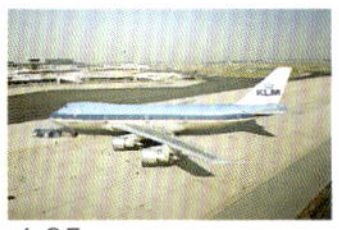
4.05
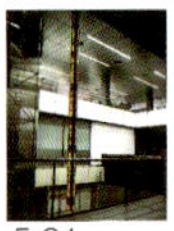
5.01
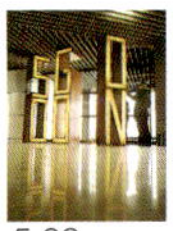
5.02
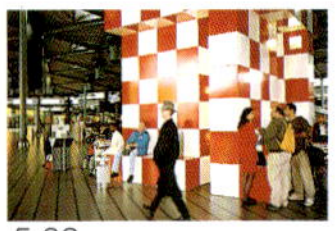
5.03
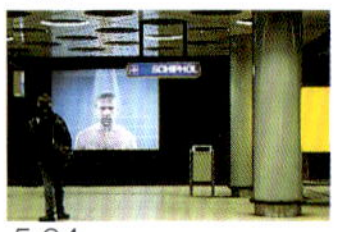
5.04
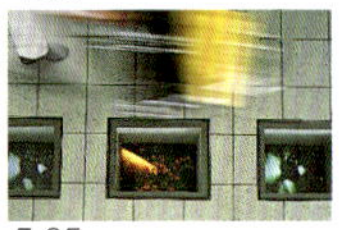
5.05
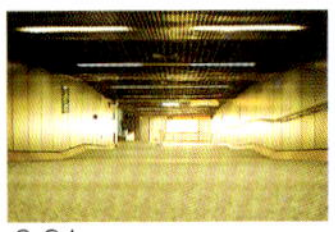
6.01
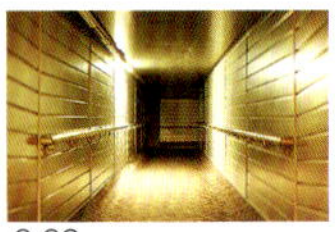
6.02
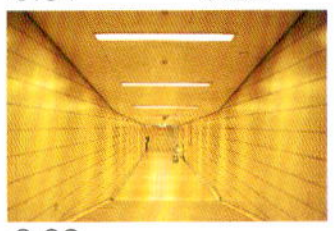
6.03
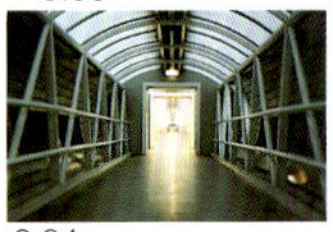
6.04
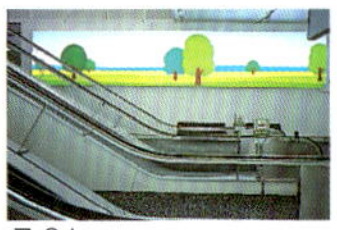
7.01
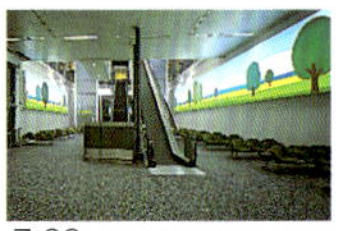
7.02
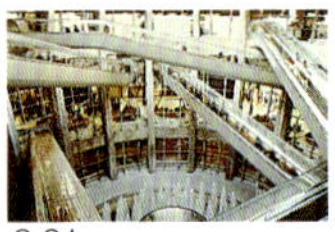
8.01
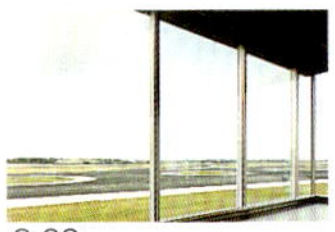
8.02
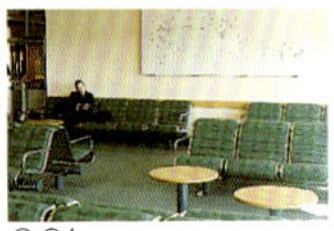
9.01
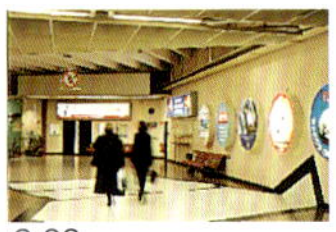
9.02
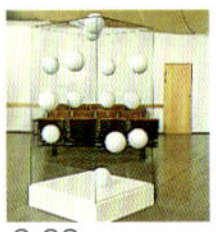
9.03
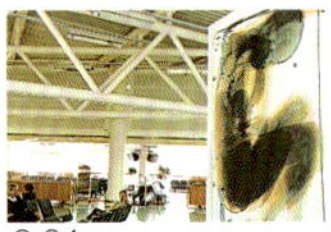
9.04
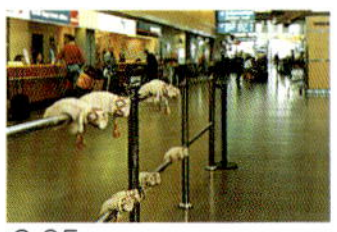
9.05
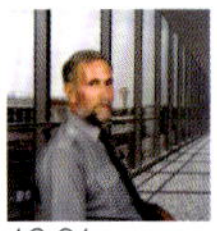
10.01
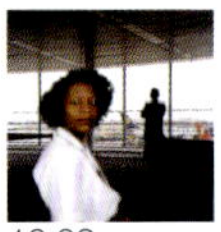
10.02

1.01–1.05 Peter Fischli and David Weiss, *Untitled*, from the series *Airports*, 1990, (courtesy of the artists)

2.01 Gabriella Sancisi, *2080G300Y (Debbie Cowlard, Retail Customer Services)*, 1997, Heathrow Point Staff Restaurant, Heathrow, BAA Art Programme (courtesy of the artist)

2.02 Gabriella Sancisi, *Pure Brilliant Flowers (Barry Horrell, Property)*, 1997 Heathrow Point Staff Restaurant, Heathrow, BAA Art Programme (courtesy of the artist)

2.03 Gabriella Sancisi, *Roughest (Sukhbinder Gill. Catering)*, 1997 Heathrow Point Staff Restaurant, Heathrow, BAA Art Programme (courtesy of the artist)

2.04 Gabriella Sancisi, *Reckless (Sheila Southgate, Transportation Policy)*, 1997 Heathrow Point Staff Restaurant, Heathrow, BAA Art Programme (courtesy of the artist)

3.01–3.02 Martha Rosler, *Untitled (JFK)*, 1990 (courtesy of Jay Gorney Modern Art)

3.03 Martha Rosler, *Untitled*, 1990 (courtesy of Jay Gorney Modern Art)

4.01–4.05 Frits Rotgans, *Untitled* (courtesy of the Netherlands Photo Archive, Rotterdam)

5.01 Jenny Holzer, *Untitled*, 1995, (courtesy of Amsterdam Airport, Schiphol)

5.02 Marc Ruygrok, *So Go On*, 1995 (courtesy of Amsterdam Airport, Schiphol)

5.03 Dennis Adams, *Coda*, 1995, (courtesy of Amsterdam Airport, Schiphol)

5.04 Mareijke van Warmedam, *Douche*, 1996 (courtesy of Amsterdam Airport, Schiphol)

5.05 Niek Kemps, *Closed Sight*, 1995 (courtesy of Amsterdam Airport, Schiphol)

6.01–6.04 Stephen Gill, *Untitled*, 1997, (courtesy of the artist)

7.01–7.02 Julian Opie, *Untitled*, 1997, Flight Connections Centre, Heathrow, BAA Art Programme (courtesy of Lisson Gallery)

8.01 Andreas Gursky, *Charles de Gaulle*, 1992 (courtesy of Victoria Miro Gallery)

8.02 Andreas Gursky, *Schiphol Airport*, 1994 (courtesy of Monika Sprüth Galerie)

9.01 Susanne Björkman, *Pleasant Journey*, Terminal 5, Arlanda, Stockholm (courtesy of Thomas Adlercreutz)

9.02 Anna Brag, *Incognito*, Terminal 5, Arlanda, Stockholm (courtesy of Thomas Adlercreutz)

9.03 Karl-Johan Stigmark, *Here*, 1997, Arlanda airport, Stockholm (courtesy of Thomas Adlercreutz)

9.04 Åsa Anderson, *While Moving—I'm Waiting*, Terminal 4, Arlanda, Stockholm (courtesy of Thomas Adlercreutz)

9.05 Christer Engström, John Håkansson, Jyrki Siikanen, *We're not a goin'*, Terminal 5, Arlanda airport, Stockholm (courtesy of Thomas Adlercreutz)

10.01–10.02 Karen Eslea, *Untitled*, 1997, Terminal 1, International Security Search Area, Heathrow, BAA Art Programme (courtesy of the artist)

Contents

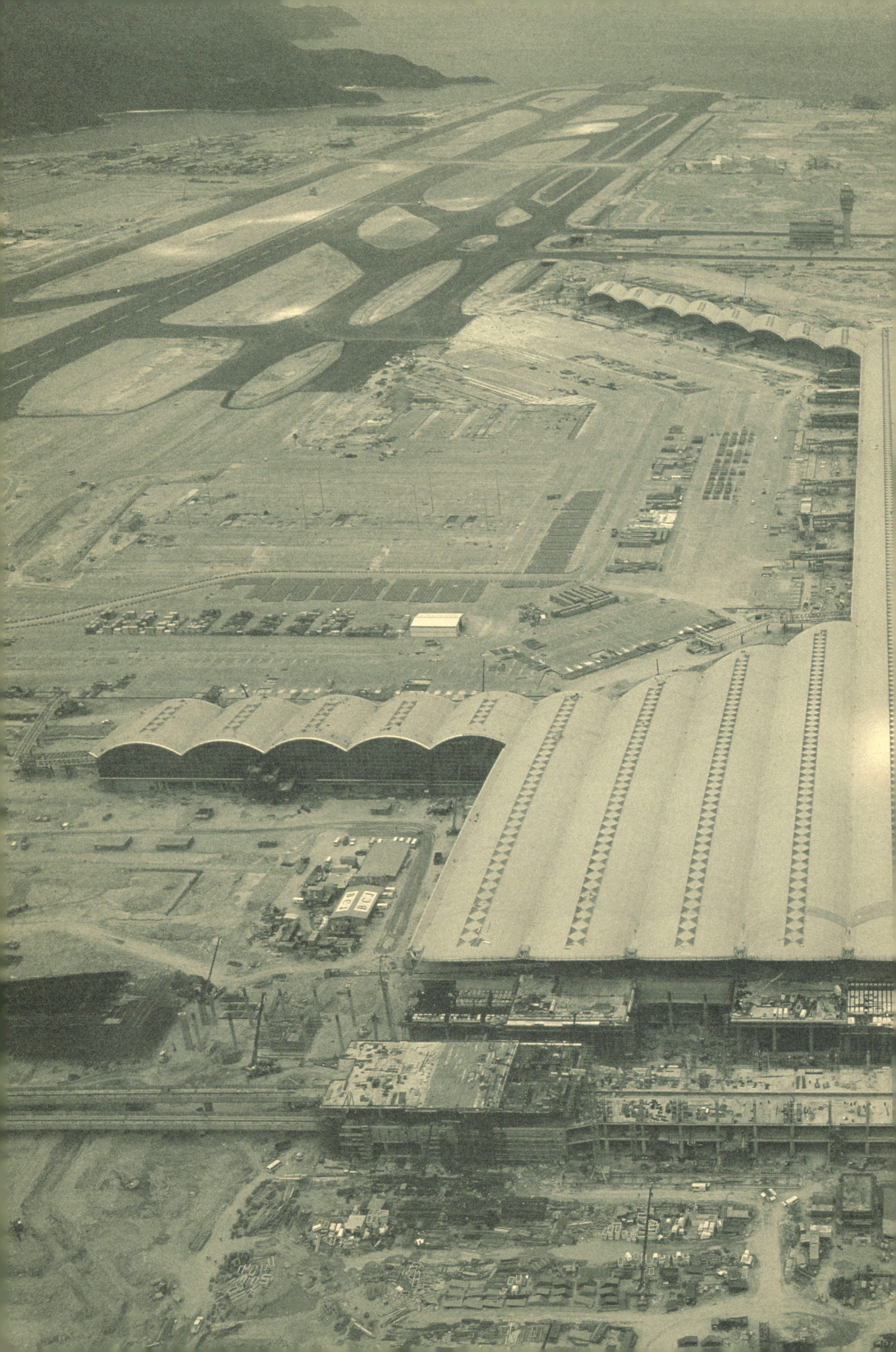

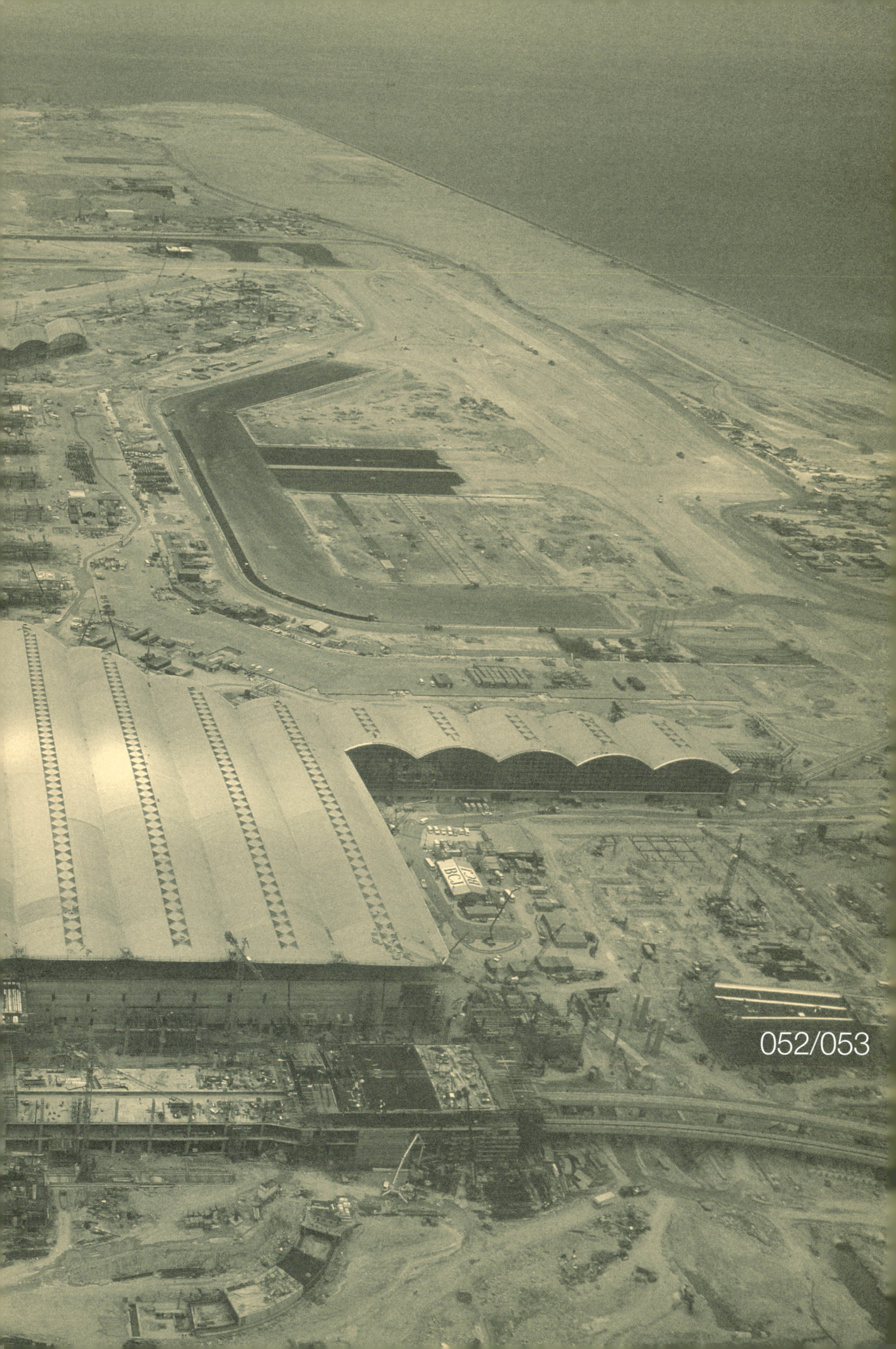

Introduction

Steven Bode
Jeremy Millar

The history of airports is the history of our century. A history of modernity and of urbanism, of flight and light and speed. A history of the future. Bringing together work by some of the most influential artists and writers of recent times, this publication offers a wide-ranging overview of arguably the most important new buildings of the twentieth-century.

During the last three decades, the popular image of the airport has altered considerably. Less the glamorous way-stations of an earlier romantic Air Age and more the functional hubs of an era of mass air travel, airports are now an established part of our contemporary physical and cultural landscape — so familiar and so frequently used (by massively escalating numbers of people) as to be virtually anonymous. Look more closely, however, and airports take on a much more interesting aspect: most notably for the way in which they seem to encapsulate so much of the texture of modern existence. Harbingers of increasing globalisation, temples to the gods of Mammon, Progress and Speed, symbols of a new-found personal freedom and mobility (as well as a creeping rootlessness and anxiety), airports are both a launching-pad and a meeting-point for many of the cultural and technological forces that are shaping the world in which we live today.

In 1967, the French philosopher Michel Foucault was invited by a group of architects to produce 'a study in space' and on March 14 of that year delivered a lecture in Paris entitled 'Des Espaces autres'. (It was published in the journal *Diacritics* in 1986 under the title 'Of Other Spaces'.) In this paper, Foucault made reference to spaces which, although sharing some of the concepts of a utopia, are 'real' and not 'imaginary' spaces. He called these spaces 'heterotopias':

> There are also, probably in every culture, in every civilisation, real places — places that do exist and that are formed in the very founding of society — which are something like counter-sites, a kind of effectively enacted utopia in which the real sites, all the other real sites that can be found in the culture, are simultaneously represented, contested and inverted. Places of this kind are outside of all places, even though it may be possible to indicate their location in reality.

In the intervening 30 years, it is the modern airport which has most closely come to fit Foucault's original description. Within their own borders, airports can often seem to resemble miniature utopias: realising our age-old dreams of flight; bringing people of all nations closer together; or, in their brightly-lit shopping arcades, promoting international capital's enduring illusion of an earthly consumer paradise.
Yet, whatever their loftier aspirations, airports are, for most of the time, grounded in mundane reality — struggling with rising passenger numbers, daunting schedules, occasionally malfunctioning technology. More than anything else, it is this basic ambiguity that most accurately distinguishes them — castles in the air that have never quite managed to escape the banalities of the world below.

Architecturally and geographically, airports also inhabit a strange kind of in-between space. Often located outside the city in the suburbs (in French, the *banlieue* — literally, places of banishment), like the out-of-town shopping malls with which they are often compared, the airport has been cited in numerous academic and architectural texts as a model for a radically new kind of social space. Lacking resident populations, and unable to put down traditional urban roots, airports have come to possess a correspondingly ghostly, liminal quality; as much a 'place' as a 'non-place'; simultaneously Everywhere and Nowhere.

This point is made, in typically witty and acerbic fashion, by Douglas Coupland in his short essay 'Hubs' reprinted here, and is further elaborated in Marc Augé's seminal *Non-Places: Introduction to an Anthropology of Supermodernity*. Coupland deftly captures the absurdities of that uniquely artificial creation, the airport hub: a 'no-place' in the middle of nowhere; 'the most metaphysically non-existent locale ever dreamt up'.

The featured extract from Augé's book records a fictional character's passage through the airport; his diary-like impressions highlighting the fleeting, fragmentary nature of this prime example of the modern 'non-place'.
In some ways, Augé's piece sets the tone for our own short contributions: Steven Bode's a series of elliptical airport observations; Jeremy Millar's a Möbius strip of text which loops back on itself in order to explore the circular nature of airport time.

The airport may be a 'non-place' but it is in no way a neutral one. Rather it is deeply encoded with meanings reflecting the orthodoxies and relationships of power. Martha Rosler's long essay 'In the Place of the Public' — brimming with amusing and polemical insights — is especially acute on the extent to which the disorientating experience of air travel and the transitory nature of the airport environment have profoundly altered our perception of public and social space. John Thackara, too, in a newly updated version of a talk given in 1994, employs a formidable array of statistics to examine the reasons airports look and perform as they do. While celebrating the airport's place as one of the few remaining outlets for grand-scale architectural innovation, Thackara also laments a dispiritingly utilitarian failure of imagination, arguing, in the end, for a new design grammar which better takes account of the complexity and interconnectedness of the modern world.

Paul Andreu, chief architect of Roissy–Charles de Gaulle airport in Paris (before the building of Japan's new Kansai International, many people's benchmark of the state-of-the-art in airport design), is well placed to discuss the creative challenges confronting architects and planners of airports today. His interview with Patrick Javault offers a fascinating behind-the-scenes insight into the design principles that animated what is still one of the most distinctive airport complexes ever built. His descriptions of the environment surrounding the airport are reminiscent of many of those to be found in the fiction of JG Ballard, in particular *Crash*, with its concrete ribbons woven around London Airport. The themes of technology, alienation and the future — so central to his influential fiction — are examined with explicit reference to the airport in 'The Ultimate Departure Lounge', a new piece of writing and one which we are honoured to include here.

The development of aviation during the early part of this century had an enormous influence on the Western imagination, particularly that of the modernist avant-garde. Pablo Picasso, Georges Braque, and Robert and Sonia Delauney were among the many artists, poets and intellectuals who visited the airfield at Issey-les-Moulineaux to watch, awestruck, some of the earliest flights. Kasimir Malevich announced that, 'If all artists were to comprehend these monstrous runways and intersections of our bodies with the clouds in the heavens, then they would not paint chrysanthemums'.

FT Marinetti's first *Futurist Manifesto* was published shortly after the success of Wilbur Wright's flights in France and Marinetti dedicated his 1909 play, *Poupées électriques*, to the American aviator. Marinetti also held 'Aero-banquets' in Chiavari and in Bologna, while his 1932 Futurist Cookbook, contained a number of flight-related recipes, such as 'Aero-food' (olives, fennel, kumquats, sandpaper, silk and velvet), 'Veal Fuselage' (veal, chestnuts, onions and sausages, all sprinkled with chocolate) and 'Piquant Airport' (salad, orange, egg, fruit, anchovies and sardines). It is perhaps best not to imagine being served any of these creations at 35,000 feet.

If, during this period, flight and the airfield were seen as sources of inspiration for artists, then more recently the compliment has been repaid. Many major airports now have schemes to commission pieces from artists especially for their buildings. Like the airports themselves, the art produced can prove mundane; however, intelligent and engaging work is being created for these potentially difficult environments, particularly at London's Heathrow, Schiphol in Amsterdam and Arlanda in Stockholm, and some of their commissioned projects have been included here. At Heathrow, an installation by Julian Opie continues his exploration of the natural environment within technological culture, his lightboxes attempting to sell us an idealised, yet utterly sterile, view of the rural idyll.

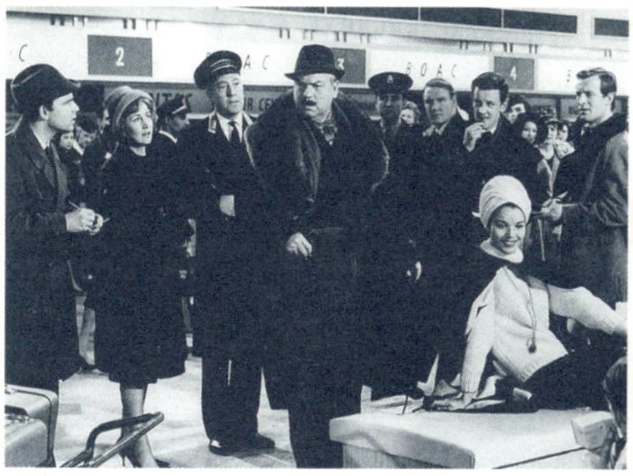
0.01

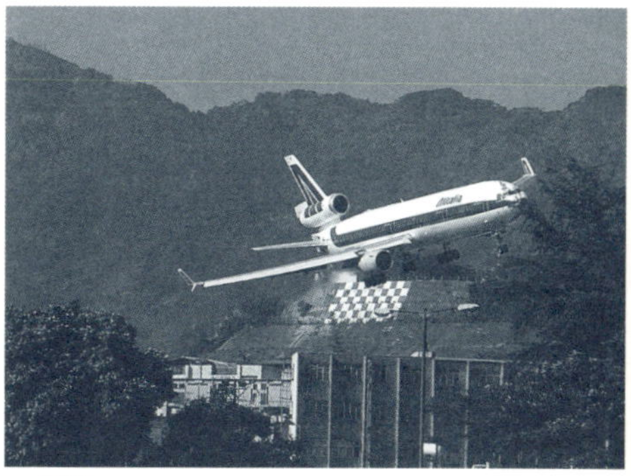
0.02

0.01 Still from *The VIPs* (Anthony Asquith, 1963)

0.02 Alitalia MD-11, on final approach to Kai Tak Airport, Hong Kong (photograph by Robbie Shaw)

Previous pages: Aerial view of Chek Lap Kok Terminal Building, Hong Kong, May 1997, courtesy of Airphoto International Ltd and Foster Asia.

As both John Thackara and Martha Rosler point out, the airport is not only a place to visit, it is also a place of work, a fact which has led to the decision of BAA's Art Programme to create a new series of portrait commissions. Both the work of Karen Eslea and Gabriella Sancisi explore the question of personal identity within a highly-regulated and controlled environment: Sancisi's sitters are placed before a backdrop showing their colour-coded level of access while in Eslea's portraits, we are caught by the eyes of security staff working in Terminal 1, their presence diffuse yet their observation intense.

At Amsterdam's Schiphol airport, the texts of Jenny Holzer, scrolling up a vertical LED display, are illustrative of the information which saturates our public spaces, even under our feet thanks to Niek Kemps' video monitors. While Dennis Adams' *Coda* may take its pattern from the aeronautical signal for an obstruction, it provides a useful place for people to meet, while waiting of a very different kind is the subject of Marijke van Warmedam's large-scale video projection on the platform of Schiphol's railway station, a strangely mesmerising exploration of slowness and the passage of time.

If Arlanda's art programme appears less monumental, it is no less interesting. Here, smaller temporary interventions are made into the space of the airport, from Karl-Johan Stigmark's ice-cream words kept in freezer cabinets within the terminal building to Christer Egström, John Håkansson and Jyrki Siikanen placing traditional mittens onto the rails behind which people wait for their loved ones to emerge from the chicane of Customs channels. Elsewhere in the building, the erotic is merged with the exotic in Susanne Björkman's *Pleasant Journey*, where a pornographic dot-to-dot drawing has been overlaid upon a world map, each dot now also providing a key to some of the world's many airports.

Perhaps the most radical art programme was developed in the late 1960s by the late American artist Robert Smithson for the Dallas–Fort Worth Airport. Smithson was an important figure in the development of what has become known as 'Land Art', art which was not simply made about landscape but which was made *in* the landscape, *using* the landscape.

The three other artists which Smithson selected for inclusion in this programme — Sol LeWitt, Robert Morris and Carl Andre — were also exploring similar issues of artistic production, issues which were mirrored in the construction of the airport itself. Here was an attempt, on the part of the architects and developers, to make space intelligible, to give it meaning, a process in which the artists wished to participate, rather than wait for its completion. Yet while the airport was completed, sadly the artists' projects were not. Smithson himself was denied the opportunity to create his *Wandering Earth Mounds and Gravel Paths*, although his essay, 'Towards the Development of an Air Terminal Site', first published in *Artforum* thirty years ago and reprinted here, is just as inspired, uncompromising and almost certainly more durable.

With the increased internationalism of the contemporary art market, many of today's successful artists no longer have to make special journeys to the airport. Travelling from a biennale here to a retrospective there, for some the airport lounge can seem almost as familiar as their studio interior. This is certainly true of Peter Fischli and David Weiss, whose early interests in the passage of 'dead time' are well-served by the terminal environment.
The photographs included here were taken during these periods of waiting and they share with it an ambiguous sense of time, a time that is mostly banal, yet which can contain moments of beauty.

The same is also true of Stephen Gill's photographs — which like a number of the images featured in this publication are also included in the touring *Airport* exhibition. Here are spaces which are at once alienating and predictable — 'dead spaces' for 'dead time' — yet which contain the potential for movement, and the potential to move us.

Although Frits Rotgans' photographs were commissioned as stock commercial images by airlines and the airport itself, his work contains more than these immediate requirements. At once studiously controlled and visually exciting, his images document the birth of the commercial jet-age, an age when international air-travel was more about the experience of glamour than clamour. Andreas Gursky may share similar formal and technical concerns with Rotgans — large colour negatives and an almost fetishistic quest for detail — yet his images betray a more familiar relationship with the airport environment. His photograph of Schiphol, of empty windows framing empty space, contains little of the excitement of Rotgans'. Even the centrifugal walkways at Charles de Gaulle no longer move us as they once did. The airport's fascination can no longer be found in its newness, and must reside elsewhere.

As we hurtle on towards the end of the century, airports are poised at a pivotal point in their history. Now their novelty has faded, we have even started to question their once-unchallenged place in the vanguard of modern development. In Great Britain, at least, environmental protests over Manchester's second runway, uncertainty over Heathrow's Terminal 5, as well as the cumulative toll of noise, pollution, traffic and the ever-present threat of terrorism, have all tarnished their aura, just as the incessant jet-blasts of millions of take-offs and landings have blighted their once-futurist architecture. However, airports are here to stay — there is (often quite literally) no getting away from them. The developed world is embarked on a journey from which there is no baling out or turning back. For anyone remotely interested in exactly where we might be heading — architecturally, technologically or culturally — the airport is still an essential port-of-call.

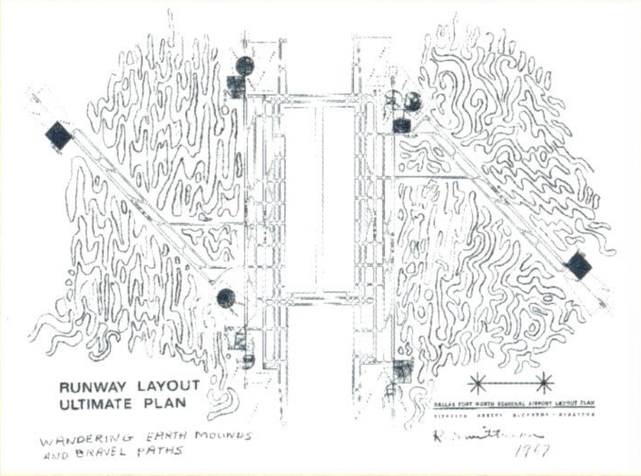

0.05

0.03 Bombed TWA airliner in Athens, April 1986.

0.04 Police storm hijacked All Nippon Airways 747 at Kakodate Airport, Japan, 22 June 1995.

0.05 Robert Smithson, *Wandering Earth Mounds and Gravel Paths,* 1967

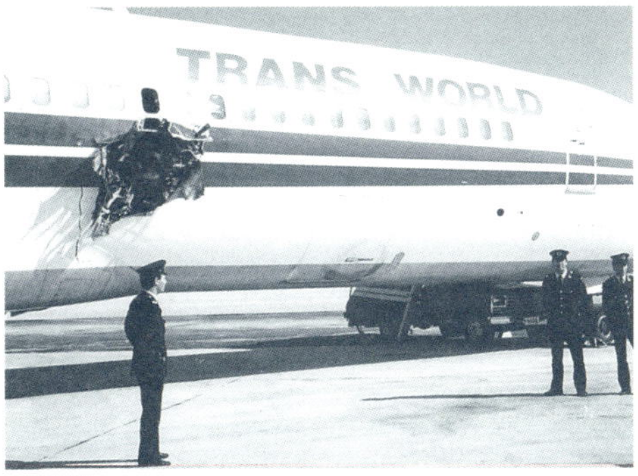

0.03

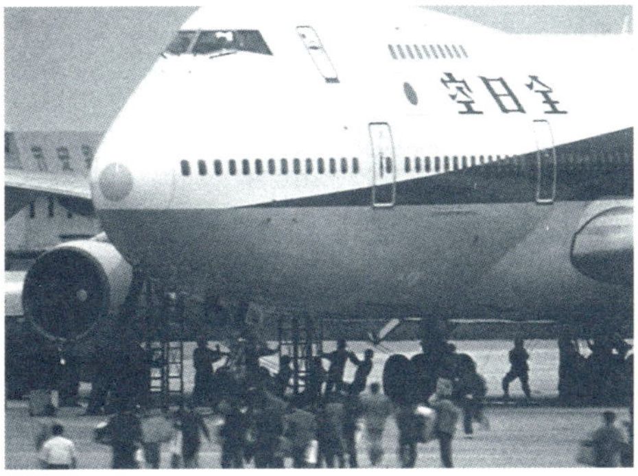

0.04

1997

Lost in Space — A Traveller's Tale

058/069

John Thackara

Lost in Space – A Traveller's Tale

John Thackara

1997

In 1994 I received an invitation from Lumiance, the Dutch lighting company, to deliver a one-hour set-piece lecture on 'the design subject of my choice'. Unlike previous lecturers in the series, I was not an architect or designer; neither was I running an innovative manufacturing company; so I did not have a portfolio of beautiful products or buildings with which to dazzle my audience. Making a virtue out of necessity, I elected not to talk about objects, or things, at all. I felt that the design of processes was just as important an issue — particularly when they bring people and technology into contact with each other. I decided to talk about airports, air travel, and the whole strange business of flying around the world.

As well as being thresholds between land and air, modern airports are gateways to complexity. Through them, we enter the operating environment of global aviation, surely mankind's most complicated creation. But in airports, although we are isolated from the rhythms of the natural world, we remain ignorant of how this artificial one works. The result is to reinforce what philosophers call our ontological alienation: a sense of rootlessness and anxiety; of not quite being real; of being… lost in space.

Aviation is typical in many respects of the way the whole world is going: saturated with information and systems; complex but incomprehensible; an exhilarating human achievement and a terrifying prospect at the same time. It's time design got to grips with these ambiguous features of our technological society. But I'll return to these broader issues at the end.

Right now, I want to focus on three design questions: why does air travel makes you feel strange? what can design do to improve the experience? and why go in person, when you can call? I believe answers to these three questions can be found by looking at the ways that different kinds of space affect the way we think and feel. The first is architectural space, a familar enough concept which is sufficiently mainstream nowadays to command generous coverage in newspapers and on television. Then there is aviation space, the 'operating environment' within which airports, airplanes, electronic signals, and people, interact with each other continuously on a global scale. Typical airport plans, of the kind you would find in an architect's office, say almost nothing about the quality of our interaction with these intangible systems and processes. I will then compare these first two kinds of space to a third, telematic space, the space of electronic communications, where all that's whizzing around is information.

In order to explain the strange way we feel when travelling by air, and the impact on us of airport and aviation space, I need to explain a bit about the aviation system as a whole, which determines what architects would call the 'programme' of an individual airport building.

Since 1993, the world's airlines carried more than one billion passengers on scheduled flights every year. That's equivalent to one sixth of the world's population. Airlines also carried 22 million tons of freight last year — almost a quarter of the total value of the world's manufactured exports. It took something like 12 million aircraft departures to carry such stupendous quantities of people and goods around the world. These were to and from about 16,000 airports in the United States alone — perhaps 30,000 in the world? Nobody actually knows: no single organisation represents them all.

But the aviation system's earthbound infrastructure is as nothing compared to the complexity of its operating environment, or aviation space. The aviation system, of which airports are one component, is distributed not just in space, but also in time. Airports exist at the intersection of airways — the space through which aircraft pass — which are densely criss-crossed, in three spatial dimensions and at different times, by the routes planes are flying, did fly, and will fly.

Aviation space is also saturated with electronic information from humans and machines, chattering out directions to thousands of aircrew — and onboard computers — at any one moment. The fact that people — passengers, aircrew, ground staff, air traffic controllers and the like — are part of the system, too, means that when it comes to complex environments, forget the banks and dealing rooms that feature so prominently on television as symbols of modern space: airports are by far the most advanced 'smart buildings' on earth.

Expansion of the system, and in particular the rate of building of new airports, is staggering. Compound growth in air travel and transport of six per cent or more has a profound impact on the phenomenology of air travel — the vague sensation that these huge flows of people and matter and information are increasing in volume and power all the time.

Once a year, *Airports International* magazine lists hundreds of new airport projects around the world. Many are in places I, for one, have never heard of — exotic towns spending untold sums on new facilities. No single world body is responsible for the aviation system as a whole. There are airlines — thousands of them: the breakup of Aeroflot produced 800 new ones in the URSS! Then there are all sorts of operators and managers of airports — some local, some national. There are supranational air traffic control bodies, but they have an uphill struggle integrating national systems. Nobody is co-ordinating this phenomenal expansion of the world's aviation hardware. It's just happening.

This stupendous investment of money and materials is not the consequence of an integrated plan to manage increasing traffic: it is a potent combination of politics and markets. Economically, aviation growth is a visceral response by the market to apparently limitless demand. Airports have become economic and political touchstones against which cities and regions measure their status in the world. In post-Cold War Europe more than 300 emerging cities or regional entities are competing with each other to attract increasingly mobile capital and jobs. For them — and for hundreds of other cities and regions around the world — an airport has become a strategic priority.

The biggest international airports and major hubs — the United States alone has 30 — are like giant pumps that greatly increase flow through the whole system. And costs are phenomenal on those places which try to keep up. A single 747-capacity runway can cost \$200m; an international passenger terminal ranges from \$100 million upwards. Once road and rail links, baggage handling systems, air traffic control systems and so on are factored in, the capital cost of an international airport quickly exceeds a billion dollars. Japan's new Kansai airport cost \$15 billion — insofar as anyone actually knows the full amount, or is prepared to say.

The ground traffic generated by all those workers, passengers, well-wishers, cab drivers and so on, is equally enormous. Los Angeles International generates more than 150,000 vehicle trips daily in and out of the central terminal area alone — excluding long-stay car parks, warehouses, nearby hotels and their suppliers. For planners, it's like designing a traffic system for a city with more than half a million inhabitants.

Airports also have huge workforces. Frankfurt airport, whose workforce is well over 40,000, is the biggest employer in the whole of Germany. London Heathrow, in order to handle more than 1,000 airliner movements a day, employs 55,000 people directly — meteorologists, air traffic controllers, pilots, cabin crew, cleaners, caterers, check-in staff, baggage handlers, engineers, firemen, police, security guards. Heathrow's staff numbers exclude more than 300,000 or more people employed by myriad suppliers. All those van drivers and sandwich makers. Airports are also the world's largest employers of dogs.

It is only because airports are multinational businesses in their own right that these sort of costs can be sustained. Indeed, commercial activity on the ground, not aircraft taking off and landing, is now one of the main drivers of airport design. Less than 50 per cent of Heathrow's earnings now come from landing fees or servicing aircraft. International transit passengers not flying spend an average of \$35 a head at Heathrow's hundreds of shops, restaurants, hairdressers — and four caviar bars. Heathrow is also the largest market for Havana cigars in the world — including Havana.

In the olden days, when airports were planned and operated as transport utilities — if only for an elite — engineers and operations people would have regarded an idle passenger as evidence of system inefficiency. Not today. Mobility is just one of the products on sale at a modern airport. So much so that to commercial managers, 'passenger discretionary time' — or 'dwell time' — the time spent by passengers killing time between flights, is a sales opportunity. Why else ask people to check in up to three hours before take-off?

The management of dwell-time to optimise commercial yield is one reason — traffic jams are another — that between 1950 and 1990, the proportion of time spent in the air by passengers on a journey has steadily decreased. As the transport economist John Whitelegg has observed, the amount of time each person devotes to travel is roughly the same regardless of how far or how fast they travel. Facilities are sited further apart, and people have to travel further to reach them than they did 70 years ago. 'Time is money, we are told, and increasing mobility is a way of saving time,' says Whitelegg, 'but how successful are modern transport systems at saving time?' If air travel is any guide the answer appears to be: not very much.

In fact, the faster we go, the less time we feel we have. Following on from the work of Ivan Illich, the German sociologist D. Seifried has coined the term 'social speed' to signify the average speed of a vehicle (and its passengers) after all sorts of hidden time costs are added in. So in addition to 'getting-to-the-airport' time — and dwell-time once you get there — Seifried reminds us about the time spent earning the money to go on the journey in the first place. Some urban designers have introduced the concept of time planning to take account of these hidden costs of travel.

Air travel purists, wedded to the fantasy that air travel denotes fast and efficient mobility, face worse disillusion ahead. London's Gatwick, for example, has developed a $40 million 'airport theme park' whose target is one million people a year — 'travellers' whose only destination is the airport itself.

Work space

Apart from shopping and 'leisure', airports are being used ever more intensively by businesses. Virtual corporations — companies that have forsaken headquarters buildings for a life on the road — are big users of airports. The growing amount of business carried out across national boundaries in the new economy has fuelled demand for meeting rooms, exhibition and showroom facilities, business centres and other non-travel-specific facilities — inside, next to, under and on top of most new airports. Airports have replaced science and business parks as the epicentre of business real estate.

These multiple programmes and agendas — operational, commercial, political — are one reason why writers have started talking about airports as cities — cities of the air. Both cities and airports cover large areas; both are a complex of intersecting transport systems, economies, buildings, and people. But there is one crucial difference: cities have inhabitants. At airports, everyone is transient. Herein lies one element of the airport's existential ambiguity.

The American writer Richard Sennett is particularly outraged that cities have become more like a pump for traffic than a place to live, and that planners can describe a local airport as a 'traffic-flow support nexus'. 'When public space becomes a derivative of movement,' says Sennett, 'it loses any independent experiential meaning of its own. On the most physical level, these environments of pure movement prompt people to think of the public domain as meaningless… It is catatonic space.'

Catatonic space

The word catatonic is horribly apt as a description of the way these great modern spaces make us feel. What is going on when they have this effect?

Any space, including artificial space, affects our minds and our bodies. But artificial environments shield us from phenomena like climate, and particularly daylight, whose cycles in the natural world expose us physically to the reality of constant change. In an optically static environment, like most airports, the body is physically de-sensitised from its sense of time.

In a brilliant essay called 'The Poetics of Light', the American architect Henry Plummer observed that 'our very sense of being is based on an experience of process, activity, and movement. We seem to find an image of our own existence in the changing lights of the natural world.' Moment-to-moment mutations of light also provide what the philosopher Henri Bergson called 'lived time' and Ernst Cassirer 'a consciousness of sequence'. I was reminded of this recently when, wandering slack-jawed around Anchorage airport en route to Japan, I accidentally stepped outside to an Alaskan night: it was literally like waking up from a dream. Startled by the cold, dank, spooky Alaskan air, I lost my bearings for a moment. Where was I? Luckily, a blast of noise and the warm embrace of kerosene fumes reminded me where I was. For a moment there, I could have been lost to nature.

Lived time, natural time, cold, dank, spooky Alaskan air time, stand in stark contrast to the so-called objective time of clocks and departure times at airports. According to the psychologist David Winnicott, loss of temporality is a feature of the psychotic and deprived individual, in which a person 'loses the ability to connect the past with the present'. The bridging of the present into the past, and into the future, is, says Winnicott, 'a crucial dimension of psychic integration and health'. So there you have it. Air travel, by scrambling your mind-and-body clock, creates the preconditions for psychosis. So that's another reason it makes you feel strange!

This will not come as dramatic news to architects. As far back as the 1930s, the celebrated Hawthorn Study analysed a connection between light and mental comfort; Hawthorn's work represents the pre-history of environmental psychology, an established branch of science for about 15 years now. It is to environmental psychologists that we owe the term 'sick building syndrome', and the development of so-called 'environmentally porous' new buildings. The smartest new structures now let fresh air and daylight in.

I have suggested thus far that the challenge posed by airports to architecture and design is threefold: the designer confronts contradictory operational and commercial agendas; s/he has to tackle the impact of artificial environments on our physical/mental state; and there is the problem of cognitive disorientation, of not understanding the system, on our mental/physical state.

The contradictory agendas of airport operators are by themselves an intractable problem facing architects and designers. Remarkably, the architect is one of the few people on earth — along with the planner and the economist — who grapples materially with the big picture, the totality of the aviation system. Almost everyone else tends to be a specialist in one bit of the system. But it is obvious, given these conflicting agendas, that the chances of an architect imposing a coherent design solution are small. I will return to the consequences of that in a moment.

The second problem — of artificial space which isolates us from natural rhythms — can be and is being tackled by letting in fresh air and daylight — just as almost any nineteenth-century parent, opening a child's window at night, would have known intuitively! Window manufacturers are making a huge song-and-dance out of the fact that their latest high-tech products, some of which are being used in airports, can actually be opened. Even where they remain sealed, letting in daylight is now a fully-blown fad in airport design.

The logic of movement

A spectacular example of this trend is Kansai International Airport in Japan which opened in 1994. It's a $15 billion phenomenon, described — even by the can-do Japanese — as 'an exceptional endeavour for the country'. To secure the 500 hectares needed for an airport with a projected capacity for 160,000 aircraft movements a year — in a country where 70 per cent of the land is occupied by mountains! — the airport was built on an artificial island. It's about 5km offshore from Osaka, where the average water depth at the site is 18.5m, with unstable clay underneath. Preparation of the site began in 1987, and involved driving one million sand piles into the seabed. They then built an 11km long seawall, which outlined the island. And filled the resulting hole with 164 million cubic metres of soil. It must have taken a lot of buckets and spades.

1.01 Route to observation hall, Kansai Airport, Customer Information Printout

1.02 Plan of Kansai Airport Island, Customer Information Printout

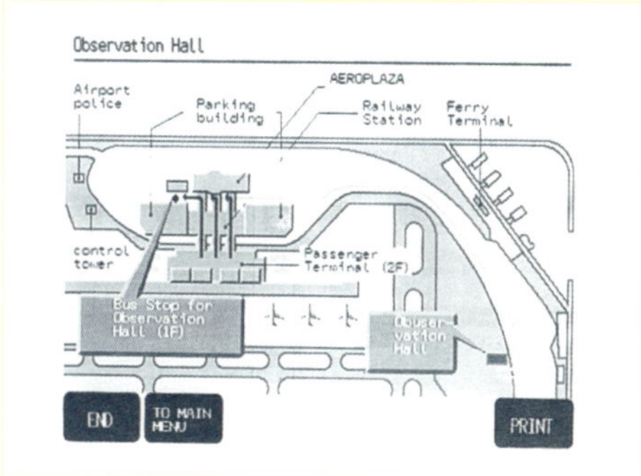

1.01

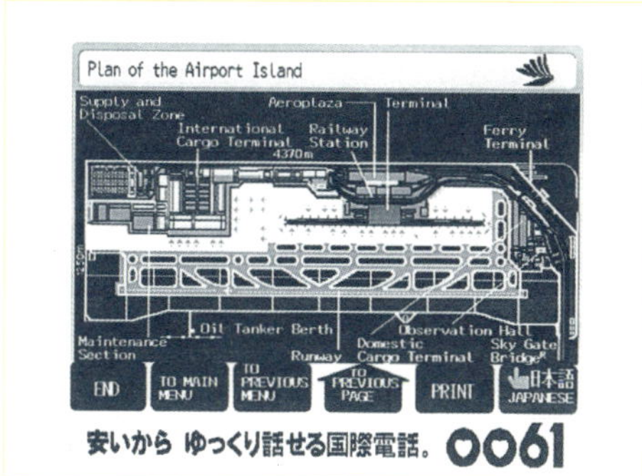

1.02

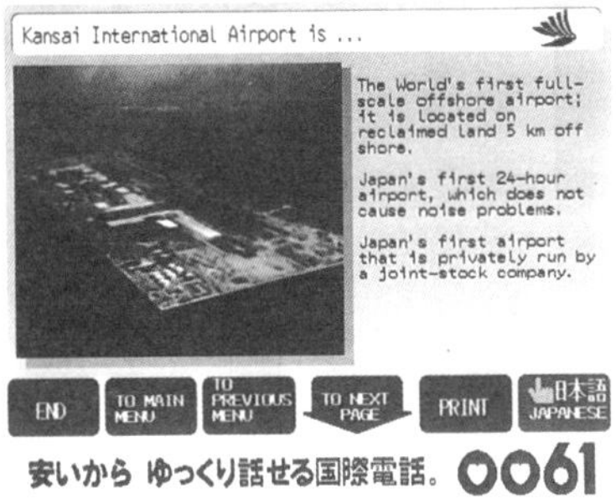
Kansai International Airport is ...

The World's first full-scale offshore airport; it is located on reclaimed land 5 km off shore.

Japan's first 24-hour airport, which does not cause noise problems.

Japan's first airport that is privately run by a joint-stock company.

END | TO MAIN MENU | TO PREVIOUS MENU | TO NEXT PAGE | PRINT | 日本語 JAPANESE

安いから ゆっくり話せる国際電話。0061

1.03

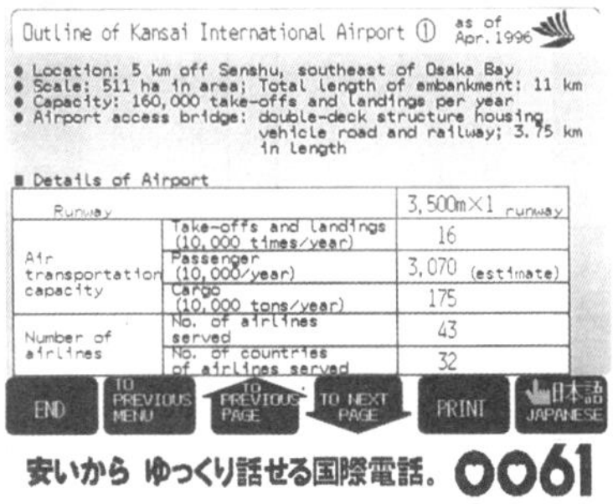
Outline of Kansai International Airport ① as of Apr. 1996

- Location: 5 km off Senshu, southeast of Osaka Bay
- Scale: 511 ha in area; Total length of embankment: 11 km
- Capacity: 160,000 take-offs and landings per year
- Airport access bridge: double-deck structure housing vehicle road and railway; 3.75 km in length

■ Details of Airport

Runway		3,500m×1 runway
Air transportation capacity	Take-offs and landings (10,000 times/year)	16
	Passenger (10,000/year)	3,070 (estimate)
	Cargo (10,000 tons/year)	175
Number of airlines	No. of airlines served	43
	No. of countries of airlines served	32

END | TO PREVIOUS MENU | TO PREVIOUS PAGE | TO NEXT PAGE | PRINT | 日本語 JAPANESE

安いから ゆっくり話せる国際電話。0061

1.04

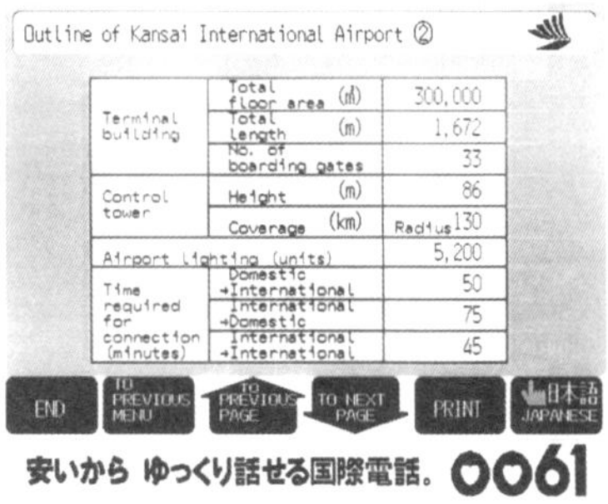
Outline of Kansai International Airport ②

Terminal building	Total floor area (㎡)	300,000
	Total length (m)	1,672
	No. of boarding gates	33
Control tower	Height (m)	86
	Coverage (km)	Radius 130
Airport lighting (units)		5,200
Time required for connection (minutes)	Domestic →International	50
	International →Domestic	75
	International →International	45

END | TO PREVIOUS MENU | TO PREVIOUS PAGE | TO NEXT PAGE | PRINT | 日本語 JAPANESE

安いから ゆっくり話せる国際電話。0061

1.05

1.03 Kansai Airport is… Customer Information Printout

1.04 Outline of Kansai International Airport 01, Customer Information Printout

1.05 Outline of Kansai International Airport 02, Customer Information Printout

Meanwhile, Renzo Piano, working with engineers Ove Arup and partners, won an international competition for the 300,000m^2 terminal. The central concept, the geometry of the main roof, was inspired by the design of an airflow, and developed by reference to fractal geometry. Renzo Piano believes that an 'air terminal should be structured as a diagram of the people moving through it. The entire building — structure, light and air movement — should complement the logic of passenger movement.' To its credit, the airport has also segregated commercial activities on another level, allowing passengers more or less uninterrupted access from landside to airside. With a main span of 82.5m, long main beams over the 300m main halls will afford travellers the pleasure of being part of a moving throng in a great space. The roof is airy and uncluttered and full of light. The design allows people to experience a drama of changing space, light and sights; familiarity intermixed, as the jury report put it, with 'bold revelations of the future'. Passengers arriving from the mainland will enter a great 'canyon' — the interface between nature and the machine — that is some 25m wide and 300m long.

At their first briefing meeting, Piano's team was presented with a 2,000 page summary of the technical briefing. As legend has it, the great man ceremoniously threw this $50 million document in the trashbin — if only to make the point that he needed to start with, and hold onto, a clear design concept. The details could be worked out later. Amazingly, the design concept survived a vast, fast, multi-billion dollar programme more or less intact — although even the Japanese ran out of money towards the end and had to trim the 'wings' of Piano's masterpiece by about half, pending later expansion.

Kansai successfully emerged as an architecturally coherent building. But the opportunity to build a new island, built on millions of sand-piles, and to spend $10 billion, is not an option for most airport developers in the world. So the third design problem I want to discuss — the cognitive dissonance that comes from being a rootless monad in an opaque system — is likely to remain pervasive in airports around the world unless new design strategies are developed.

Countless modern writers, from Karl Marx to Baudelaire to Richard Sennett, have written about the alienation you feel in modern cities. Urban anxiety is part of our culture — *Blade Runner*; MTV videos of wild creatures singing songs amidst burned-out cars; the lurid urban advertising used by law-and-order politicians during elections. All these media use urban angst as their backdrop. But psychologists have only recently addressed the phenomenon. They have now discovered the importance of what they call 'situated understanding' — a phrase of Hubert Dreyfus — the fact that having a clear mental picture of an artificial environment contributes to mental health.

When it comes to giving us a 'clear mental picture' of our environment, architecture has not exactly excelled itself in recent years: in most airports one is situated in a box — and it feels like it. After a pre-history involving utilitarian brick buildings on the edge of fields, airports once seemed destined to become the architectural equivalent of modern cathedrals. Eero Saarinen's TWA terminal in New York had a particularly strong impact on the public imagination and became for many critics a symbol of modernity. But as Reyner Banham so memorably observed, the TWA terminal was obsolete before it even opened. Designed for fleets of propeller-driven Lockheed Constellations, by the time it opened the first jets — Comets and Boeing 707s — were in use and the terminal's airside had to be encrusted with jet-blast deflectors. Today, Saarinen's masterpiece at JFK has almost disappeared: you glimpse it every now and again, cowering between great lumpish buildings like a lost child in Times Square.

Planners, besieged by data, can't really help but think in terms of boxes. Boxes contain lots of space, can be packed together, and stack up nicely. And frankly, a well-made box is preferable to artworks like Roissy–Charles de Gaulle in Paris. This monument to system complexity looked stunning on paper — but turned out a nightmare to use. I must have been to Roissy 40 times; it's nice, as you glide down those capillary-like tunnels into the featureless aorta of the main building, to imagine oneself in a Jacques Tati movie. But I still have to think twice, and sometimes ask at Information, where to catch the railway shuttle.

Sim city without batteries

When complex systems are not hidden or disguised — for example in the vast, cathedral-like dealing rooms built by Japanese banks in the 1980s — the geometry and atmosphere of the space is determined by the technology, not by a designer. Architecture really doesn't have a language for unstable contexts of this kind — still less for ones like airports where large numbers of people, as well as data, are passing through. As the architect and critic Bernard Tschumi points out in *Architecture and Disjunction*, 'three thousand years of architectural ideology have tried to assert that architecture is about stability, solidity, foundation, when it is the very opposite: like modern scientific knowledge, buildings are constantly on the verge of change'. And as Donald Schon put it in *The Reflective Practitioner* back in 1971, 'design is now increasingly taking place beyond the stable state'.

Beyond the stable state

Some architects have at least acknowledged the problem that confronts buildings and urban spaces in an era of speed and change. The Dutch architect Rem Koolhaas talks about the 'incoherence or, more precisely, randomness that is the underlying structure of all architects' careers. They are confronted by an arbitrary sequence of demands — parameters they did not establish, in countries they hardly know, about issues they are only dimly aware of.' We have dismantled urbanism, says Koolhaas, leaving only architecture —'more and more substance is grafted on starving roots'.

The trouble is that although Koolhaas the critic understands the problem, Koolhaas the architect can't do much about it. An extremely macho 'hundred crane man' during construction of Euro-Lille in France (quantities of cranes are a measure of how big a building project is) his project celebrates space, change and movement but does virtually nothing to to give passers-through a cognitive sense of place. You feel like one of those tiny humanoid figures architects use to decorate their models — sleek, but blind.

Signs of the times

Some airport managers do try out new tools and techniques to make complex space more inhabitable. Schiphol in Amsterdam, for example, installed a large Jenny Holzer artwork in one particularly vapid void. Cryptic words and phrases flow up and down the 20 metre-high stack of digital displays all day long. Jenny Holzer's use of typography and digital displays has a particular resonance for anyone contemplating the notion of 'semiotic pollution' in the sheer volume of information swirling around us. I guess these are the first artists to have spent a lot of their lives staring at departure boards. But this large, strong, clearly-conceived and subversive object is pitiful in the context of Schiphol as a whole. Phenomenologically, it is inert. It is powerless to communicate amidst the silent roar of people, movement and information that pervades the airport.

Cartography also fails in such contexts. Maps represent one of the fundamental tools by which we make sense of the world; as cartographic historian Stephen Hall has explained, 'they mediate between an inner mental world, and an outer physical world, of which the map-reader may have no direct experience'. By that definition, maps should be an excellent antidote to the cognitive fog that surrounds us in vast artificial environments such as an airport. And it is true that the best maps and charts do inform you where you stand in relation to the whole. But what they do not do is convey a sense of movement, of flow, of process — which is the experiential reality that you are aware of, but cannot see, in places like airports.

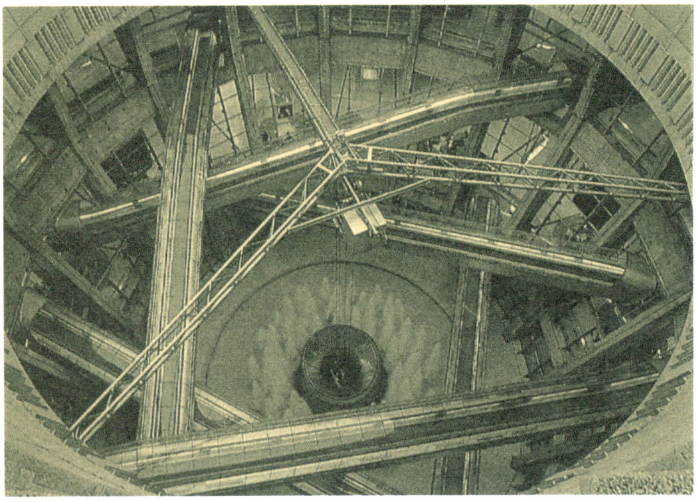

1.06
Construction of moving walkways,
Roissy – Charles de Gaulle, Terminal 01

It is not the role of signs, either, to reveal the fundamental structure of a system. Their role is to control and optimise flow, to induce your movement in a particular direction at a particular time. They are the graphic design equivalent, for humans, of the metal strips on the floor that robots follow blindly around automated factories. Don't get me wrong. I love good signs. When I arrive back at Schiphol from any other airport in the world (except possibly for the new bits of Frankfurt, whose Grundig digital signs are also beautiful). I get real pleasure from the sheer design quality of the banks of video information screens, and those large yellow signs. If one is going to be processed by a system, better to be processed by an elegant, even beautiful system than by a bad one.

But I return to my point that neither maps, which are representation, nor signs, which issue instructions, can help us understand the system as a whole. Visual displays to explain complex processes do exist — the French make particularly beautiful ones for their nuclear power stations; and the Japanese make wonderful, high-resolution digital displays for banks and dealing rooms that are a sheer pleasure to watch — but neither airport operators nor architects seem have thought about presenting information to the public using new media in a creative way.

Slow space

The same cannot be said of artists. Throughout the twentieth century artists have intervened in a variety of ways into man-made space: futurism, cubist collage, Duchamp's readymades, Dada, constructivism, surrealism, Fontana's 'spatialism', 'happenings', Fluxus, land art, arte povera, process art, conceptualism. These groups and ideas all confronted the movement, energy, dynamism, and sheer process-ness that modern man encounters in the modern places we have made. They treated the deadness and catatonia of modern public space both as a rebuke and a challenge. Their aim has been twofold: to create reflective, liminal or 'slow' space on the one hand; and to animate space, to give it a narrative content, on the other.

In recent years a new generation of media artists has emerged with new tools and new ideas. Jeffrey Shaw's piece *Legible City*, for example, is a quite remarkable idea: the participant bicycles down 'virtual streets' where instead of buildings, you pass words. Shaw worked with a writer on the project, and together they created a template for the words based on the grid and actual buildings of Manhattan. If you turn a corner, you move from one narrative — or sentence — into another one. Keiici Irie, one of the most brilliant of the new young architects in Japan, used sound to animate and delineate space in a project called *Movable Realities* in which you passed through 'cones' of sound, each of which plays a different sound sequence.

Again, in a show called *T-Zone* which we did together in London and Glasgow, Irie created 10m high slabs of glass behind which were video cameras which captured your picture as you walked past and replayed them with a delay, on small monitors. In Glasgow we had to turn the thing off because the frequencies were interfering with air traffic control at Glasgow Airport. (Just in case you were wondering what possible connection this had with airports!)

Another Japanese artist, Toshio Iwai, who designs games for Nintendo and installations for the Group Of Seven summit, intervenes in space with crisp, evocative and visceral combinations of computers, projectors and various interfaces. I do not mean to be over-literal about this, but one could at least imagine an enriched design scenario for airports which combined the latest mapping and computerised cartography with the spatial sensibility of the best artists, and simply bring the places to life.

Let me remind you of the three questions I posed at the beginning: why does air travel makes you feel so strange? how might design improve the experience? why go in person, when you can call?

My reason for mentioning media artists followed my reluctant conclusion, concerning question two, that architecture and design by themselves lack the motivation and the tools to improve our experience of airport space. My thought was that perhaps different specialisms, like cartography or media art, might be able to add a new dimension to the articulation of these spaces.

The trouble is, I'm not completely naive: it's highly unlikely that airports and their design can be influenced in such interesting ways — let alone by artists. Some enlightened airport operators do try to make their facilities cleaner, easier to use, more humane. Schiphol exemplifies this. Sometimes they even hang art on walls, or put sculptures in the concourses. But apart from the fact that most concourses are semiotically stronger than most art, this is not really the point. The fundamental logic of airports — their basic 'operating software' — is to process passengers, not to enlighten them. Even Schiphol suffers gravely from the fact that no person, and no team, is responsible for the perceptual integrity of the airport as a whole.

Greedy space

But there's another, quite different reason why my contemplation of radical design scenarios for airports ran out of steam. Aviation as a whole is already far too greedy a consumer of energy — and space. If we are serious about striving towards a sustainable world economy, and given population and other trends, we have to increase the energy- and matter-efficiency with which we live on this planet by a factor of 20. Getting a bit better each year will not be enough. In this rather daunting context, there's no way our world can afford the continued mad growth of aviation. If we are serious about a sustainable economy then aviation will have to contract.

It sounds implausible, but consider this: matter is more expensive than energy; energy is more expensive than information. It is almost infinitely cheaper to move information than people or things. So why not fly less, and communicate more? Hence my third and final point: the telematic alternative. Rather than try to 'cure' the alienating effects of airports — for example, by radical artistic intervention into airport space — should we not be looking for alternative ways to achieve the same ends as air travel, without the obscene consumption of energy that we now know aviation entails? Hence my third question: why go in person when you can call?

From aviators to avatars

Despite all the hoopla about highways of the mind, the capacity of information and communication technology to recreate what it's like to be in a meeting with people somewhere else is a long way off. A lot of the whizzier demonstrations you see or hear about are either faked, or cost $10,000 an hour. But whether or not the technology will actually deliver distant verisimilitude now, or later, is not the main point. Existing forms of communication already deliver perfectly satisfactory results to billions of people everyday. POTS they call it in the trade — or 'Plain Old Telephone Service'.

If the aim of air travel were simply to exchange information, then we wouldn't bother doing it. The trouble is — to state the obvious — that's not why we do it. It's that mind-body business again: experientially, there never will be an alternative to actually 'being there'. Now I know that — and you know that — but the terrifying thing is that the world's telecommunications companies don't appear to know that. On the contrary: they're spending vast amounts of money in the search for systems and networks that will reproduce as closely as possible the sensation of 'being there'.

At Germany's huge GMD national computer laboratories, for example, one team has harnessed together a row of super-fast Thinking Machines computers in order to increase the perceptual depth of its 'virtual conference room'. GMD's idea is to recreate, as closely as possible, the experience of sitting round a conference table — only with the people opposite you being located in different parts of the world. Most major TelCos are engaged in similar experiments — mindless to the fact that most of us find real meetings, let alone virtual ones, futile enough.

Skip Ishii, a researcher at Japan's NTT, is a leading critic of Being There-ness as the strategic aim of TelCos. Ishii points out that the human eye has something like 40 million receptors in it. Many millions more receptors are to be found in our ears, up our noses, in our skin and on our tongues. So even if you could capture the smells, sounds, tastes and feel of a place, digitise them, and send them down a wire — you'd still never get near the sensation of Being There. Why? Because we humans are not so dumb. Our minds and our bodies are one intelligence. We'd just know, that's why.

So why bother trying? Well, there's big business in all this. Assuming, as the industry does, that two billion people will be flying annually by 2005, and that 20 per cent of that number will be travelling on business, as forecasters predict; that's 400 million business travellers who might be persuaded — or told by their boss — to take the superhighway of the mind instead of flying.

As a matter of fact, this is already happening. Sales of video-conferencing equipment and services in the United States climbed from $350 million in 1992 to $7 billion in 1997— and the graph continues to rise. But the real growth is in the Internet, and there the graphs are not shooting upwards for the reasons the TelCos imagine.
The geometric explosion in usage of the Internet is despite the fact that it is actually rather difficult to use, and is many years away from 'Being There' verisimilitude. Most of what you send or receive is boring old text. Visual trickery will come: as we have seen, industry is busy developing high-bandwidth networked computer graphics and real-time simulators. But funnily enough, the prospect of virtual reality 'coming true' is not what is turning on one million new Internet subscribers a month, now. Simulation, per se, has already lost its allure.

No. What drives the explosion in Internet usage is something else, a new quality to existing communication, the quality of connectivity.

Connectivity is the capacity of the communication networks to connect everything and everyone, to everything and everyone else. Unlike the telephone, whose great advantage is its intimacy as a medium — you use the phone, but you don't think about it — the Internet very positively conveys the idea of shared communication space. So although the engineers and bandwidth junkies will continue their quest for 'Being There' verisimilitude, the more interesting task for design is to enhance the communication quality of cyberspace by more artful and indirect means.

The promise of proxemity

To give you a flavour of what this might involve, let me tell you about a project called *The Poetics of Telepresence* which the Netherlands Design Institute did with two English designers, Tony Dunne and Fiona Raby. Their idea, which was to look at the effect of fusing physical and telematic space, was inspired by the obscure (outside Umberto Eco books) social science of proxemics. Proxemics looks at how different spatial relationships — standing close, standing apart, eavesdropping — change the whole tenor of the way we communicate. Dunne and Raby extrapolated from these findings to ask: why should video-conferencing always be face-to-face? They developed scenarios in which each person sits inside a box in which the weather in the other person's country is represented, and listens to the person's voice. They also asked, why limit contact to speech or sight? We could use radio to trigger heat devices remotely, or to emit smoke or smells. (I particularly liked the idea of a 'hot air button' on my telephone, so I could politely let the person at the other end know she or he was talking nonsense.) Temperature is highly evocative of the body: to recreate an intimate atmosphere of co-presence for a call, why not make the area warm?

The big telecom companies emphasise 'purposive' communication — exemplified by all those ghastly television advertisements with dynamic business persons doing deals on their mobile telephones. But a lot of the most important communication is informal, accidental, and happens by chance. In the brain, intense activity takes place in liminal parts of the cortex that nobody understands, but which we know are important.

In offices, the water cooler or coffee machine tends to be more important than the boardroom as a communication nexus; so why not create similar reflexive spaces and street-corner moments in cyberspace? Dunne and Raby came up with ideas whereby telecommunications might allow you to 'bump into' people in distant spaces.

New ways by which people might be represented in telematic space include the use of 'avatars'; these are images or symbols (the word has origins in Hinduism) which either literally or metaphorically represent a particular person. Microsoft have an avatar team whose experiments include Miro-like squiggles that co-habit so-called chat-spaces with others of their (i.e. our) kind. An English team is developing 3D whole-body scanners that will be installed rather like passport photo-booths in public spaces. Having digitised your body, you will be able to send it out on the Internet on your behalf where it will meet and hang out with other avatars.

Speed is God; Time is the devil

The thing about air travel is that it affords you the illusion of compressing space and time. But, as John Urry has observed, 'speed turns nature into landscape' — and we have no real idea what this unprecedented explosion in mobility and telecommunications portends. It took centuries for information about the smelting of iron ore to cross a single continent and bring about the Iron Age. During the time of sailing ships, it took years for knowledge and technologies to spread around the world. Just 100 years ago, 99 per cent of all people lived their lives within a 50 kilometre radius of where they were born.

All that has changed — and in a couple of generations. The telegraph and radio made it possible to deliver information point to point, simultaneously. Radio, television and satellite increased the communicational footprint. Now we have the Internet and World Wide Web and nobody really knows what the interaction of this new medium with the old ones will mean in the medium term for the nature and dynamics of knowledge.

We tend to scoff nowadays at nineteenth century medical experts who warned that the acceleration of life, and use of the telephone, would cause serious mental degeneration. We think it quaint that the word 'phoney' should derive from early descriptions of the communicative quality of telephones. But how sophisticated are we, really, today? We seldom step back and think critically about the aviation system as a whole, for example, preferring to pass our days either mindlessly passing through it — or working intensively on small bits of it: flying aircraft, managing passenger manifests, delivering canapes, designing avionics, staring at air traffic control screens. There are thousands more functions in the system, and millions of people work on them day and night. But aviation is so complex that we find it hard to grasp as a totality. Even social scientists hold back. They will wax indignant about the impact of television, or of the computer, but I have yet to hear a behavioural critique of aviation — even though aviation has transformed the way we experience 'here' and 'now' and 'there' and 'then'.

I set out to explore a common activity, flying, and to provoke you to look and think about it differently next time you do it. My proposition is that in the modern world — of which airports and air travel are a paradigm — ignorance is not bliss. We need new design languages, a grammar of complexity, to describe the contemporary world — not as it used to be, and not as the engineers would like us to see it, but as it actually is: a world of global computer and communication networks; of distributed intelligence; of interactivity; of connectivity.

In the seventeenth-century we were exposed by science to the fact that — to cut a long story short — the world is not flat. Today, to cut an even longer story even shorter, the world is more complicated than it used to be. But we made it, and we can still understand it. We have to, if we are to control it.

Hubs

Douglas Coupland

070/073 1995

Hubs
Douglas Coupland
1995

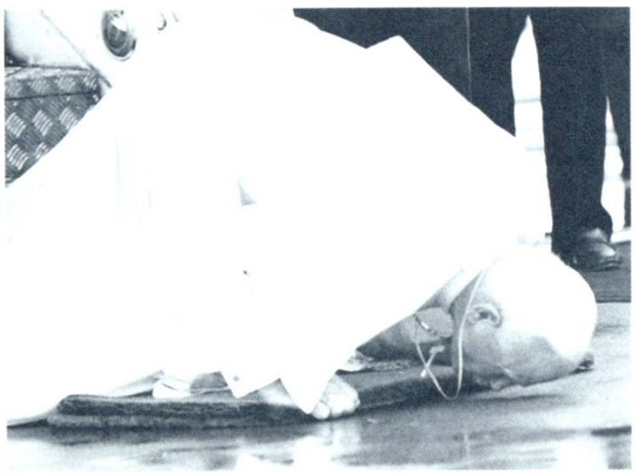

2.01

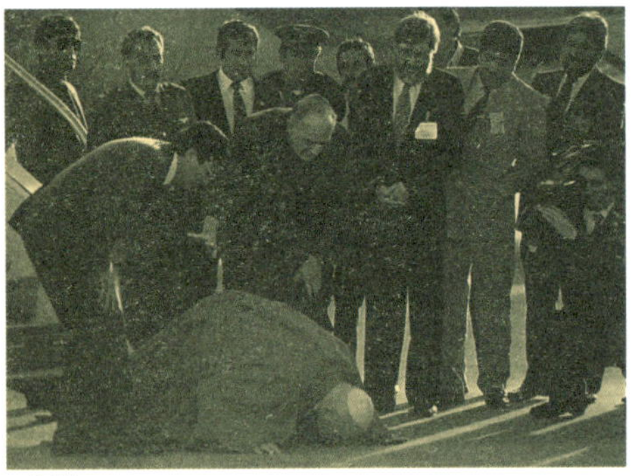

2.02

2.01 Pope John Paul II kisses the ground, London, 1990

2.02 Pope John Paul II kisses the ground, Vilnius Airport, Lithuania, 1993

2.03 Pope John Paul II kisses the ground, London, 1990

2.04 Pope John Paul II kisses the ground, Jakarta Airport, Indonesia, 1989

Images courtesy of Associated Press

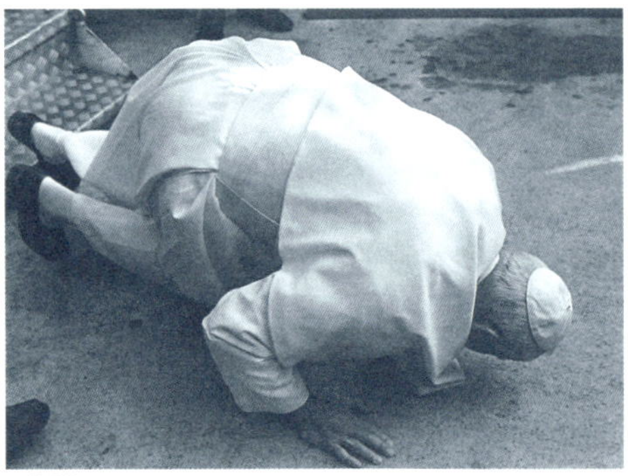

2.03

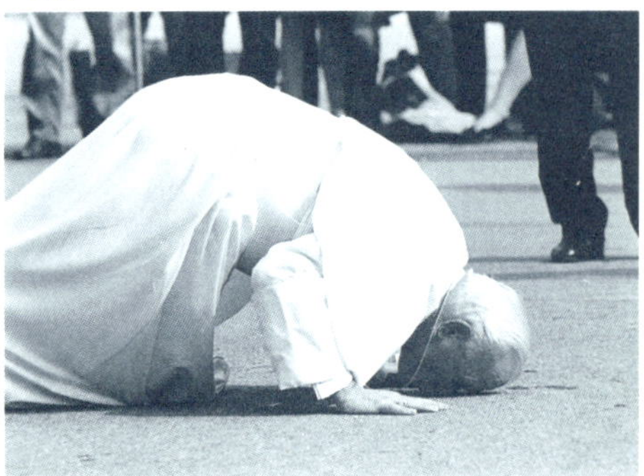

2.04

I remember once hearing of Pope John Paul II, who, while in transit to Asia, back in the mid 1980s, stopped to refuel in Anchorage and got off the jet for a stroll. I imagine the Pope descending the steps from his Air Italia DC-10, and kissing the tarmac of Anchorage International Airport, as is his custom.

Just think: the Pope blessing an airline fuelling stop, a 'hub' of sorts — consecrating a place that isn't technically a 'place'. For the Pope to kiss the Anchorage tarmac is like him taking a laboratory ampule containing a perfect vacuum, and blessing the pure nothingness inside.

Numinous ritual and the emptiness of the universe collide. The act itself seems somehow pointless: an empty gesture made to an empty arena; a mime's wall; a fan letter written to a character created by a now-dead author; the class clown facing the chalkboard, pretending to be making out with someone, arms writhing. Certainly Anchorage itself is a place — a magnificent thriving spectacular city of a place — but Anchorage International Airport (particularly if you're halfway between JFK and Narita) is definitely not a place. It is a pit stop, an in-between place, a 'nowhere', a technicality — a grudging intrusion into the seamless dream of teleportation that is transcontinental jet flight. The hub is essentially an anti-experience born of technological necessity and the imperatives of petroleum, flight schedules, the curvature of the planet, and geographic accident. Hubs are nowheres, with their security apparatuses, landing and fuelling infrastructures, and pictograms both patronising and incomprehensible.

The unspoken ethos is one of keep-up-with-the-Joneses anti-regional sterility.

Hub signage almost exclusively employs the Helvetica type font, a font specifically engineered to have no personality. Hub food is always vacuum-packed and seems to strive for unitised, stainless placelessness. The buildings feel so sterile that they could only be the precise opposite: incubators of great plagues; fathers of all microbial lies. But airline hubs — more so than airports — are complete nowheres.

This nowhereness both attracts and repels; seduces and frightens. The hub is the embodiment of a certain dimension of capital-P Progress — that dimension equating progress with comfort, the dimension that views progress as those technologies that separate our senses from the world as it was created by nature. The hub is where we experience the horrific torpor of Extreme Progress, where Modernism is fully integrated into a universe of Smarte Kartes, nubbly maroon fabric chairs, non-specific accents squawking across grand halls that flights with numbers four digits long are currently boarding. The hub is a dead-number office for damned digits, where numbers like 1388, 1490, 1218 are abandoned and thrown away, only to reappear with Sysyphian regularity.

Almost everyone in the western world has served time in a hub: Salt Lake City, Denver, San Jose, Dallas. We all know the emotional limbo that hubs and fueling stops represent, the sense of life's narrative having been suspended — the petrified-in-amber feeling implicit in the process of transit. Yet unlike Cecelia Brady's enigma-strewn fueling stops of *The Last Tycoon* — all romance and bonding and Tennessee moonlight — today's hub is a dispassionate nodule; the one place a citizen actually buys a copy of *USA Today*; a world of time-stand-still. Barcelona chairs atop decaying synthetic carpets in colour schemes long passé; cheap-seat travellers in Disney-wear, spilling diet beverages onto cracked chair modules aligned into conversation-thwarting rows; businessmen in navy-blue off-the-racks, wondering if they'll be upgraded as they eat corrosive pizza slices — they are serenaded by ESPN and anointed by the odour of a million Marlboro Lights.

Chicago's O'Hare Airport serves 66.5 million passengers a year, but only a fraction have Chicago as its destination. O'Hare is perhaps the most metaphysically non-existent locale ever dreamt up. While the airport is physically 'there' (after all, it can be measured, surveyed, telephoned, and driven to) it somehow seems not to exist at all.

This sounds contradictory, but it is not. O'Hare is the acme of metaphysical nonplaces dreamed up: the realisation of technology's secret goal of placing Plexiglas sheeting between ourselves and the world.

Jets and turboprop commuter planes may well be the vessels in which drama occurs, but the hub is the stopping of time; human biology divorced from narrative and nature.

O'Hare, like all good hubs, is a highly efficient structure for the processing of the individual, not a forum for the engagement of the individual soul. Do you have a disease? Are you violent? Are you American? Are you on United Airlines? Are you upgraded to first class or full-fare first class? Do you want a coffee, a drink, or a gate number? O'Hare exists to deal skillfully with these issues — not to provide you with a natural Arcadia. Connection to the world is what happens at your destination, not at your hub. O'Hare is like what happens to you just after you die and before you get shipped off to wherever you're going, what happens to you while your final destination is being determined. It is not judgment; it is transit distilled — like crack — pure neutrality made concrete — extreme.

Frequent flyers touch down in O'Hare many times a month, accumulating overall tallies that perhaps stretch into weeks, if not months, of their lives in and between terminals B and C. Almost everybody knows of the Dante-esque, quarter-mile-long people-moving conveyor belts, ever-revolving beneath the tarmac; the otherworldly voices imploring you to: 'keep – moving – keep – moving'. Yet oddly, these hours on the conveyor belts in terminals B and C don't count as life on earth, but more as hours put toward some sort of pre- or post-life limbo. For life begins again at take-off — when one looks out the windows at the sky and at night, the universe itself is also a vacuum. And so perhaps the universe is holy and (while no Catholic, I) just maybe back on the apron at Anchorage, the Pope may have had a magic idea — knees to cement, aviation fuel evaporating into the sky, hot steel above — kissing the nothingness.

The Airport Town

Interview with Paul Andreu

1991

074/083

The Airport Town

Interview with Paul Andreu 1991

Interview with Paul Andreu, director of Architecture and Engineering at Aéroports de Paris.
Interview conducted by Patrick Javault

Patrick Javault: You started work on Roissy Airport in the mid-sixties, at a time when Orly had the only architecturally designed air terminal in France. Who inspired your ideas? What did you use as a reference, both architecturally and otherwise?

Paul Andreu: My initial reaction was a negative one, which was not very productive, as negative reactions rarely are. It was a reaction against Orly, and, above all, the use made of it. They organised a homes exhibition at Orly which proved so successful that all the access routes got blocked up, meaning that the passengers were late, and some even missed their flights. At the time, many of us reacted against this. Above all, an air terminal should be efficient. We should be more concerned with its principal function, and not with the number of visitors. I also had one other very positive point of reference, which was the two air terminals designed by Saarinen. I have always loved them, especially the TWA Terminal at Kennedy Airport. It came in for a great deal of criticism at the time, especially from those at Aéroports de Paris, who considered it neither functional nor extendable. They found a thousand things wrong with it. However, in my opinion, there was nothing wrong with it. And, in fact, this terminal has not aged badly at all; it has certainly done better than some of those considered functional and extendable at the time. I found that it had an amazing feeling of space, and all the proportions were well thought out and exactly right. It was technically highly ambitious, and not all of its aims were achieved. Saarinen's dream was that the building would have no façades, that these would be replaced by curtains of air. Many of the other aims were achieved, but the building as a whole was not well received. The critics wanted something simple and prosaic, and the hallucinogenic nature of the TWA Terminal disturbed them. To tell the truth, the architecture itself disturbed them, despite some strikingly beautiful features, like the curvature of the bridges leading to the satellites which meant that all sense of perspective was lost. When you go in, you cannot see the end of the tunnel. Instead of this horrible impression of a fixed perspective, you genuinely get the feeling that you are going somewhere. The space inside has been organised with incredible sensitivity; for example, the waiting room has just been added to the main building slightly below street level so as not to impair the view of the main area. Such sensitivity is very rare in a field where there has, until recently, been none. I never regarded this as a formal model (it was too much of a prototype to be a source of inspiration) except in the broader concepts, in the spirit which closely combined extreme functionality, generous open spaces and sheer poetry.

The idea that gradually emerged in the planning of Roissy 1 was to create a comfortable air terminal where passengers would not have far to walk. We found that Orly had very long 'fingers', and that its creators seemed obsessed with the distance covered by the pedestrians. We wanted to create a more comfortable, less tiring environment. I also wanted, and this desire intensified as the planning progressed, to discover and to demonstrate the truth — the truth about structures, the truth about function and the truth about materials. As the airport terminal represents an intersection between cars and aeroplanes, both the aeroplanes and the car park had to be visible. I did not find it embarrassing that, at long range, the terminal could be mistaken for a car park surrounded by aeroplanes.

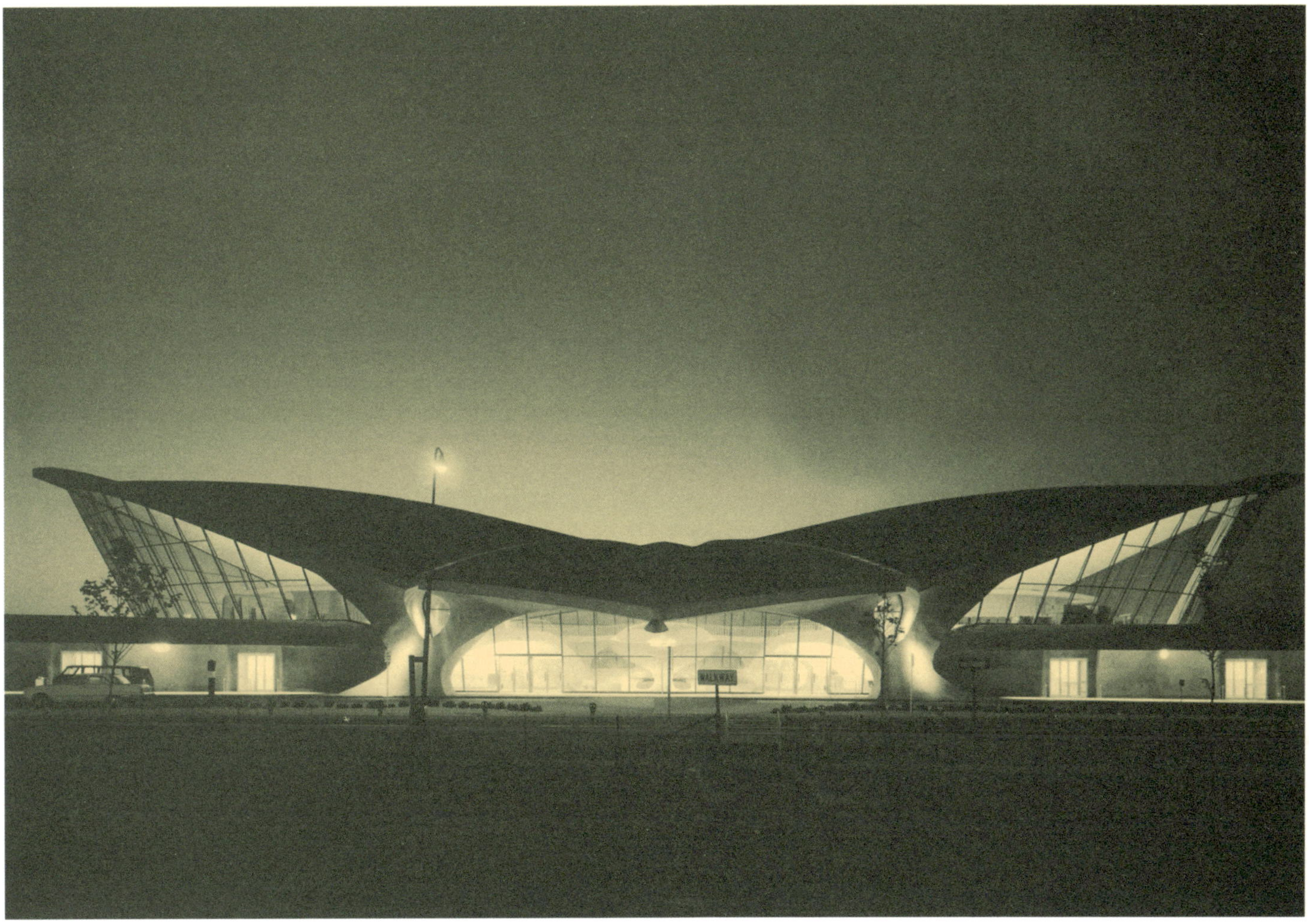

3.01
TWA Terminal 5, Kennedy International Airport, New York, Courtesy TWA

On the contrary, I found it gratifying, and for the same reason I rejected false floors that covered up structures, shaftsand cables. Instead, I aimed to study these elements to see how they could be turned into interesting or aesthetically pleasing features. Although this attitude was not entirely deliberate to begin with, it gradually became the motto for the project in the planning stages.

Patrick Javault: Did symbolism, in particular the idea of the circle, play an important role?

Paul Andreu: No, that came later, or, to be more precise, we discovered it later. To begin with, the circle was the solution to an organisation problem we had. As we wanted to reduce the distances the passengers had to walk, we needed to find a way of arranging the aeroplanes. After a few attempts, we came up with a sort of double wraparound arrangement, whereby aeroplanes were wrapped around the satellites, and these satellites were wrapped around the terminal. This meant that 28 aeroplanes could be arranged at a minimal distance from the centre of the terminal. Organising the whole thing as a circle allows the greatest number of aeroplanes to be in contact with the building. Of course, this arrangement did cause some traffic complications, which we had to deal with later. That is where the circle came from. Then I decided to carry this shape through to the whole of the interior of the building. Initially we sought to design a conventional building within this circle of aeroplanes — a building which would look circular, but would not function like a circle, a building which was highly asymmetrical inside, or even a square building. I found that this inconsistency would have been annoying and nonsensical. As soon as the decision had been made to arrange the aeroplanes in a circle, the roads and the building should have also been designed as a circle. We went into detail on a number of different versions, which are difficult to describe today. For example, in one version, we had three exterior ramps and a crazy sort of maze of roads that was in front of the terminal and hid it completely, in another, the terminal was in front and paths led off to all the satellites.

The result of all this was a highly complex hybrid. With the motto 'let the circle be a circle', which, to me, signified respect for concepts and the search for coherence and truth, I took the maze of roads from in front, and wrapped them around the terminal. The terminal became as much an intersection as a building, and this symbiosis of the elements of transporting both cars and passengers allowed us to completely accommodate the function and the density of traffic to which we had aimed.

Patrick Javault: So the circular shape, which has been associated with travel and transformation, emerged as the result of a functional analysis?

Paul Andreu: Yes, we organised the circuits later. We came up against a problem at the level of the purely functional analysis. In a convergent system, the convergence must stop somewhere. You cannot go right into the centre, as that is the very place where you lose all sense of direction, like a compass needle spinning at the North Pole. What is more, you cannot concentrate too much traffic there as, by definition, the centre has no area. Therefore, we removed the centre by making a hole in the circle. Then we did two things, we allowed light into the centre of this very large, very dark building, and we created an area where all the changes in level were shown in a unique perspective, in the light. Initially the level was changed by means of conventional escalators. We moved on thanks to a comment from the managing director of Air France, Pierre Donatien Cot. He asked me if the escalators could not go in a straight line, so as to avoid having to turn at the landings, and running the risk of forming bottlenecks.

So we came up with the ideas of an empty space at the centre, and crossing this space in a straight line. They led to this highly complex design involving six moving walkways that link up the three main storeys of the terminal. The design was simple enough on paper, but actually developing it in reality proved very complex and forced us to further the limits of our research, which up to then had been purely functional. It was this shape which was to dominate the design of the air terminal entirely. The changes in level, which were functionally important as the terminal's features were spread out over three levels, had to take place in an unusual environment, there had to be total symmetry with respect to this environment. The centre was to be empty apart from these lines which could cross but not touch, and this proved a source of fascination throughout our research.

After about half an hour discussing the air terminal, we would invariably end up talking about this space, we just kept coming back to it, as if were some sort of primordial place, a place for breaking off with old traditions, for moving on. Obviously, it is always difficult to know what projects will involve, and in general it is not what you would have wanted it to be. It is a totally different thing to what you discover during the project, and read about once it is completed. I am convinced that projects create themselves as much as they are created.

So there is a large discrepancy between what I can tell you today, and what I knew during the project. Based on the reality of the programmes and the demands of the technology, I was fumbling around in the dark for something that the original sketches had allowed me a glimpse of, but which I had immediately forgotten. As my guide, I had a motto of craft and design that was both theoretical and practical.

Patrick Javault: You mention Saarinen, who achieved a very distinctive architectural style when he designed the TWA Terminal. But with Roissy, you get the opposite feeling, almost a feeling of self-effacement.

Paul Andreu: I had no wish to produce gratuitous effects. Moreover, when I did try to do so, it did not work. I can remember one particular instance when I was looking into some external poles and I indulged in some superficial details. We had already torn up loads of ideas; they were not right at all because we were trying to express many things with these poles which were not part of their substance. And the day that we gave up on the style and the message, and decided to give these poles a shape which was consistent with their construction and their function, we got a positive result. Without a doubt, in this way we managed to avoid designing something that would have been nothing but banal in the long run. There are very few shapes which merely have an exterior form, or merely have a cultural form. For the most part there is a direct relationship with their construction or their function. But they are not a direct consequence thereof. In many cases, a gratuitous decision has been made at some stage. In the whole of the first phase of the development of Roissy, and especially of the terminal, there is no absolute justification for the fact that slopes are systematically added to the facings of walls and other objects. It is always possible to come up with justification after the fact, by saying, for example, that it allows the light in better, but this is not true. There is no justification apart from a moment's whim. However, and this is more important, there is a degree of consistency in the use of formal terminology.

It is as a result of this consistency that a world has been created which is composed of a system of familiar signs. And, especially when studying the Roissy project by means of another, in a vision which combines all the exterior and interior spaces, it is this system which allows a strong communication between them, because they are fruit of the same thought and expressed within a coherent mental space.

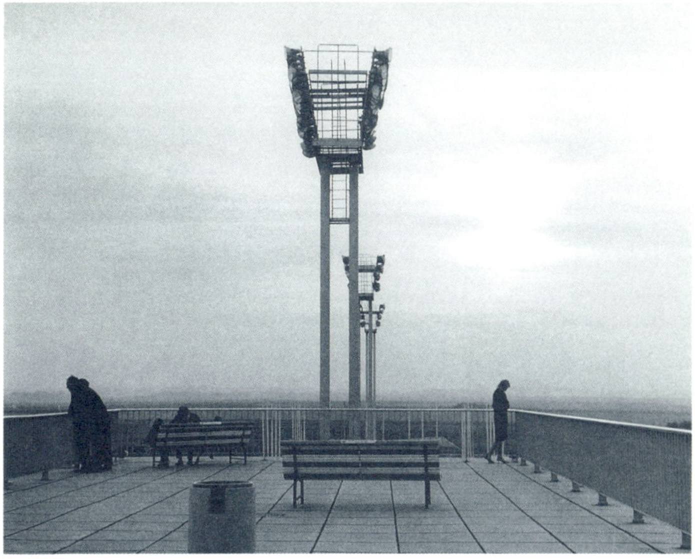

3.02

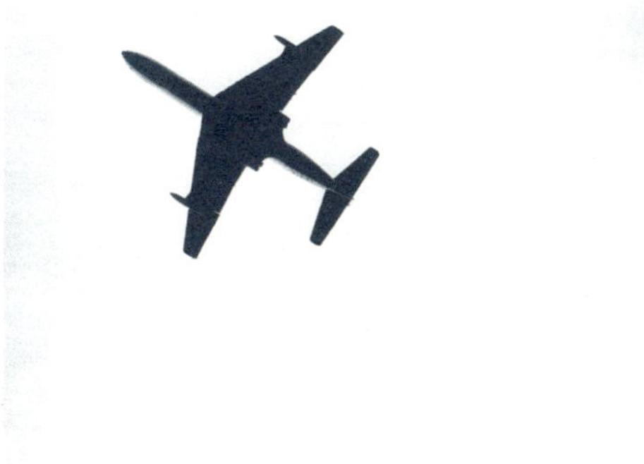

3.03

3.02 Still image from *La Jetée*
(Chris Marker, 1962)
Courtesy of the Artist

3.03 Still image from *La Jetée*
(Chris Marker, 1962)
Courtesy of the Artist

Patrick Javault: Can the architecture of Roissy also be recognised from the air?

Paul Andreu: Yes, perhaps, but it is more real in representations — photos or drawings — than it is in real life. A bird's eye view, even of an airport, is not familiar to us. The other day I was arriving in Paris on a route I am not used to and I saw something round and seemingly very large emerging from the fog. I have always been intrigued by anything round, and I really wondered what this unknown building was. Just at this moment, I spotted that it was Roissy 1, and that the satellites were obscured from view. I found this a very gratifying experience.

In fact, the aerial view is very revealing, like mantras and the patterns by which space is organised. I hardly think that the Forbidden City was designed with the view from above in mind, even if the emperors did have a special relationship with what was up there. The justification for the wish to organise space, to sketch it out exactly, is the search for a mental order which is perceived as progressive and mysterious by means of multiple sensations provoked by the routes.

The aerial view unravels the mystery but does not reduce the intention to sketch out the essentials: the succession and the capturing of effects and sensations. At about that time, I remember reading *The Hidden Dimension* by Edward T. Hall, in which he discusses all the various ways of perceiving space. They are all very different. The simplest, and the least interesting, is to have a constant perspective and watch a building grow — a metric organisation of space — the building is located by its façade and its position in the field of view. But there are other, more topological methods. For example, you can read space by perceiving the relative, changing positions of two objects, without being influenced by their size, and judging their superposition by which partially obscures the other. As a vision of space, it is at least as effective as the first method. I tried this sort of approach at Roissy 1; I wanted the relationships between objects to be such that they could be regarded less in terms of their dimensions, and more in terms of a relational system of reciprocal positioning in space.

More by luck than judgement, all the main objects at Roissy 1 turned out to be round: the station is round, from a distance the control tower is round, the water tower is also round, and the thermo-electric power station, which is important because of its size, is also round in shape.

These objects vary little according to the perspective taken, whether you are in front or behind, to the right or to the left. You do not find out where you are in this space by the fact that you are in front of the principal, secondary or lateral façade, but by the overall shape formed by the buildings as a whole: i.e. the tower is in front of the terminal, or the tower is behind the terminal.
Of course size is also a factor, but it is not the orientation of these objects that allows you to locate yourself. In my opinion, this gives a space which is richer, more cinematographical.
At the time, I used to say, somewhat incorrectly, that I was making use of all three dimensions. I thought, and I still do, that perspective which consists of moving straight towards a building reduces space to two dimensions. Once the relative size of the object had been ascertained, that is it: you know everything, you can sketch the geometrical shape of the object.
What I wanted at the time, and what I've always wanted for nearly all my projects, and this is a legacy from the TWA Terminal, was the universality of space, with the real and imaginary lines of the building passing through it in every sense. That is what moves me about certain Roman and Gothic churches. To me, architecture is not all about signs or meanings, but space and the sheer poetry associated with it, and the pleasure, the sensuality of moving through this space with one's body, one's vision or one's thoughts.
It is for this reason that I had to wait so long to get any decent photos of Roissy 1. I could not find any that looked like it did in reality, or at least how I consider it looks in reality. They did not capture the movement; they had no concept of the passing of time.

Patrick Javault: You have said that the best way to prepare passengers for the violent upheaval involved in making an aeroplane journey is to play it straight with the materials. Do you dislike deceptions?

Paul Andreu: It all has its roots in a very interesting investigation, the like of which has never been repeated, into the psychological state of aeroplane passengers. They noted that catching an aeroplane is never as innocuous and banal as catching a bus. It is always something out of the ordinary, even for frequent travellers. Whatever form the technology takes, it is not natural to be up in the air, even temporarily, as it only ever lasts a short while. I do not know if this effect is different for the cosmonauts who spend long periods of time in space. In any case, being on an aeroplane, being up in the air, flying is an extraordinary dream and something that defies known laws. It is the myth of Icarus, the knowledge which allows you to go beyond your limits. At the same time it is the sin of excess because you overdo it, you want to go too far, you get your wings burnt and you fall back towards birth and the sea.

On the basis of this analysis, we came to the conclusion, rightly or wrongly, that we needed to reassure the passengers, or rather not to add to the stress they find themselves in. There is no point in broadcasting music or sounds, this would merely induce artificial excitement into the genuine excitement they were feeling already. I am, and always have been, strongly opposed to muzak and pastel shades: why not just give them Valium as they come in! On the contrary, I needed to create a real world, a world in which the passengers can come face to face with themselves, their joys and their fears, without losing out on a single opportunity of discovery, even though, at the end of the day, these opportunities are fairly rare. The passengers needed to be in a strong, peaceful, almost maternal, environment. The circular forms should be reminiscent of the softness and the strength of the maternal bosom, without being claustrophobic. To this end, everything had to be truthful; the materials, the colours, the floors. What is more reassuring for someone entering into a building than a concrete beam which says, I can hold weight, I am here to hold the weight of the building, everything is fine, just don't worry.

This demand for truth in materials dominated everything else in the analysis phase. Perhaps someone else would have taken another approach based on the same psychological analysis. The important thing was to articulate a personal position of principle with the real situation of the passengers, and to try to combine these two factors by regarding them as indissociable from one another. This is what justifies the position of architect, he must be present and committed at all times, yet nothing must depend entirely on it.

The building is made for others, but should escape them, go beyond them. At least then it will not be average; the worst things, in my opinion, are those that are average. You will have something that goes beyond its creator's ego. To tell the truth, I hate the creator's absolute ego just as much, which must, at all costs, be evident, deliver a message and be recognised. They fly in the face of marketing ideals, which claim to encapsulate the average 'public opinion'. This method does not achieve results because two people generally have little in common, three people have even less, ten will have almost nothing, and what a hundred people have in common is something so negligible that it may be able to help to sell certain things, but it can certainly not contribute anything creative. By definition, creativity is the emergence of something which does not exist. And marketing, at least in its narrowest and crudest form, consists entirely of trying to pinpoint that which already exists, therefore it is worth nothing.

3.04 Still image from *La Jetée* (Chris Marker, 1962) Courtesy of the Artist

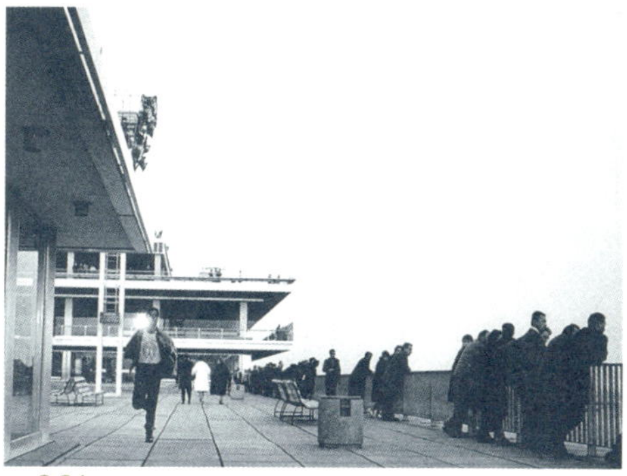

3.04

Patrick Javault: Has designing air terminals for non-western countries forced you to think about other types of cultures and other standards?

Paul Andreu: Their concepts of speed and relationships in space are not the same, but it is always difficult to comprehend exactly how they differ. There is often not enough time to get to know people well. They are often not even aware of these differences themselves. Most often, they want to demonstrate how westernised and close to us they are. So you have to go back to your original ideas, to your intuition.

When I went to Jakarta, I asked the people there what recent buildings they would recommend that I saw.
They sent me to see some pieces of architecture that were rather mediocre, but which were all found within gardens. In all probability, my hosts were not considering the architecture, but the gardens. This proximity to nature was worth much more to them than the construction. This made me decide to design a very special air terminal which was a garden as much as a building. These works overseas have forced me to ask myself a few questions, and have prevented me getting stuck to one particular style. I have little taste or comprehension for many works with links to postmodernism and historicism. On the contrary, I believe in the existence of specific architectural vocabulary, whose aim is not to copy, but to identify and study, as they form the foundation of a contemporary creation. It was not cultivated architecture that interested me most, but simple, traditional architecture.
If you want to form a link with them, it is often the most recent constructions that allow you to discover what is subsequently expressed in an elaborate way in the most developed structures.
It is not necessary to adopt their system and transform their methods of construction; in my opinion this equates to total betrayal, or to treating them with a lack of respect.

On the contrary, in a movement that is constantly changing, you need to understand the original thought process, the perception of space that decided how exactly the available means would be utilised, and then research how this thought process can be developed today, bearing in mind the technology, the workforce and the economy of each country.

I was lucky in that these foreign contracts forced me to address these questions, and to run the risk of straying from what I already knew and of what I was sure.

This period of my life has passed now, but it played an important role in the cycle of my work because it gave me a clear understanding that you must not be restricted to one idea, or to one way of working. I also learnt that I loved space, and that epiderms are merely secondary considerations. On the basis of this, I have always resisted the contemporary trends for superficial affectations. I have a great deal of faith in the maxim of elevation and depth, and in the corruption of surfaces.

All these overseas projects allow me to escape the little world I had created for myself with Roissy 1, which I had feared, for a while, would trap me completely.

Patrick Javault: An airport could be seen as a sort of idealised town. Have you never wanted to work in towns?

Paul Andreu: Yes, I have wanted to for a long time. Perhaps a part of my dream is in the process of coming true. It is true that many town functions can be found in an airport. But it is not a town, merely a part of one. Airports form a centre of movement from which the heart of the town can be dispersed. There are several elements which contribute something to the town; the facilities, the shopping centre, and the airport. I have always felt a sort of nostalgia for both the town and, naturally, for the beauty of wide open countryside which need not conform to any rules. I have gradually got closer to the town. The Grande Arche is still a quite a long way from the town centre, but it is nonetheless in the town.
At the moment, I have been given the opportunity of doing some work on the Avenue de Tolbiac. We shall see…

I'm excited by the density and complexity of the town because, by developing new methods and making them economically viable, towns have to allow new, vibrant, poetic spaces to flourish. I would like to be able to continue here what I have started elsewhere, but it would need to be more in-depth because the population is even denser.

Patrick Javault: You have been working on Roissy for twenty-five years, and it is now almost on the scale of a town. You are just starting on the third phase of the project; can you give us a broad description of it?

Paul Andreu: Roissy 1 was a sort of eternal crystal, Roissy 2 is a plant which grows in stages. As the plan was that its eventual capacity would far exceed that of Roissy 1, it needed to be built in a series of stages, hence the modular structure and the system of expansion. There is a sort of framework of roads, like a tree-trunk or the stalk of a plant, to which the traffic modules, which are all very similar on the outside, but totally different inside, are attached.

You could also use a different metaphor and say that, on a functional level, Roissy 1 is a centralised state and Roissy 2 is a confederation. All Roissy 1's units are more or less identical. In contrast to this each module of Roissy 2 is different and specifically adapted to a type of traffic or passenger. Today we are in the third phase, which is both a sequel and a new chapter. The broad plan for Roissy is basically like a game of rugby. The game is the same for all air terminals, but what is interesting is seeing which way the ball bounces, as it is always unpredictable and exciting.

The TGV is going to come to Roissy, which it has not done before. The station at Roissy will be on the line connecting all the TGV lines around Paris, and will be linked by train to all the major French cities as well as some European capitals, such as Amsterdam, Brussels and London.

This place will form a strong link between rail and air travel. It will be a railway station and an air terminal in one, and each will be complete in itself. It will be unprecedented, a totally new transport building, and I am sure that it will add something to the very concept of transport.

We have also taken advantage of the advent of the TGV to improve the local rail access to Roissy. At the moment this access is in the middle of the airport, between the terminals, and this is not satisfactory. A second station, to be built parallel to the TGV station, will lead directly into Terminals 2 and 3. The internal transport systems around the site itself will also leave from the same point, which will allow the whole terminal area to be joined together, so that all the terminals can be linked to each other, the railway stations and the car parks.

The TGV and regional train stations will be perpendicular to the axis of Terminal 2, after the first four modules of the terminal. It is a very complex web of routes, encompassing the travellers' buildings, which will have two large white glass walls looking out over the sunken platforms. From these, you will be able to see trains, planes and cars in one glance… It will be Sant'Elia's dream made real at last.

We are investigating the possibility of a new terminal beyond that, but still on the same axis. This terminal, which we have called Terminal 3, will have an infrastructure of routes similar to, but more advanced than, Terminal 2. At the moment we are planning on having two traffic modules, which will be larger than those in Roissy 2, 360 metres in length instead of 230 metres. The aeroplanes will be arranged along two large glass halls, perpendicular to the body of each module.

In terms of the function and the architecture, everything is based on the contrast between these two curved areas; the concrete model and the glass halls, or 'peninsulas' as we call them. Roissy 3 will follow on from the movement towards the light embodied by the interior of Roissy 1, but Roissy 2 has been a major stepping stone along the way.

Roissy 3, with its peninsulas open to the sky, unfolds in completely diffused light in which the very structure and the solar protection screens should be about more than mere density. And in this light, the light of a journey already begun, the passengers will wait on a level that we would like to suspend in mid-air, like a flying carpet. Perhaps the journey will seem more real in this motionless place than in the aeroplane itself, where you battle to close the blinds to make it look more like a cinema. Perhaps the journey will already seem complete after a brief glance at the curves along the length of the surfaces, as the aeroplanes come and go, and as you eventually make a move to get up and go.

Prologue from Non-places

084/087

Marc Augé
1995

Marc Augé

Prologue – From Non-places Introduction to an Anthropology of Supermodernity, Verso, London 1995

On the way to his car Pierre Dupont stopped at the cash dispenser to draw some money. The device accepted his card and told him he could have 1800 francs. Pierre Dupont pressed the button beside this figure on the screen. The device asked him to wait a moment and then delivered the sum requested, reminding him as it did so to withdraw his card. 'Thank you for your custom,' it added as Pierre Dupont arranged the banknotes in his wallet.

It was a trouble-free drive, the trip to Paris on the A11 autoroute presenting no problems on a Sunday morning. There was no tailback at the junction where he joined it. He paid at the Dourdan toll-booth using his blue card, skirted Paris on the périphérique and took the A1 to Roissy.

He parked in row J of underground level 2, slid his parking ticket into his wallet and hurried to the Air France check-in desks. With some relief he deposited his suitcase (exactly 20 kilos) and handed his flight ticket to the hostess, asking if it would be possible to have a smoking seat next to the gangway. Silent and smiling, she assented with an inclination of her head, after first consulting her computer, then gave him back his ticket along with a boarding pass. 'Boarding from Satellite B at eighteen hundred,' she told him.

He went early through Passport Control to do a little duty-free shopping. He bought a bottle of cognac (something French for his Asian clients) and a box of cigars (for himself). Meticulously, he put the receipt away next to his blue card.

He strolled past the window-displays of luxury goods, glancing briefly at their jewellery, clothing and scent bottles, then called at the bookshop where he leafed through a couple of magazines before choosing an undemanding book: travel, adventure, spy fiction. Then he resumed his unhurried progress.

He was enjoying the feeling of freedom imparted by having got rid of his luggage and at the same time, more intimately, by the certainty that, now that he was 'sorted out', his identity registered, his boarding pass in his pocket, he had nothing to do but wait for the sequence of events. 'Roissy, just the two of us!': these days, surely, it was in these crowded places where thousands of individual itineraries converged for a moment, unaware of one another, that there survived something of the uncertain charm of the waste lands, the yards and building sites, the station platforms and waiting rooms where travellers break step, of all the chance meetings places where fugitive feelings occur of the possibility of continuing adventure, the feeling that all there is to do is to 'see what happens'.

The passengers boarded without problems. Those whose boarding passes bore the letter Z were requested to board last, and he observed with a certain amusement the muted, unnecessary jostling of the Xs and Ys around the door to the boarding gangway.

Waiting for take-off, while newspapers were being distributed, he glanced through the company's in-flight magazine and ran his finger along the imagined route of the journey: Heraklion, Larnaca, Beirut, Dhahran, Dubai, Bombay, Bangkok... more than nine thousand kilometres in the blink of an eye, and a few names which had cropped up in the news over the years. He cast his eye down the duty-free price list, noted that credit cards were accepted on intercontinental flights, and read with a certain smugness the advantages conferred by the 'business class' in which he was travelling thanks to the intelligent generosity of his firm ('At Charles de Gaulle 2 and New York, Club lounges are provided where you can rest, make telephone calls, use a photocopier or Minitel... Apart from a personal welcome and constant attentive service, the new Espace 2000 seat has been designed for extra width and has separately adjustable backrest and headrest...'). He examined briefly the digitally labelled control panel of his Espace 2000 seat and then, drifting back into the advertisements in the magazine, admired the aerodynamic lines of a few late-model roadsters and gazed at the pictures of some large hotels belonging to an international chain, somewhat pompously described as 'the surroundings of civilization' (the Mammounia in Marrakesh, 'once a palace, now the quintessence of five-star luxury'; the Brussels Métropole, 'where the splendours of the nineteenth century remain very much alive'). Then he came across an advertisement for a car with the same name as his seat, the Renault Espace: 'One day, the need for space makes itself felt… It comes to us without warning. And never goes away. The irresistible wish for a space of our own. A mobile space which can take us anywhere. A space where everything is to hand and nothing is lacking…' Just like the aircraft really. 'Already, space is inside you… You've never been so firmly on the ground as you are in (the E) space,' the advertisement ended pleasingly.

They were taking off. He flicked rapidly through the rest of the magazine, giving a few seconds to a piece on 'the hippopotamus — lord of the river' which began with an evocation of Africa as 'cradle of legends' and 'continent of magic and sorcery'; glancing at an article about Bologna ('You can be in love anywhere, but in Bologna you fall in love with the city'). A brightly coloured advertisement in English for a Japanese 'videomovie' held his attention for a moment ('Vivid colours, vibrant sound and non-stop action. Make them yours forever'). A Trenet song, heard that afternoon over the car radio on the autoroute, had been running through his head and he mused that its line about the 'photo, the old photo of my youth' would soon become meaningless to future generations. The colours of the present preserved forever: the camera as freezer. An advertisement for the Visa card managed to reassure him ('Accepted in Dubai and wherever you travel… Travel in full confidence with your Visa card').

He glanced distractedly through a few book reviews, pausing for a moment on the review of a work called *Euromarketing* which aroused his professional interest:

The homogenisation of needs and consumption patterns is one of the overall trends characterising the new international business environment… Starting from an examination of the effects of the globalisation phenomenon on European business, on the validity and content of Euromarketing and on predictable developments in the international marketing environment, numerous issues are discussed.

The review ended with an evocation of 'the conditions suitable for the development of a mix that would be as standardised as possible' and 'the architecture of a European communication'.

Somewhat dreamily, Pierre Dupont put down his magazine. The 'Fasten seat belt' notice had gone out. He adjusted his earphones, selected Channel 5 and allowed himself to be invaded by the adagio of Joseph Haydn's Concerto No.1 in E major.

For a few hours (the time it would take to fly over the Mediterranean, the Arabian Sea and the Bay of Bengal), he would be alone at last.

4.01–4.06 Video stills from *Geneva Express*, Graham Ellard and Stephen Johnstone, 1997
Courtesy of the Artists

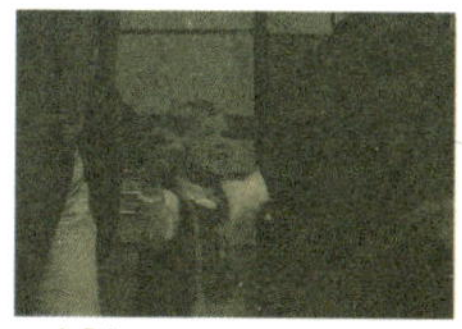
4.01

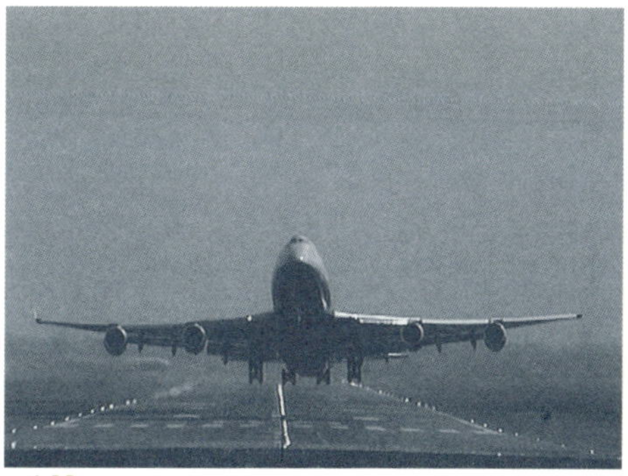
4.02

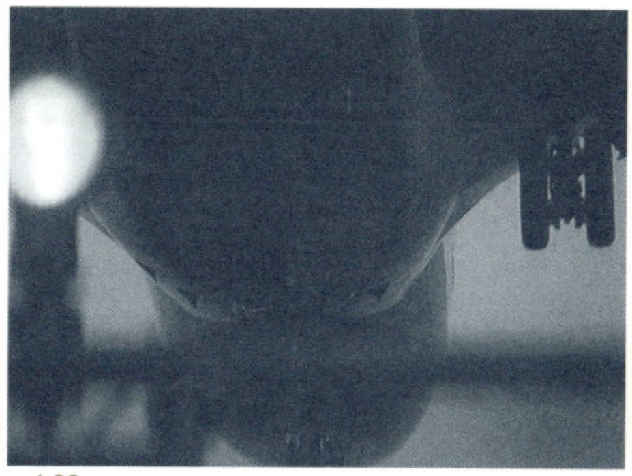
4.03

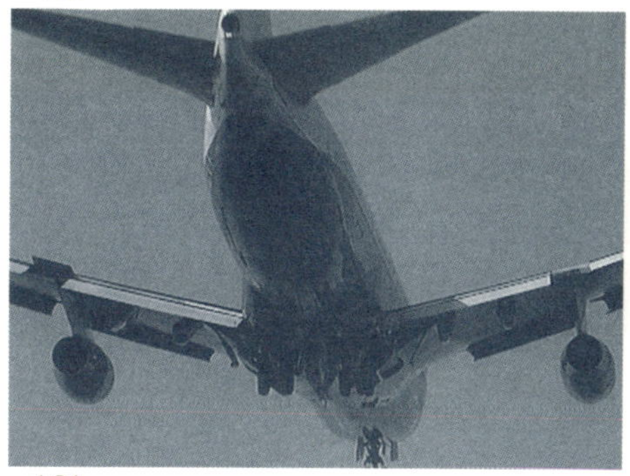
4.04

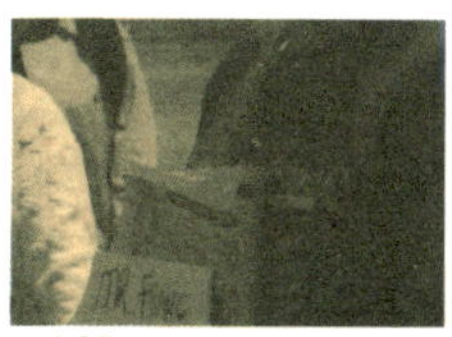
4.05

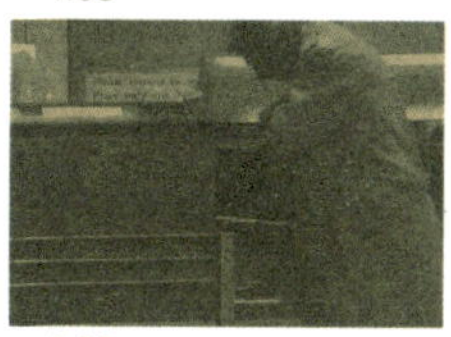
4.06

Martha Rosler 1993/6

In the Place of the Public

As a teenager at the end of the 1950s, however, I was lucky enough to sail the Atlantic and the Mediterranean on a scholarship voyage. In the 1960s and 1970s, I drove across America a number of times. In the 1970s, when many travellers were already flying, I still couldn't afford it. Instead, I traversed the country in long-distance buses, experiencing the bald regimentation suggestive of custody for minor crimes — trips which I photographed in black and white. By the end of the 1970s, though, the art world required a lot of jetting about by artists, for shows and lectures. As an artist whose fare was paid for by various institutions, I all but abandoned the buses for airplanes.

I offer this history as typical of the possibilities awaiting an upwardly mobile city dweller in the postwar United States. Air travel was both an entry into and an emblem of a very different world from that of bus stations and ground-level transportation.[3] Nowadays, the airport represents entry into the world of 'everybody', those whom mass media, advertisers, and everything else address; the riders of the bus are those whom time and fortune have forgotten. Long-distance bus travel[4], like poverty, is not respectable in the United States.

In the past fifteen years, living an artist's life, I have frequently found myself flying on commercial airlines. I found myself in the company of the besuited and the befurred, of those in trench coats carrying attaché cases and garment bags or those in leisure wear toting skis or pedigree dogs. I discovered that at many small airports the flyers included the same people who might have been riding the bus[5]. I changed my black-and-white film for colour, and my serious 35-millimetre camera for a less-weighty pocket version. I became interested in the ephemera and experience of this form of travel, so different in time, space, and (self-) organisation from train and, particularly, bus travel. I flew during crises that stranded travellers for hours while planes were grounded wholesale for investigation of stress points and cracks. I flew during the breaking of PATCO, the association of air-traffic controllers whose crushing marked the opening onslaught of the Reagan administration. I flew during strikes (of airlines other than the ones I was flying, of course) and during the bankruptcies and takeovers occasioned by the cancellation of the anti-trust regulations governing the industry. I flew during periods of war and bad weather. And I continue to fly, and to photograph. I continue, no doubt indefensibly, to resist researching airports beyond the elements and experiences accessible to the ordinary traveller with ideas in her head and a camera in her hand. In a time in which production in advanced industrial societies is increasingly characterised by metaphors of transmission and flow, I am interested in the movement of bodies through darkened corridors and across great distances but also in the effacement of the experience of such travel by constructs designed to empty the actual experience of its content and make it the carrier of another sort of experience entirely.

This totalised industrial representation of air travel and its associated spaces as 'a world apart' is different from that of any other form of mass transport. Walter Benjamin, unexpectedly, ends 'The Work of Art in the Age of Mechanical Reproduction' with a pocket analysis of architecture: 'Architecture has never been idle. Its history is more ancient than that of any other art, and its claim to being a living force has significance in every attempt to comprehend the relationship of the masses to art.'[6]

Architecture, Benjamin continues, is 'appropriated' not only through sight but through touch; it is experienced by the body as presence, through 'distraction', or habitual use, not through optical contemplation. Likening the new art of cinema — composed of fleeting images — to architecture, undeniably solid and three-dimensional, Benjamin holds out the hope of the education of the senses as a means to combat the fascist aestheticisation of politics through spectacle.

Despite the focus of his essay on the social effects of photography and film, Benjamin could hardly have anticipated the more recent, allied invention of virtual reality, a computer simulated 'environment' or 'architecture' that envelops the spectator in a sensory phantasmagoria of (apparently) spatial, auditory, and tactile cues[7] — in other words, 'experience' — that revokes the solidity of 'the real thing'. Virtual reality, like 'cyberspace', the broader conception of a computational environment, exists more in the promise than in the fulfillment; but it is not news that in the organisation of physical space and the design of buildings in advanced industrial society there are elements that relinquish presence or presentness in favour of signification: the so-called Empire of Signs. Those who seek cyberspace dream the future by literally moving space to the plane of the imaginary.

How far can one advance a discussion of air travel and its associated spaces, structures and experiences by broaching the subject of virtual reality? Not far, perhaps. Nevertheless, as one of the quotations that open this essay suggests, Henri Lefebvre — followed by a host of commentators — has shown how space is produced by the relations of production, mapping political economy onto the physical world.[8] Cyberspace too, although only a simulation, is thrown up by the collective imaginary of late capitalism, a translation of Lefebvre's 'abstract space' to an intangible realm.
In describing the role of processes of image reproduction in contemporary society, the situationist Guy Debord[9] has argued that 'the spectacle' is created by the mode of production and is not a technological accident, nor a freely created spectral other world standing against 'the real':

The spectacle is not a collection of images, but a social relation among people, mediated by images…
The spectacle cannot be understood as an abuse of the world of vision, as a product of the techniques of mass dissemination of images. It is, rather, a Weltanschauung which has become actual, materially translated…
The spectacle, grasped in its totality, is both a result and the project of the existing mode of production.[10]

Ultimately, Debord and Benjamin are on the opposite sides of the question of technological optimism, but in terms of diagnostics, Debord's proposition that 'this society which eliminated geographical distance reproduces distance internally as spectacular separation'[11] seems to intersect with Benjamin's concept of fascist aestheticisation.

The history of flight is not separate from the history of information management[12] — nor from that of image production and, ultimately, of 'simulation'. The flight simulator was an embryonic start toward virtual reality. Its sensory inputs were multiplied in the interest of training military pilots. As soon as it became practicable, video was incorporated into flight-simulator training, and video and flight simulation have developed in tandem. According to Captain 'X', air-traffic controllers, who spend their free time playing video games, are able to handle their jobs only through a process of de-realisation: If they thought of the radar blips as planes with people in them, they say, they would not be able to last a single day[13].

The recasting of movement as information flow is a consequence of excess complexity. In the brief compass of the present essay, I want to invoke some features of air travel and airports[14] that, among other things, touch on matters of simulation and representation. I reiterate that I frame my discussion not from the point of view of an expert, an outside observer, or even a student, but from that of a traveller[15]. That is, a traveller and an artist (an itinerant, to be precise, on the European-American circuit).

In 1834, the American Transcendentalist poet and philosopher Ralph Waldo Emerson reported on an English train ride. He described railroad travel as a salutary drug of sorts, disconnecting the traveller from place and loosening the perception of stability — or the stability of perception — with its streaks and blurs of motion and allowing for a new (transcendent) perception of nature, indeed as something like a catalogue of ideal forms:

One has dim foresight of hitherto uncomputed mechanical advantages who rides on the rail-road and moreover a practical confirmation of the ideal philosophy that Matter is phenomenal whilst men & trees & barns whizz by you as fast as the leaves of a dictionary. As our tea kettle hissed along through a field of mayflowers, we could judge of the sensations of a swallow who skims by trees & bushes with about the same speed. The very permanence of matter seems compromised & oaks, fields, hills, hitherto esteemed symbols of stability do absolutely dance by you.[16]

Back home in the States, railroads were soon extended across the 'empty' continent, linking scattered communities and regions. Emerson's optimism, however, encapsulated in his responses to the railroad, gave way to disenchantment. In 1840, six years after his initial euphoria, he wrote, 'The railroad makes a man a chattel, transports him by the box & the ton, he waits on it. He feels that he pays a high price for his speed in this compromise of all his will. I think the man who walks looks down on us who ride.'[17]

Even in his earlier account of the train's perceptual effects, Emerson had noted the rapid habituation to this technological marvel that the English — both travellers and roadside observers — had achieved. A century later, the celebrated American aviator Charles Lindbergh lamented his own loss of poetic perception resulting from his habituation to flight.

All histories of art's vacillating responses to technology invoke the early twentieth-century effusions on modernity offered by the Italian Futurists that ended up affirming the technology of death. A well-known passage by Filippo Marinetti, quoted by Benjamin, celebrates death from the air as wholesaled to Ethiopian villagers in the Italian rehearsal for the Second World War:

War is beautiful because it initiates the dreamt-of metalization of the human body. War is beautiful because it enriches a flowering meadow with the fiery orchids of machine guns.
War is beautiful because it combines the gunfire, the cannonades, the cease-fire, the scents, and the stench of putrefaction into a symphony.
War is beautiful because it creates new architecture, like that of the big tanks, the geometrical formation flights, the smoke spiraling from burning villages…[18]

In the Place of the Public: Observations of a Frequent Flyer

Martha Rosler

1993/6

You've the effrontery to tell me I must go to Kansas City to get to New Orleans. You people are rewriting geography! You're mad with power.[1]

Capitalism and neocapitalism have produced an abstract space that is a reflection of the world of business on both a national and international level, as well as the power of money and the 'politique' of the state. This abstract space depends on vast networks of banks, businesses, and great centers of production. There also is the spatial intervention of highways, airports, and information networks. In this space, the cradle of accumulation, the place of richness, the subject of history, the center of historical space, in other words, the city, has exploded...[2]

I grew up standing at the front window of New York City subway trains fantasising an effortless, unencumbered, but noisy flight through the tunnels. As a small child in postwar America, I rode the railroad from the East to the Midwest and back, and on many shorter adventures, and I developed a typically archaising love of trains. Unlike absolutely anyone I knew, in my neighbourhood where almost no-one could afford to own a car, when I was three years old I flew to Chicago with my mother and brother — an ostentatious trip paid for by my profligate aunt; I exulted even over the deafening noise of the propeller as we climbed aboard the plane from the runway. But for many years thereafter, even as the newly proliferating private automobiles were driving passenger railroads out of business, I did not — except for a recreational helicopter flight — fly again.

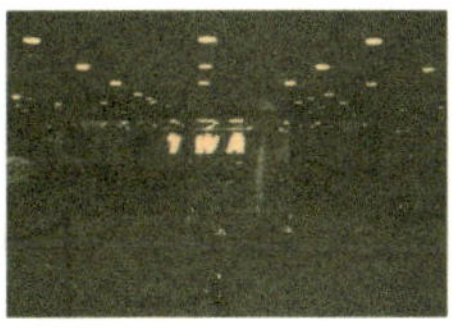

5.01

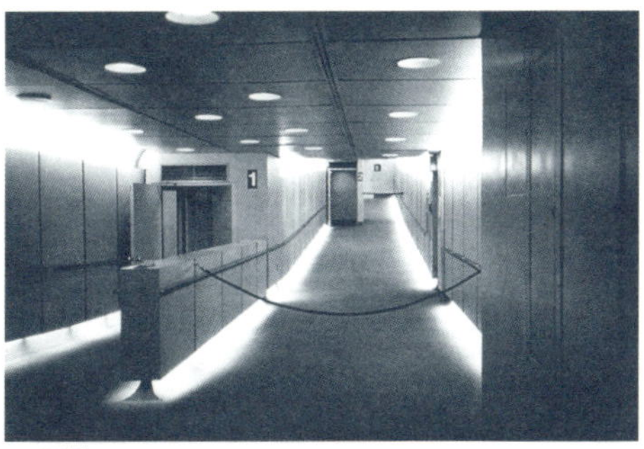

5.02

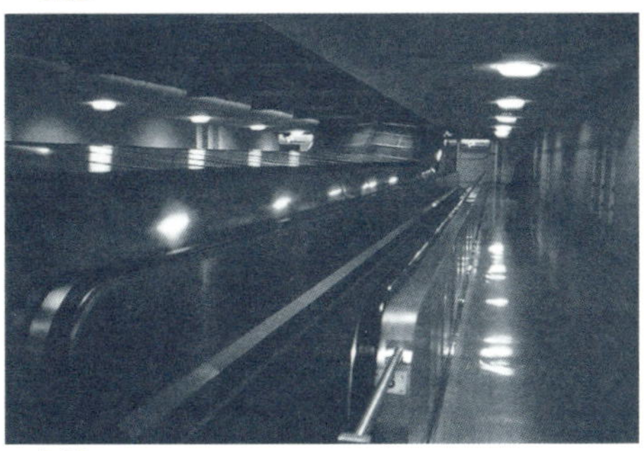

5.03

5.01 Martha Rosler, *Untitled, (John F Kennedy Airport)*, 1990

5.02 Martha Rosler, *Untitled, (John F Kennedy Airport)*, 1990

5.03 Martha Rosler, *Untitled, (Madrid Airport)*, 1990

All images courtesy of Jay Gorney Modern Art

088/109

War — and its pornographic appreciations — helped dampen technological optimism, even among artists, until it was giddily reawakened by the 'global village', mirage of postwar communications technology, and, more recently, by cyberspace. Such fictive 'spaces' created by instantaneous transmissions are compensatory for the destabilisations and fragmentations (the clichés of urban life) produced by the global expansion ('globalisation') of production and of markets. Despite industrial interest in a yet-to-be-realised technology of environmental simulation, at present the play environments of cyberspace are created by and for restive young men who find few places for mastery among actually existing social relations.[19] But even today the computer and telecommunications networks that join discontinuous actual places into working units create a functional cyberspace, however primitive and lacking in simulation cues. (It is worth noting the collision between the detective-fiction cyberpunk underworld of simulation games invoked two sentences back and the banal space of the operational office interior.) Manfredo Tafuri has noted that 'the technological universe is impervious to the here and the there. Rather, the natural place for its operations is the entire human environment — a pure topological field, as Cubism, Futurism, and Elementarism well understood.'[20]

The movements of industry and information that link discrete areas of the world and simultaneously create localised discontinuities in ways of life and daily experience are not most notable for their transitory perceptual effects — particularly those affecting the eye and perhaps the sense of balance — and they have their greatest effects on those not aboard the train (so to speak). Furthermore, there would be nothing surprising in the observation that, once again, the technology of speed represents a flight from the urban toward an Edenic pastoralism that leaves the losers off the train, immured in the city's immiserated sprawl. The scale of social and psychic frag-mentations occasioned by the globalisation of advanced industrial production and distribution is incomparably greater than those produced by train, plane, or space travel; yet these movements of individuals are symptomatic.

After a century of fascination with the ever-increasing speeds of transportation and information, our particular civilisation finds speed alone not particularly discomfiting, indeed possibly reassuring. Motion parallax, no longer confusing, is simply another special effect of travel. Unlike a pet cat trapped in a moving vehicle, we have learned to cope with rapid passage across the ground and the water, in conveyances powered by complex hidden mechanisms. Jet travel, in contrast, introduces a dislocation or destabilisation so complete that it is well to suppress the realisation of where one really is in favour of illusion. The technological development of illusionism has adequately kept pace with the technological development of motion, and it appears that those who have a taste for conjuring up the future prefer to do so through simulations rather than through anything as normalised and apparently orderly as jet travel.

The possible euphoria of actually flying, of being in flight, is not capitalised on by those whose business it is to keep us from excessive curiosity or from panic while travelling in commercial aircraft.[21]

The determinism of speed has no meaning in the sky, and the detachment brought about by the dream of flying helps organise each person into private space, making us the perfect audience for the in-flight movie, the perfect suckers for the unrelenting babying inflicted on us by cabin attendants. Airlines have only just begun to take the opportunity to beguile travellers with video and flight-simulation games and other electronic flight-related diversions. The illusions that are provided in mid-air replicate, by and large, the banalities of everyday life, or worse, the experience of institutionalised infancy in an imperfect womb.

The dignity of both passenger and attendant is left at the gate. Confined in spaces so small no-one in control of their circumstances would willingly endure them, passengers are pacified by promised diversions of food, drink, movies, music. For the shopping addict in withdrawal on long flights, airlines offer sales of high-end trinkets, perfume, electronic toys. As the specialness of flight — which once gave rise to expectations of special treatment, special food, special entertainment — gives ground to the ordinariness of air travel, the ordinary passenger does not hesitate to submit to the ordinary fare of homely television, complete with advertisements and 'news' reports, in the newly domesticated space in the air. The domestication of air travel attests to the falling rate of profit in the sky.

Look out the window of the plane during flight. Below is a vague array of generic sights: rivers, mountains, agricultural parcels; towns and cities; cloud cover and horizon. Rising sun, setting sun, a plane or two flying above or below. Except for the occasional wonder of the world, the scene lacks impact; it is dreamlike but without compelling narrative. You might object that a trip across the ocean in a commercial liner is not different, only emptier and longer. But on the ocean one sees the water and the waves (and feels their impact), one remembers maps and globes, one recognises one's place in a microcosm with a daily round of events, on a voyage that makes no pretense of instantaneity. Flying intimates that there is no journey, only trajectory.[22]

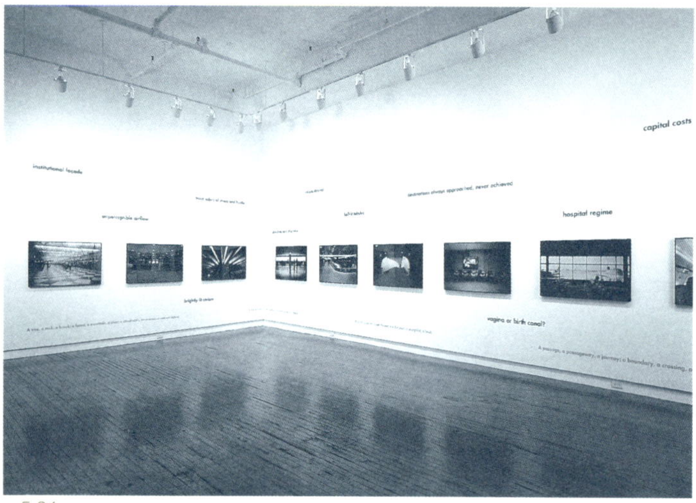

5.04

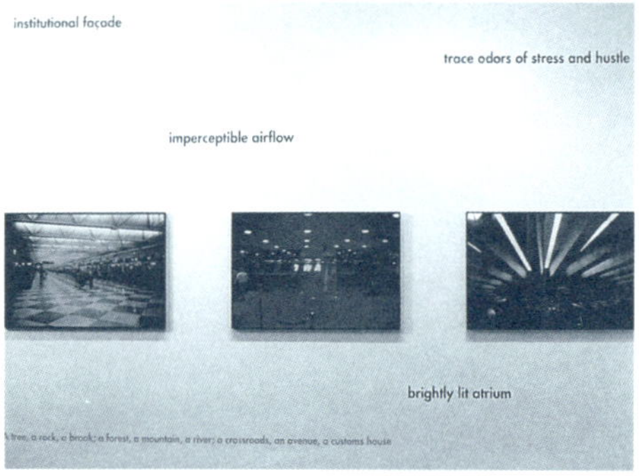

5.05

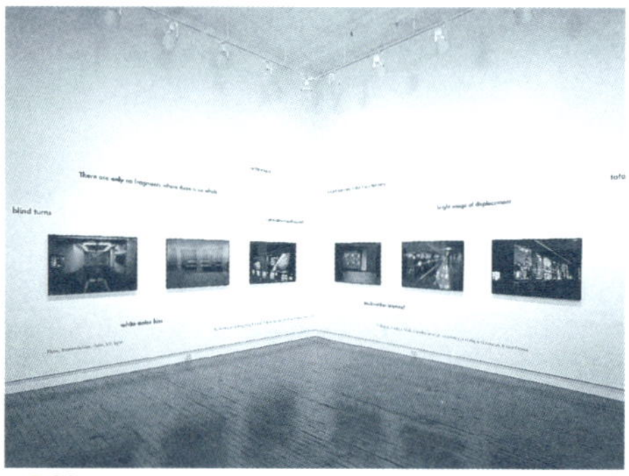
5.06

5.04 Martha Rosler, *In The Place of the Public*, installation view, Jay Gorney Modern Art, New York, 1993

5.05 Martha Rosler, *In The Place of the Public*, detail, Jay Gorney Modern Art, New York, 1993

5.06 Martha Rosler, *In The Place of the Public*, installation view, Jay Gorney Modern Art, New York, 1993

All images courtesy of Jay Gorney Modern Art

Look at the maps at the back of the airline guide: the arrows dominate the featureless shapes on the map. Less to identify with here than with the image of the globe from outer space. One US airline used to show the image out the cockpit window at take-off on their DC-10s; do they do so still? It is the rare passenger who pays attention to the cabin attendants' demonstration[23] of safety equipment, rarer still the one who obediently follows along in the safety guides outlining emergency procedures. Better to become absent-minded about such matters and about where one is.

Denial is a powerful psychological mechanism in air travel as it is in much of the rest of everyday life. Deny speed and elevation. Deny the thinness of the airplane's aluminum skin providing warmth, oxygen, protection. Deny the totality of air crashes, the dangers inherent in aging air fleets, the possibility of incompetent or inadequate maintenance. Deny the terror of completely relinquishing control to the hidden men/machines up front. Deny the small chance of hijacking or the larger one of 'pilot error'.

Deny the absurdity of the space into which you are shoe-horned. But think now about this particular physical space. The bit of social space hurtling through the air that is the airplane is regarded by its masters as very expensive real estate, and the smallest margin of comfort above the outrages of cabin class is expensively obtained. (There is a certain historical irony here, since Le Corbusier referred to airplanes as little flying houses [!] and attempted to adapt some principles of aircraft production to house design and production.)

The physical expansiveness of the gasoline-hungry Boeing 747s, although more a matter of vista than of bodily allowance, was supplanted in more recent US airplane production by the crampedness of the more fuel-efficient 757s.[24] In terms of comfort, the European Airbus is little better, though the Boeing 767 is. Even under the best of circumstances, the commercial airliner certainly is nothing like the ocean liner or even the railroad train, which gather their inhabitants in communal spaces for dining or recreation and do not insist on strapping them to their beds; rather, it is much like the least wonderful specimen of that despised proletarian hauler, the long-distance bus.

If the plane is like a bus[25], however, the journey is not very much like a bus trip — although each of these conveyances aspires to a hospital atmosphere under the firm hand of those who control levels of light, noise, and temperature, and periods of eating and sleep. But in the plane the smooth-faced attendants are professionals, and there is no getting off this particular 'bus', no physical escape for the duration. In the United States, long-distance bus drivers surely regard themselves as stern patriarchs, lecturing their passengers, likely to be working-class travellers and students, about rules and whatever else strikes the driver's fancy.

Pilots may serve, fitfully, as invisible tour guides and weather reporters, but rarely as guards. (As Captain 'X' explains, once the captain appears, there is no higher appeal, and if that appearance fails to bring order, what then?) The cabin 'stewards' of the airways, although modelled after obsequious servants on old-fashioned pricey ocean liners, also read out and enforce the rules.

As the commercial flight industry developed, the pretty young female nurses of air travel's beginnings[26] were transformed into smiling beauty queens (sometimes male) with a disposition to serve you food and drink and tuck your little self under a blanket. The flight crew called the women 'menu items' and saw them as providers of sexual services. As commercial flying grew older, so did its flight attendants, and the airline owners' fantasy of docile glamour ('Coffee, tea, or me?')[27] was beaten back by the organisation and professionalisation of this still overwhelmingly female labour force.[28]

Despite distraction and denial, the body cannot escape the mundane physical dangers — or the rather remote catastrophic ones — posed by flying, and many affect the crew above all. The frequent changes of time zones and of work schedules upset circadian rhythms (though it is claimed that a recently publicised pill, perhaps containing the brain chemical melatonin, will somehow adjust the body clock). The food, even in first class, offers poor nutrition, and alcohol consumed in thin, dry air is more intoxicating than an equal amount drunk on the ground. The dryness of the cabin atmosphere disposes to respiratory ills and diseases but also to dandruff. Air travel means exposure to an alarmingly high degree of cancer-causing cosmic radiation; at forty thousand feet, the average exposure is two hundred times greater than at ground level, and solar storms can greatly increase the dose[29]. Ventilation aboard airplanes is often inadequate because outside air must be heated before it is released into the cabin, which requires a great deal of jet fuel; therefore, many aircraft mix fresh with recirculated air. This recirculation of the cabin atmosphere means repeated exposure to whatever pollutants, pathogens, and vapours may be present, including 'side stream' cigarette smoke. Most of the moisture in the air is that expelled by fellow passengers. It is certain that respiratory ailments have been passed around, as cholera has been.[30]

The carbon-dioxide-laden air (at thirty times recommended levels) may precipitate fatal blood clots; less cataclysmically, it causes excessive fatigue and fuzzy-headedness. Atmospheric pressure aloft is typically as low as that at a ground altitude of nine thousand feet. The descent of small planes, even the workhorse Boeing 727s and 737s, may bring about motion sickness. As the plane descends, air pressure decreases, and while many passengers may suffer minor ear discomfort; those with colds or blocked eustachian tubes risk severe pain or even burst eardrums. And fully-loaded planes appear statistically more likely to crash than lighter, less crowded ones[31]. Finally, the plane is itself a disease vector, as the cholera case demonstrates; it has been hypothesised that AIDS was first brought to the New World by an Air Canada steward who contracted HIV in Africa. Because transportation links are multiply redundant, such diseases will inevitably arrive everywhere in fairly short order (or may even have been here already), but it suits the mythology of the present to locate the transmission of HIV aboard a jet.

For passengers on long flights — aided by the blankness of the environment, the paucity of reasonable pastimes, the heightened effects of alcohol, the poor air, the white noise generated by the engine, the cessation of the stress of running for the plane, of 'making one's connection' — the impulse is to go to sleep. Infatuated couples, mothers (or fathers) and their discomfited infants, people with high metabolisms or active hormones as well as compulsively occupied businessmen — those who can or must ignore the imperative to hibernate — run against the trend. In any case, aggression, along with the body, must be folded into a very small space. Stewardesses claim to prefer male over female passengers, and their favourite type is the frequent-flyer businessman: the person, in other words, created by the system at hand.[32]

Even though the realities of class division and ranks of privilege are replicated on virtually every flight (Virgin Atlantic calls its front-of-the-plane seating 'Upper Class'), the imaginary ability of those at the back to sit in the more expansive, well-tended front negates the impulse second-class passengers may feel to invade or to destroy.

What defines first-class accommodations on airplanes, where every passenger is a captive? Greater leg and arm room, recliners with sliding foot rests, wider aisles, fewer fellow travellers, quicker boarding and deboarding (no need to wrestle one's bags down narrow aisles deep into the plane's interior), more convenient and roomier storage space, closer bathrooms, first choice of business publications, excess obsequiousness and pampering by the crew, hot towels, non-proletarian (and almost tolerable) food, salt and pepper shakers, and wine from corked bottles rather than the screw-top variety offered in the back — that is, the rest — of the plane. (But the likelihood of survival after a crash is less at the front of the plane.) When second-class passengers, allowed entry into the forward first-class precincts by virtue of their frequent flyer 'upgrades', caused concern and annoyance among snobs who felt invaded by the less well-dressed or well-behaved, many airlines responded by importing an intermediate class from international flights[34] into the domestic schedule, namely, 'business class' (petit bourgeois?)[35] Upgrades thenceforth would allow cabin-class passengers into business class but never into first class, the airlines pledged. For those international jet-setters who disdain absolutely the company of their social inferiors and who can pay the price for speed, there is the SST, the Concorde. (One wonders if its toilets are less revolting at the end of a flight than those on any ordinary long-distance plane.)

One of the great blessings of railroad and subsequently plane travel was the inaccessibility it afforded the traveller: no phones. The perpetually plugged-in lower-level executive or criminal of today cannot abandon the telephone, carrying it into restaurants, on the road, on the street, in the train, and, along with computers and fax machines, into the air.[36] Phones are implanted in seat backs on some aircraft. Fax modems will soon be able to link computers, phones, and land terminals with their flying users; these functions, moreover, will likely be combined into a single pocket-size instrument.[37]

This telephone slavery completes the circuit of physical passage from point A to point B. As the plugged-in body moves through real space, the plugged-in mind, in the loop of information in transmission, has no respite. How does this condition differ from that of the social offender who, under house arrest, must wear an electronic bracelet? Alternatively, a passenger dons the headphones provided by the cabin attendants or those of a personal Walkman.

This interval that might be used for private purposes or socialising, for anything at all, is recast as a duality: produce or consume, work or be distracted (or become inebriated or unconscious). This never-terminated hook-up — an ad hoc version of cyberspace, after all — reflects the auditory horror vacui of all formerly silent public spaces, from elevators to restaurants to dentist's offices, places that used to be without piped-in sound, a condition of auditory freedom now apparently forbidden. An apparent exception may be the air terminal, which unlike the airplane or the telephone 'hold' mechanism, has not yet been deemed conveniently colonisable by 'easy listening'.

Eventually, the plane lands, the traveller arrives. At 'major destinations', airport traffic, on the ground and in the air, is often congested. Airports are planned yesterday and built today to serve tomorrow's planes arriving and departing at tomorrow's volume. In the United States only one new airport, in Denver, has been built in decades[38], partly because of the difficulty of persuading local communities to accept the disruption of ground and air traffic.

As with roadways, adequate planning is almost impossible because the future of aviation cannot be properly forecast, based as it is on geopolitical and business trends rather than merely on the logic of technological change. Overcrowded airports mean periodically clogged terminals, delayed departures and arrivals, heavy road traffic, crowded air space.[39] Captain 'X' blames air congestion not on planes but on communication: 'The real problem is radio congestion. We're flying near Mach 1 [the speed of sound] while using old-fashioned voice communication.'[40]

In the United States, the air-travel market was given free rein by the deregulation process begun in the late 1970s and strengthened in the 1980s by Reagan's policies[41]. But the deregulation of American carriers, while allowing many former bus riders to fly, also forced most travellers to spend longer on the plane and in the terminal, for during this period the airlines extensively developed the 'hub' system of organisation. In the hub system each airline is based at a particular city, seldom one that is a likely destination for many passengers — such as Raleigh-Durham, North Carolina. Passengers must first fly to this city and then, usually by changing planes, fly to their destination city.[42] Because of the local monopoly, people who begin or end their trips at the hub city must pay higher-than-average prices. Others pay the price of boredom or stress, waiting for or running to catch the connecting flight.

Because most air-travel accidents occur during take-offs and landings, increasing the stops along the way also increases the physical risks. (New classes of privilege are constantly being created, including the ability to fly the shortest and most direct way without stopping en route or changing planes.) Diminished service to unprofitable locales forces people onto the very small, more dangerous 'commuter' planes. It also often costs significantly more to fly to small cities than to higher-volume destinations. The airline industry is now poised on the brink of true globalisation, as airlines from various countries enter operating agreements and perhaps eventual mergers — the first moves toward the formation of international airlines operating out of 'megahubs'.[43]

Far from participating in a grand display of arrivals and departures, air passengers are politely hustled onto and off the planes, preferably through narrow 'jetways' that channel them from terminal to plane or vice versa. These blank-walled, elevated walkways share something with the elevated shopping arcades, or skywalks, in malled-in America.

It is the denial of the space below, the space that surrounds them, their demarcation of separateness and privileged passage, the nature of the (dis)embarcation. Were we, understandably, to apprehend these passageways as conduits to a netherworld, we might locate the space of the plane as the bowels of the earth, the subterranean erupted upward; invoking the crossing of Charon, a plane flight becomes an encounter with death. Or the bowels of the body: the airport itself can be apprehended as a series of blind passages and darkened tubules along whose walkways passengers move in an approximation of peristalsis. Out on the field, the airplane, often bearing a female name, lies quiescent, serviced by shuttling fuel tankers and 'honey wagons' (trucks that siphon off the toilet wastes), food trucks and cargo carriers. These evocations of the body are the closest approach to the possibly female in the phallocratic regime of flight.[44] That this regime calls to mind structures of domination replicates the relationship of air travel to the land, to the sky, and to the earth itself.

The airport suggests the meeting point of theories of time and of space, of schedules and mappings. The airport is a multidimensional, multifunctional system whose overriding concerns are operational. To state the obvious, airport design requires a consideration of a set of flow trajectories in vertical space, a dimension normally regarded as more or less stable. The most intensive period of airport construction (in the United States, at least) coincided with stripped-down functionalist modernism.

It would be interesting to compare airports built in the early postwar period with those built more recently, when the dominant metaphors of flow dynamics shifted from water to information — and the model of passenger terminal from railroad terminal to shopping mall. Airports, unlike railroad terminals, are located not in the heart of an urban milieu but on the peripheries and so are not subject to the same siting and façade considerations as other major structures.

Further, they are often under the control of different agencies from those responsible for town or city planning. Falling under the rule of the technocrat, they do not encode capital the way large urban structures do.[45]

Since the airport is conceived of as a web of functionalities, the idea of an architecturally imposing gateway structure, while certainly present, is secondary.

The conception of the façade is also altered by the possibility that ground travellers may, in the best circumstances, approach airports not from roads but from trains, preferably underground — though this is rarely so in the United States. Increasingly, they are approached by people getting off one plane only to get on another. That the airport venerates technical efficiency, rather than the state (or the public interest, to be sure) has resulted in structures whose experiencing subjects are atomised. Inside the terminal buildings, each atomised subject is in fact the same consumer created by so many other commercial transactions: an irrationalist, operating in the realm of desire.

Even excluding retail stores and landside services, the terminal at a major airport is a typically schizophrenic space, given over to the instrumentalities of schedules and movement as well as the equal imperative of pacification.

5.07 Martha Rosler, *Untitled, (John F Kennedy Airport)*, 1990

5.08 Martha Rosler, *Untitled, (John F Kennedy Airport)*, 1990

All images courtesy of Jay Gorney Modern Art

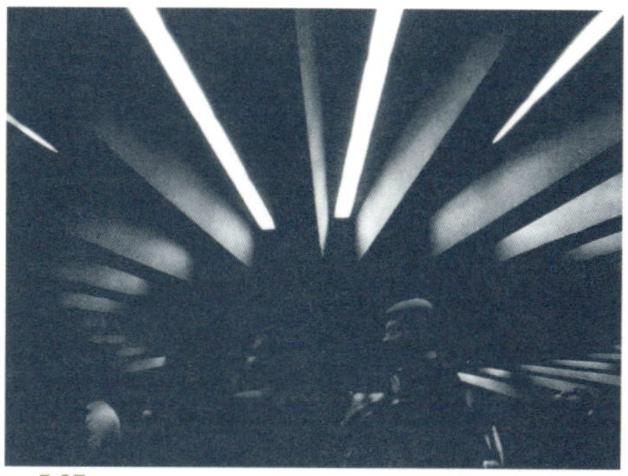

5.07

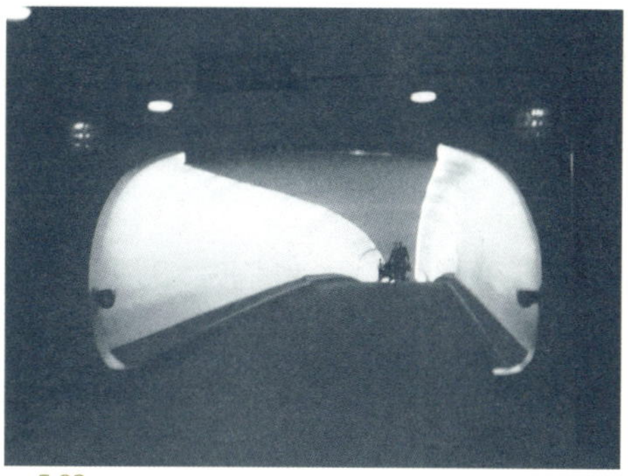

5.08

5.09 Martha Rosler, *Untitled, (Vigo, Spain)* 1990

5.10 Martha Rosler, *Untitled, (Vigo, Spain)* 1990

All images courtesy of Jay Gorney Modern Art

As a site of commercial exchange, the airport consists of terminal, hangar and airstrip (runways, taxiways, and ramps) along with ancillary buildings and access routes, a complex system of structures around which flows an endless cycle of production, construction, demolition, maintenance, and other forms of labour. The airport as passenger destination provides an array of services, the most fundamental of which may be toilets, telephones, and food, as well as access to air and ground transportation. The airport is the site of prominent security, immigration, and customs processing and, less visibly, of other police facilities and functions (of which more below). The airport is enmeshed in this web of customs, security, and ticketing procedures, this trafficking of food, fuel, mail, cargo, baggage, reading matter, sundries, souvenirs, and cash.[46]

The volume of air freight at commercial airports is likely to be greater than that of passenger travel. Kennedy Airport has an 'animalport' and huge cold-storage food lockers. Stationed at every airport are fleets of ground vehicles, including emergency vehicles. At large airports, the passenger terminal is further served by passenger pick-up and drop-off areas, parking lots for private vehicles, bus and taxi stops, car-rental agencies, and internal transportation routes.

The notion of the terminal as a passageway for travellers vies with the conception of it as a city on a hill, an enclave amid wastelands. Many international airports offer a wide range of services including lodging, meeting rooms and clubs, health centers, medical and dental services, amusement areas, even supermarkets. Singapore's Changi Airport advertises its 'city within an airport'[47], and Frankfurt airport (Rhein-Main), Europe's second largest, calls itself one of Germany's largest economic enterprises.[48]

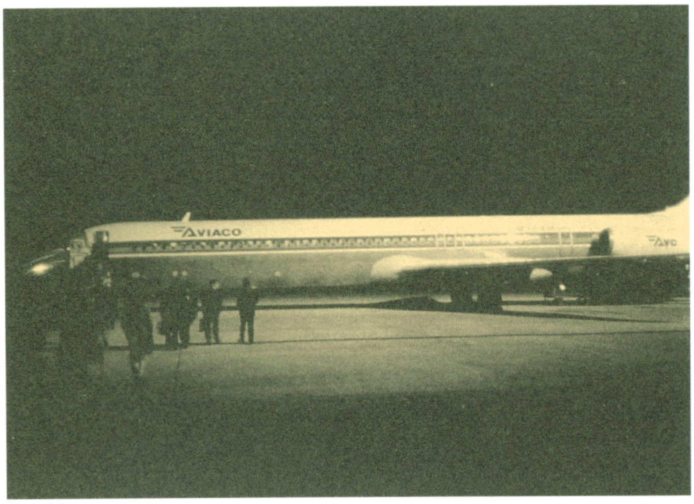

5.09

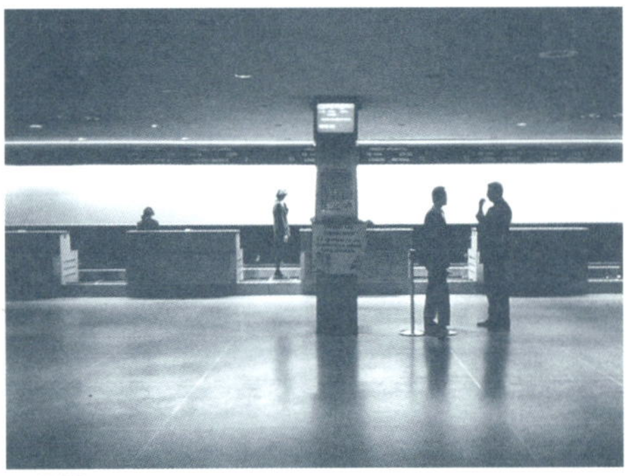

5.10

In the midst of the ceaseless activity of passengers and flight crews, the bulk of the airport labour force remains unseen or unnoticed by visitors. Executive offices house the administrative staff. The control tower holds the famous yet unseen air-traffic controllers — flow masters in whom the public mind has accumulated all the stress associated with flying so that it can be expunged from the image of the pilot and the passenger alike. Inside as well as outside, in interior tunnels and machine spaces, in unfinished cubicles behind nubby-carpeted walls, pushing baggage on and off wagons and conveyor belts, running X-ray machines, news shops, and food kiosks, driving little vehicles, pushing cleaning carts through the hallways or engaged in cleaning, changing bulbs, fixing escalators, or doing carpentry, terminal workers enter in and out of visibility to passengers. Airport workers, like in-flight workers, wear quasi-military uniforms, from officer to grunt. Most are local residents who virtually never get off the ground.

Except for a few high-profile terminals, the airport may not be usefully described in terms of 'architecture'. Airports reflect the thinking of engineers, underlining the historic split that turned architects into a profession of more or less willing mandarins. While the airport does not escape its conception as a system composed of a linked series of operational 'modules' — a term interestingly incorporated not only into the lexicon of space travel but also of the 'architecture' of the computer 'environment'[49] — it is useful to elide the distinction between architected and engineered space. Architecturally, the terminal is conceived as a hangar or shed. Many terminals celebrate the functionality of glass and steel, elements not only considered essential to the construction of the terminal itself but understood as signalling the fabric of the plane and the act of navigation. Façade elements are de-emphasised in favour of an interior that is often defined by glass but without the triumphalism of the Crystal Palace; but many airline terminals forgo even the orientation outward. Central areas or concourses range from the humdrum to the grandiose, with little in-between. Huge aimless spaces are marked off by rope-and-stanchion arrays to keep order among those lined up at ticket counters.

Away from the central hall, acoustic tiles in grim tracks, self-effaced flooring, fluorescent-lit low-ceilinged corridors are ubiquitous. The accountant and the crowd-control manager are the gods supplicated within.

Allowed past security checks, ticket holders hurry to the gates. For passengers there is no immediately intuitive logic to the terminal layout, which is often described in terms of 'fingers'. Such biomorphic analogies notwithstanding, the fingers may be on far too many 'hands' to make obvious sense. Airplanes do not rest like ocean liners in a great public arena, and airport bays and piers do not replicate the docks of ships. Instead, they run up and down terminal buildings placed alongside the runways rather than along the 'natural' juncture of ocean and land. You get off a plane and rush to catch another. So often, the departure gate is far away. You race along those fingers to a different bay. You run along or ride on a moving walkway, or you ride in a cart or in a wheelchair. (The suspicion lingers that the architect, the terminal owner, the leasing airline — at any rate, someone — harbours a certain satisfaction at 'showing off' the whole property to the captive audience of travellers). This mystification of place and space appears to conflict with the operational aim of routing people efficiently. Passengers are directed by reductive signage no more inflected than road signs (though the latter are meant to be grasped at high speed), to areas designated more like the rows in parking garages than like public streets. In the airport, as in the giant shopping mall or immense natural-history museum, an aerial schematic map tells you, 'You are here'.

At Kennedy Airport, Eero Saarinen's biomorphic 1962 TWA terminal, while attempting an inspiring interior, is probably more comprehensible from the air than on the ground.[50] At Chicago's O'Hare Airport — America's busiest — Helmut Jahn's celebrated late-1980s United Airlines terminal organises our perceptions in a straight-ahead interior runway with a big sky. If the great railway terminals created a pseudo-sacral public space with soaringly meaningful overheads, the United terminal is mausoleum-like, a reminder of individual insignificance. And that authoritarian black-and-white checkerboard floor! But Jahn, although predictably megalomaniacal, can be held accountable only for his design, not for its emptiness.[51]

Underground, those passing from one concourse to another are enfolded in an astounding fun-house of serially flashing neon lights and overhead reflections flanked by back-lit pastel walls of moulded plastic curves. Filling the ears is an a cappella sound mix of abstract melodic phrases studded with directives and warnings such as 'Walk! Walk!' and 'Walkway Ends! Walkway Ends!' enunciated by a perky female voice. I don't know whether this extravagant fairyland has colonised the dim tunnels through which I had in past years seen homeless pushing their carts or whether that Stygian space still exists in some other territory of O'Hare underground.

Like the airplane itself, the airport is not organised as a signifying space that creates a public — unless we accept their message equally to be docility, homogeneity, replaceability, transitoriness. This is a 'public' constituted only as a regulated flow. The internal spaces of airline terminals preclude collectivity or immanence. Rushing and waiting is the pattern of travel; yet, as William Whyte has pointed out, the seats in most airport waiting areas are individual buckets screwed to the floor in rigid patterns that create and enforce isolation, in the effort to prevent sleeping.[52] The terminal is full of television monitors, and full of people gazing at them. Some list arrival and departures, some blare out television shows, and some are 'personal' sets attached to moulded plastic chairs (more modules) into whose space a person slips, slips in a coin, and takes her choice. The airport is organised to offer instructions for motion without having to sound a human voice.

At many large airports, planes are not announced. When instructions are given, disembodied voices override human ones. I heard a Midwestern airport manager describe the monorail that shuttles passengers between terminals at his airport: The vehicles must come and go rapidly, only 90 seconds apart. But people tended to hold open the doors for stragglers. The airport tried using a recorded male voice to admonish riders to let the doors close, but it was soon ignored. A female voice was tried with similar effect. At present, an artificially generated voice like that of the computer Hal in Stanley Kubrick's movie *2001* is used, and it works. The machine speaks for itself.

Theme restaurants and pseudo-sidewalk cafés, which mimic public plazas under terminal roofs, are common in large airports. But the airport is so far removed from the public plaza that the right to solicit money for charity or to hand out political and religious leaflets, a right considered fundamental in the United States, was uniformly denied until reinstated by the Supreme Court. In this effort at a tidy order free of political or religious displays, airport authorities revealed their conception of the facility as a private space much like a store or a home.[53] 'Public spaces' are rethought as 'non-private' spaces, spaces of consumption and control or spaces of disorder, characterised by homeless people, crime, vehicular traffic.

In countries less dominated by the reign of commodities, in the peripheral reaches of the Empire of Signs, the totalisation of the airport as singular unified space is less advanced. In Johannesburg, commercial signage has until recently been minimal, the modest bit of art is commemorative bronze statuary, and passengers ascend and descend the planes via staircases rolled onto the runway. This has been a society in which consumers know themselves, and the State has other preoccupations than facilitating consumption. (Tourism is another matter: there is a full-scale replica of a Dutch Colonial façade in one corner of the high-ceilinged terminal, behind which tourist information/propaganda is retailed to travellers.) Sheremetyevo Airport in Moscow has recently come under contract from some European company or other, and there are a few gigantic electrically lit signs announcing Duty Free shops, and glassed-in display kiosks of electronic goods. All commercial signs are, of course, in English, the premier language in which consumers are confirmed, if not created. The balance of the terminal is shrouded in gloom, and the processing of passengers is archaic, bureaucratic, paranoiac. The duty-free shop as yet stands alone as the mirage of capitalism.

A new terminal at USAir's hub in Pittsburgh includes a shopping mall,[54] apparently still the only model to which an air terminal can aspire. (European airport shops tend toward the up-scale boutique; less democratic?) The huge terminal also contains a 'meditation room' designed by a New York artist and works by other internationally known artists, among them Robert Morris.[55] Many US airports incorporate art, much of it mandated under municipal 'percent for art' programs. A *New York Times* article called attention to the differential between the potential audiences at airports and at museums.[56] Unconcerned with the private-property argument about airports, the *Times* treats these works as examples of public art. It compares the Chicago O'Hare airport's sixty million passengers and uncounted other visitors in 1990 to the four and a half million who visited New York's Metropolitan Museum of Art. The elision of the difference between travellers passing art works and (paid) visitors to a traditional museum tells. What also tells is the article's description of a planned Baudrillardian simulation in the Denver hub in the Rockies: '…the facility will use its multi-million-dollar art budget to bring the essence of Colorado to the many transfer passengers who never venture outside the airport. Among innovations planned are a light sculpture that will cast changing Colorado cloud formations onto an atrium roof, and a 60-foot-long water sculpture reproducing nearby mountain landscapes.' The terminal earnestly approaches the status of the enormous room, the prison-house of culture, described by people as diverse as the poet e.e. cummings and Theodor Adorno.

This conception of the airport as museum is municipally imposed and does not follow the logic of the resident airlines, which naturally want to colonise your mind with notions of big and little trips. The works of art — often screwed to the wall like fire hoses, in thick Plexiglas cases — generally seem negligible, out of place, absorbed into the 'architecture' like inexplicable 'beauty marks' or eruptions on its office-interior skin. Airlines, as I have suggested, want terminals to be more like virtual than actual spaces. Airport corridors are generally no better lit than the average department store, with similar intentions — to cast you inward to the psychological space of desire. In the airport, desire is always infinitely deferred, and meaning is elsewhere and otherwise. Back-lit photos lure us to Tahiti or Cincinnati (unless we are in Tahiti or Cincinnati), to Disneyland or the Eiffel Tower, to Marlboro Country or to the land of financial accumulation, telephones and computers, or of remote outmoded forms of transportation, such as a canoe trip in rural Africa — sometimes both simultaneously. Travellers are even reminded through photographs of the existence of other planets. All are equal possibilities for fantasy destinations, all for some reason more interesting than the view awaiting the flyer outside the window of the terminal or the plane.

This sameness blanketing the world to uneven depths (and with however many rents in the fabric), this global neo-imperialism, reassures and defeats the traveller. The crippling comforts of the advanced world appear in many guises in far-flung locales. No news here; this has been true for a century or more. But the businessman linked to global networks never shucks those bonds, no matter how invisible and revocable they seem. Everywhere is anywhere when you retain the means to 'phone home' (or fax or modem home) at will. Then there is no 'there' there. 'The economic organisation of visits to different places is already in itself the guarantee of their equivalence. The same modernisation that removed time from the voyage also removed from it the reality of space.'[57] Photography and the creation of (commodified) space, which share a common cultural origin, continue to develop together; preservation efforts, always a project of elites, are being carried forward via electronic digitisation of images, the latest linkage of photography and computerisation.

Projet Patrimoine 2001 is in the process of photographing two hundred 'cultural and natural wonders', beginning with Cambodia's ravaged Angkor Wat, and making the images 'instantly available worldwide through digital transmission'[58] as well as through CD-ROM.

If at the airport profit and crowd control are the prime movers, surveillance is the constant practice. Surveillance may or may not be accomplished with the aid of hidden cameras, as in urban luxury high-rises or government buildings. There is always in place some dangerous and insidious Other to be invoked, and the entire international air-travel system now appears organised around the spectre of the international terrorist, a sufficient excuse for the remilitarisation of flight.[59] Especially in certain European capitals, terrorist explosives must be guarded against.[60] Yet ordinary armoured-car robbers of airport payrolls and payments,[61] not to mention baggage thieves and pickpockets, are more likely to be the interlopers at American airports — thieves and those with no homes. One aim of policing terminals is to prevent homeless people from seeking shelter at the airport.[62] In this task, US airport managers are fortunate, because airports, unlike ground-transportation terminals, are located well away from urban downtowns. O'Hare is one of the few US airports that can be easily reached by rail from the city.

The airport, like the modern corporate space, cleanly embodies Foucault's observations on the ways that information is used to organise and control people. Information, a necessity for every traveller, is not easily obtained. With any change in schedule or plans, whether caused by accident, mechanical failure, bomb threat, or weather, the system breaks down, and the flow of passengers stops. The oldest model of bureaucracy — information constriction, information sadism — takes over. A plane begins to taxi down the runway but for some reason it turns back to the gate. Told almost nothing, the passengers are left sitting for an hour in the darkened, unventilated plane, or they are asked to step back out into the terminal. Or assume you hear about a paralysing storm before you leave for the airport. You attempt to telephone your airline. After an interminable period on hold, you are told by a bored clerk that he or she 'knows nothing'. It is not, of course, possible to obtain the number of the airline or anyone else at the actual airport. You arrive there to discover that your flight has been delayed indefinitely. People are standing in long lines or in clumps trying to find out what is occurring, with almost no effort at co-operation from the airline employees, who stand behind counters, manipulating computer terminals, and decline to make eye contact. Hours pass. Food and drink are rarely offered. Sometimes hotel accommodations are offered, but regardless of the nature of the emergency, information is as far as possible withheld.[63]

On the other hand, the search for impersonal information on the part of the authorities extends to a microscopic level. High-technology bomb detectors, 'thermal neutron analysers', have been announced as being readied to search luggage at international gateways in the hunt for plastic explosives. (This announcement was made to placate the families of the people killed in the bombing of Pan Am Flight 103 over Lockerbie, Scotland, but the reality is that the machines tested so far don't work.)[64] More routinely, all hand luggage (and much checked baggage) is scrutinised by means of X-ray machines and hand searches, and people must pass through magnetic metal detectors or are physically searched. More personally, customs and immigration officers, inspecting people and documents, apprehend illegal entrants and turn them back. Dogs and men wearing bullet-proof vests and cradling semi-automatic weapons patrol many European airports, and photography is often forbidden. At international gateways, extraordinary measures are taken in the search for illegal drugs. Dogs accompany customs agents in cargo areas, and passengers on suspect flights are detained and searched, sometimes X-rayed for condoms or balloons of cocaine or heroin and held in custody until their bowels are voided.[65] (True story: detained passenger balks, waiting customs agent falls asleep, balloon bursts, detainee dies.) Drugs have been uncovered in the structural spaces of airplanes and in the luggage of flight crews.

The employment of people as (illegal) drug couriers represents a theatrical sectioning of the population, with the cast of the hour never knowable in advance: sometimes women with small children are the 'mules', sometimes very young girls, sometimes middle-aged women, sometimes old people, making the job of customs inspectors possibly less boring. Planes and passengers from suspect places — most of Latin America, Jamaica, Nigeria — are heavily scrutinised. Because of that, when in 1990 an Avianca plane with 73 people aboard crashed at Kennedy, out of fuel because it was kept circling during a busy period, it was rumoured — perhaps falsely — among customs rank-and-filers that the plane was kept aloft to satisfy customs' requirements for a clear stretch of time in which to search the plane and the passengers, and probably the crew, for drugs.

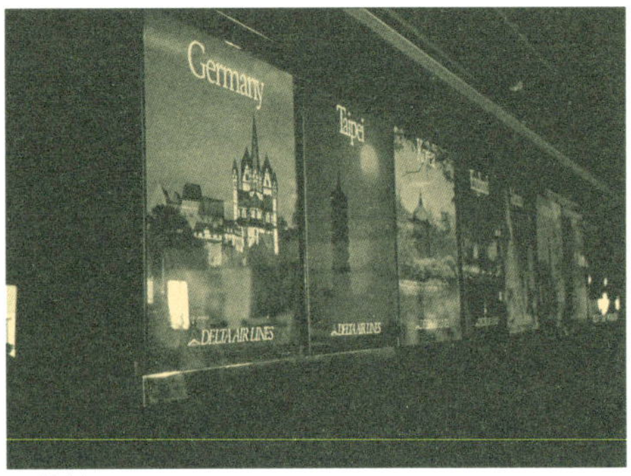

5.11

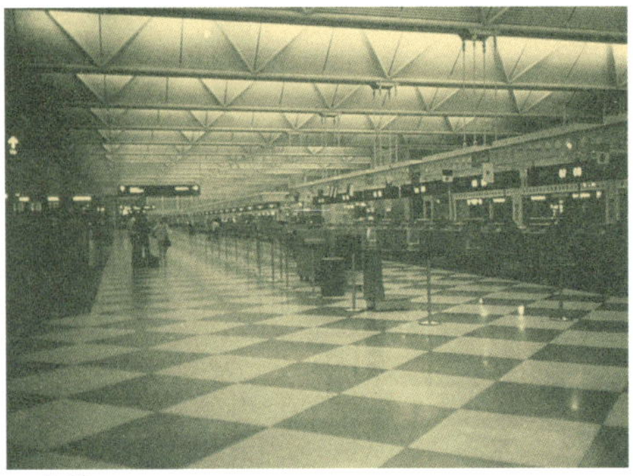

5.12

When catastrophe befalls a plane carrying a large number of Americans, when such a plane crashes or blows up, routine is left behind. Along with emergency services, news and information are marshalled for various purposes. The machinery of containment is deployed by the airline and the State, human-interest stories are written and grief is exploited by news agencies, blame is sought as a cathartic act. With crashes of international flights, the rationalist efforts of state agencies are offset by sudden suspicions of conspiracy and secret terror. Pilot error, the preferred explanation,[66] is not particularly reassuring to travellers, traffic-controller mistakes or mechanical failure even less so.

Foreign acts of aggression may suit state purposes. Worst are the suspicions or confirmation of sabotage. Sabotage, formerly perpetrated by persons seeking life-insurance gains, is now inescapably the purview of international terrorists, almost all Muslims. Mass paranoia, generally repressed, surges around such incidents, fuelled by the families of victims, who brush aside explanations offered by the State. As time passes, the families' dragnet is cast wider and wider, invoking hidden plots and counterplots by intelligence and other, unnamed clandestine forces, involving explosives and drug smuggling, agents and double agents. This was as true of the Soviet downing of KAL flight 007 over Sakhalin in 1983 as of the still-unresolved bombings of Pan Am Flight 103 over Lockerbie in 1988 and the recent crash of TWA flight 800 out of New York in the summer of 1996.[67]

5.11 Martha Rosler, *Untitled, (Philadelphia)* 1992

5.12 Martha Rosler, *Untitled, (United Terminal, O'Hare)* 1990

5.13 Martha Rosler, *Untitled, (Madrid)* 1990

5.14 Martha Rosler, *Untitled, (Seattle)* 1990

All images courtesy of Jay Gorney Modern Art

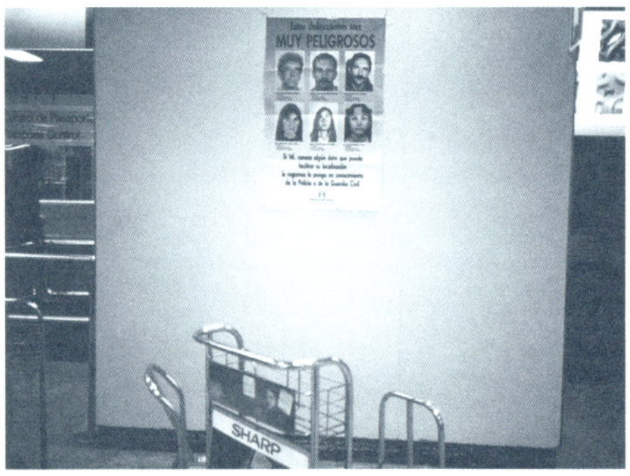

6.13

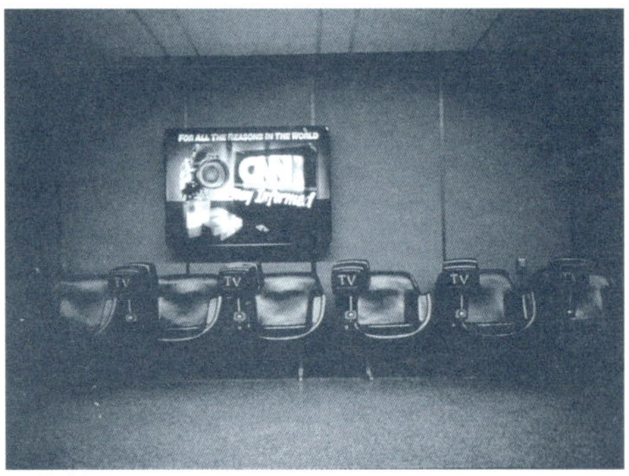

6.14

What of the airport as a gross physical, a geographic, entity? The airport's presence on the land is generally that of a wound near water. Airports serving large cities are often many miles from town, and the Cincinnati, Ohio, airport (so designated) is located in Kentucky. Airports are tremendous colonisers, rendering the land they occupy and the surrounding areas into wasteland. Like the ground under a city, the airport bulldozes and flattens out the spaces of nature. It brings the land as close as possible to the condition of perfection, in which geometry has conquered diversity or incident. As in Isaiah, every valley is exalted and every mountain brought low. But unlike the time of the second coming and unlike the space of the city, the airport remains a gash immured in temporality.

Air travel wrecks more than the land on which the airport sits; aside from the chemical pollutants inevitably introduced into the surrounding landscape, human and animal life in a wide area around the airport is disturbed by airport noise. (But money talks, and pilots are often required to loop about in the air, giving up a direct route in or out of the airport in order to preserve the quiet of wealthy homeowners below.)[68] Land values around airports and in the flight path are depressed[69] and working-class dwellers are annoyed and sometimes killed by overflights, as in San Diego in 1978 or Amsterdam in 1992, and in many incidents with far smaller death tolls.[70]

Airports, like all modernising modalities, serve the needs of capital above all and leach away resources from those who are not integrated at a sufficiently high level into the political economy. Airports, highly valued real-estate, devalue the real-estate all around them. And airports, like shopping malls and other spaces of social formation, are both consequences and causes of a shrunken public space, a space that no longer adequately functions as a genuine accumulator and circulator of persons and ideas but rather of consumers and non-consumers, or threats to consumption. Just as in suburbia or in inner cities, and on the streets below the skywalks and the outer perimeters of the indoor malls, service workers can be seen waiting for hours at bus stops or riding for hours to and from work, because car ownership is presumed to be 'universal', the ubiquity of air travel underdevelops more modest forms of transportation, such as the railroad and the long-distance bus. Some cities, like St. Louis, sink millions into light-rail lines to the airport while neglecting internal transport in the highly segregated city. Lefebvre again:

Abstract space reveals its oppressive and repressive capacities in relation to time. It rejects time as an abstraction — except when it concerns work, the producer of things and of surplus value. Time is reduced to constraints of space: schedules, runs, crossings, loads.

Time has disappeared in the social space of modernity… Economic space subordinates time, whereas political space eradicates it because it is threatening to existing power relations. The primacy of the economic, and still more, of the political, leads to the supremacy of space over time.[71]

A grand reconception of the entire Kennedy Airport in New York, which would have involved building an immense central terminal (Henry Cobb, architect, of Pei, Cobb, Freed & Partners) in the midst of the existing scattered terminals, was commissioned in 1984 and scrapped in 1990; the next couple of years saw recriminations over monies already spent by the Port Authority on even the barest traffic-flow improvements. The reigning paradigm always casts its meanings back through time; wherever possible those meanings are newly embodied in social practices, in landscape, on the face of the city and its structures. On the way to the commuter railroad that takes me to work from within the 'new' Pennsylvania Station in New York City, an enormous, hideous pit with low-ceilinged, dreary areas uncomfortable in every detail, I pass a series of photographs of the old Beaux Arts-neoclassical Pennsylvania Station (McKim, Mead & White, 1906-10) razed by the Pennsylvania Railroad in 1963. The face presented to the street — the architect's face — of this terminal, meant to replicate the Roman Baths of Caracalla, was that of monumental classicism and stability. Inside, at track level, the traveller saw a paean to engineering, at last a Crystal Palace of soaring steel. Without romanticising the 'lost' edifice, one may still invoke this grand advertisement for capital as the epitome of the public space, the physically embodied metaphor of an imperial people — as is the still-standing Grand Central Terminal on the other side of town. In these terminals one realises oneself, for good or ill, as part of a totality.
In contrast, in the airport, the space on which the new Penn Station clearly is modelled, everything and everyone is weightless, anomic, and the appeal is to consumerism, not to sociality.[72]

There is no middle ground between imperial citizenship and the vacuum.
In the contemporary Penn Station, the station for moles, as one descends the escalators one is confronted by an enormous panoramic lighted advert-isement that appears too close and is now groping toward its destiny as the backdrop of giant television sets bearing 'news' and stock quotations. There are no other signifiers of importance.
In comparing the two terminals, there is hardly any need to ask oneself, 'Where would I rather be standing?'[73]

After Penn Station's demise, Grand Central Terminal (Warren & Wetmore, arch.; Reed & Stern, eng.; 1910–13) was saved by New York's Landmarks Preservation Commission in 1978, which had to pursue its owner, the near-bankrupt Penn Central Railroad, all the way to the Supreme Court to keep it from knocking the terminal down in favour of yet another unnecessary office building.[74]
One may draw one's own conclusions about 'preservation' values from this — but not without the acknowledgment that both terminals, the carceral and the grand, house populations of people who would otherwise have to sleep in the street. Their passage across the landscape is in inverse proportion to the speed of those above them. The space created by capital perpetually re-creates its own underworld, its own space of 'underdevelopment' and immobility, its own wasteland.

…the twentieth century is a century which sees the earth as no one has ever seen it, the earth has a splendor that it never has had, and as everything destroys itself in the twentieth century and nothing continues, so then the twentieth century has a splendor which is its own and Picasso is of this century, he has that strange quality of an earth that one has never seen and of things destroyed as they have never been destroyed.[75]

How is it that we are confronted with a choice between the intrusive reminders of capital's aspirations toward total domination and the blank-eyed emptiness of anywhere/nowhere?

1 The words of an irate traveller in Arthur Hailey's best-selling novel *Airport* (New York: Doubleday, 1968; Bantam ed., 1969), pp. 20–21.

2 Henri Lefebvre, 'Space: Social Product and Use Value' in J.W. Freiberg, ed., *Critical Sociology* (New York: Irvington, 1979), pp. 285–295. Compare the passage as it appears in Lefebvre's *La Production de l'espace* (Paris: Editions Anthropos, 1974), in a new translation by Donald Nicholson-Smith, *The Production of Space* (Oxford, UK., and Cambridge, Mass.: Blackwell, 1991), p. 51: 'Capitalism and neocapitalism have produced abstract space, which includes the "world of commodities", its "logic" and its worldwide strategies, as well as the power of money and that of the political state. This space is founded on the vast network of banks, business centres and major productive entities, as also on motorways, airports and information lattices. Within this space, the town — once the forcing-house of accumulation, fountainhead of wealth and centre of historical space — has disintegrated.'

3 In the late 1960s, struck by the growing hegemony of air travel and the internationalisation of Euro-American style skyscrapers, I produced some collages with airplane-centered themes. One four-by-six-foot collage was based on aerial photographs of International Style cities and airports around the globe. I filled the sky above this everywheretown with airplanes high and low and surrounded the enclaves with bulldozed earth. Although no bombs and no destruction were in evidence in this work, the image of the B-52 haunted this, the Vietnam War, period in which the work was made.

4 Tour buses are another matter entirely.

5 It wasn't until later that I realised that deregulation of transportation, which had made air travel accessible to the bus riders, also made it necessary, since so many bus routes were abolished along with the competition. And still later I realised that many bus riders' time in the air market would be relatively brief, as short-hop fares rose precipitously, thus diminishing people's options and increasing the cost in terms of both money and time.

6 Walter Benjamin, 'The Work of Art in the Age of Mechanical Reproduction' (1939), in *Illuminations,* Hannah Arendt, ed. (New York: Schocken, 1969), translated by Harry Zohn, p. 240. Originally published in *Zeitschrift fur Sozialforschung* (1936).

7 The term 'virtual reality' was coined by one of its inventors and promoters, the American Jaron Lanier. The creation of this simulated body of experiences, which is being developed in conjunction with the military-industrial complex, generally involves the donning of goggles or a helmet with tiny video monitors and a glove containing elements that allow the wearer to see and apparently to touch and manipulate objects not present in the same space or not existing in the real world. The synchronicity and multiplicity of these cues serves to 'inform' the experiencing subject that s/he is 'in' the other space. The term 'cyberspace' was coined by the science-fiction writer William Gibson in the mid-1980s in his *Neuromancer* future-dystopia novels and refers to a vision of an entire world based on computer simulations. There is a certain irony to the fact that these nightmarish and paranoiac visions of a future far more bleak and disorienting than Orwell's *1984* are likely to be realised through the intervention of the military. For visions of this future unencumbered by such dark speculations, see, among other sources, Michael Benedikt, ed., *Cyberspace: First Steps* (Cambridge: MIT Press, 1991). Benedikt is a professor of architecture; the book is inflated, but less annoyingly so than Howard Rheingold's breathless *Virtual Reality* (New York: Simon & Shuster, 1991). The military, the aircraft industry, the entertainment industry, the architecture/real estate industry, and advocates for the disabled are particularly interested in VR.

8 The production-driven progression of metaphor making was dramatically underscored in the summer of 1992, after this article was completed, by the official opening by the administration in Washington of the 'information superhighway', the newly capitalised road to the intertwined information-based technologies of the future. Although the phrase has by now become common, we have yet to hear where it will be located on the map of labour, on the one hand, and profit-ability, on the other.

9 Guy Debord, *La Société du spectacle* (1967), translated as *The Society of the Spectacle* (Detroit: Black & Red, 1970; rev. ed., 1977)

10 *The Society of the Spectacle*, props. 4–6; n.p.

11 *The Society of the Spectacle*, prop. 167; n.p.

12 On the most concrete level, commercial flying was financially kept aloft by flying the mail, nationally and internationally.

13 See Captain 'X' and Reynolds Dodson, *Unfriendly Skies: Revelations of a Deregulated Airline Pilot* (New York: Doubleday, 1989). The captain is a pilot for a commercial US airline. To avoid mistaken impressions caused by my linking the discussion of virtual reality with comments by Captain 'X', I stress that the pilot's book evidences not the least interest in flight simulation or virtual reality.

14 My experience is limited largely to North American airports and airlines and a number of mostly Western European ones, though my experience in Russia and with Aeroflot reveals a number of differences that now appear to be giving way to capitalist cost accounting and marketing techniques. On another note, although some airports (the St. Louis airport and San Diego's Lindbergh Field, for example) make much of the relationship between flight and fight, I pay little attention here to the relationship between military aircraft and hardware, space exploration, and commercial aviation, except to note the intertwining of military and civil aircraft development and the ancillary command, control and communication systems. This all-pervasive relationship is of a piece with the rest of the military-industrial-academic domination of postwar life in the industrial nations.

15 About the design of planes, for example, I know little beyond the immediately observable. The ubiquitous 'streamlining' of the utopian 1930s was borrowed initially from aeronautical theory as actualised in ships, planes, and dirigibles, and subsequently extended to high-speed trains. It was then adapted to home furnishings and appliances. 'Speed,' wrote Norman Bel Geddes — along with Raymond Loewy, an indefatigable formulator and populariser of the streamline style — 'is the cry of our era, and greater speed one of the goals of tomorrow'. (Norman Bel Geddes, *Horizons* [1932]; quoted in Richard Guy Wilson, Dianne H. Pilgrim, and Dickran Tashjian, *The Machine Age in America, 1918–1941* [New York: The Brooklyn Museum and Harry N. Abrams, 1986]. Streamline styling, an evocation of speed rather than a functional necessity, had a greater influence on the plane's interior than on its exterior and was most comfortable producing fortress-like, inward-looking interiors, windowed with glass brick instead of clear glazing. It was passionately adopted by science-fiction illustrators as well as the architects of the New York World's Fair of 1939. It seems ideal for planes and for contemporary terminals.
But streamlining, along with the religion of progress which it symbolised, is past history. An astounding remnant, perhaps a 1950s 'moderne' reworking of streamlining, is the air-controllers' tower at La Guardia, oldest of New York's commercial airports. This tower rises like the sepal of a flower, swelling tumescently upward to a windowed top much broader than its base and covered along its sharply curved shaft with a myriad of tiny windows. The more subdued utilitarian functionalism of the 1960s was made homey in the 1970s. By the 1980s it was doo-dadded up with minor evocations of opulence. My favourite airplane decor accent of the period was a line drawing of a castle woven into the napless carpeting covering a bulkhead wall.

16 Emerson's journal entries are cited and discussed in John Kasson, *Civilizing the Machine: Technology and Republican Values in America, 1776–1900*, pp. 114–116. See also Leo Marx's classic work, *The Machine in the Garden: Technology and the Pastoral Ideal in America* (New York: Oxford University Press, 1964). Kasson invokes Charles Lindbergh's description of his first plane flight: 'Trees become bushes, barns, toys… I lose all conscious connection with the past. I live only in the moment in this strange, unmortal space, crowded with beauty, pierced with danger.'

17 Ibid, pp. 116–118.

18 Filippo Marinetti, quoted in Benjamin, 'Work of Art...' in *Illuminations*, pp. 241–242. I am leaving out Marinetti's, and others', celebrations of the speed of automobiles, because one is likely to drive the car oneself, whereas I am concentrating here on multi-passenger vehicles driven by 'professionals'.

19 One wonders what the implications are of the fact that when the industry in question is information transmission, techonological development may arise from an initial beginning in fantasy projection, in the space of desire, rather than in 'reality'-oriented problem solving. Magic versus science, the predictable antipodean choices.
For a consideration of the encoding of computional space as private (real) property, see the discussion of 'hacking' as trespassing versus the computer invader as 'a polite country rambler' traversing 'picturesque fields', in Andrew Ross, *Strange Weather: Culture, Science, and Technology in the Age of Limits* (London: Verso, 1991), pp. 82 f.

20 Manfredo Tafuri, 'The Crisis of Utopia: Le Corbusier at Algiers' in *Architecture and Utopia: Design and Capitalist Development* (Cambridge, Mass.: MIT Press, 1976), p. 129.

21 The airline industry, like the auto industry, initially chose to focus consumers' attention away from the technological in favour of strictly ancillary issues — styling in the case of cars, food, and other forms of babying in the case of air travel. The increased competition for (especially business) travellers did, however, spur airlines to compete in terms of a real-world consideration, although still an abstraction, namely, on-time statistics, as well as inevitably, the all-too-real question of fares. While the statistics are not easily decipherable, the fare 'structure' is subject to manipulation rivalling that of computerised stock-market trading and full of deceptive advertising and gimmickry.

22 On trans-oceanic flights, many airlines display a cartoon-like arc and plane over a city-marked map on the plane's monitors when other programming is not being shown. A friend of mine, a commercial pilot, told me of an incident in which the passengers witnessed their own plane crashing thanks to such a transmission displayed during landing. Is this a bit of folk-lore of the skies?

23 On some airlines, including Lufthansa, this demonstration is carried out not by the living attendants — safety officers, Ralph Nader calls them — but by images of such persons, or of computer animations, on the plane's monitors.

24 At the same time, in response to a recession in the airplane (and aerospace) industry, Boeing, the world's largest aircraft manufacturer, and the four largest European manunfacturers moved toward jointly building an eight-hundred-seat passenger jet. Fittingly, this 'superjumbo' would primarily service links to Asia from the United States and Europe, and there is some likelihood that Japanese companies would be included in any joint-production venture. One wonders whether airport runways and terminals would have to be adapted to accommodate the superjumbo.

25 Some pilots have been heard to complain that flying commercial jets is too much like driving a bus, because technology is usurping too many decisions; others, of course, welcome the technological advances; one said that finally there is a plane that flies itself — namely, the brand-new 777.

26 It appears that the first attendants were male baggage handlers, but an enterprising executive at Boeing, as a public-relations maneouvre, developed the idea of recruiting young nurses for the job. The conversion of a male to a female workforce is typical of the second, or take-off, stage of a mass-service industry and follows the pattern of such jobs as office workers, bank tellers, and telephone operators.

27 A recent incarnation of this geisha fantasy is the cloyingly saccharine Singapore Girl, the advertising persona of Singapore Airlines.

28 Now that flying is the established mode of travel, the airline industry has made its first tentative overture to the flying public to capitalise on the nostalgia effect similar to that which overtook rail travel, leading to the creation of special trains and trips for 'railroad buffs'. The English entrepreneur Richard Branson (who so far has catered to youth-culture individualists) seeing the link between recorded music and air travel (and sex?), founded both Virgin Records and Virgin Atlantic Airways; he also floated a plan to create an entity called Vintage Air Tours. Despite the relatively early date in the history of commercial flying, Branson's plan is, in effect, for a historical theme park in the sky. This isn't nostalgia for the pioneer days of the Red Baron or Lucky Lindy, this is a yearning for the imaginary unproblematic docility of regularised commercial air travel — and its stewardesses — circa 1940. Destinations appear incidental, but the charter venture was intended to fly between Orlando (site of Disneyworld — where else?) and Key West. Fifty-year-old magazines will be provided by attendants in pillbox hats and seamed stockings. But will it fly? See 'The Perfect Transport for a Flight of Fantasy', *New York Times*, December 4, 1992.

29 Matthew L. Wald, 'New Estimates Increase Radiation Risk in Flight', *New York Times*, February 19, 1990.

30 Seth Mydans, 'Cholera Kills One and Fells Many on Flight', *New York Times*, January 21, 1992. The flight to Los Angeles was from Buenos Aires by way of Lima, Peru. After this article was completed, a small furor arose in the media over questions of in-flight air quality and the possible effects upon health. See, among many examples, Martin Tolchin, 'Frequent Fliers Saying Fresh Air Is Awfully Thin at 30,000 Feet', *New York Times*, June 6, 1993, p. 1, and Martin Tolchin, 'Study Says Flight Attendant Infected 23 with TB', *New York Times*, October 21, 1993, p. 17.

31 Malcolm W. Browne, 'Fatalities Higher on Crowded Jets', *New York Times*, November 1, 1991.

32 Considering the plane as a job site, one imagines the stress caused by the uncertainty of employment consequent on the global changes in the airline industry, especially for US crews. See note 41, below.

33 The other class is not 'lower' but the industry-wide designation 'economy'.

34 This does not mean that there are no disruptions. Naturally enough, there are many — many of them alcohol-related. Lately, the *New York Times* has been publishing articles about 'unruly passengers', such as the highly-placed executive who defecated on a food cart and similar incidents in which men drunkenly assault cabin attendants and discharge bodily functions as provocations in common areas.

35 This expensive fare class is also trumpeted, of course, on the basis of snob appeal. For example, in newspapers on October 15, 1991, United Airlines announced 'Connoisseur Class', marked by wider seats, 'sophisticated CD audio', 'where fine wines, spirits, and award-winning cuisine are artfully prepared and presented'. Captain 'X' writes that 'since we've had lower fares, the caliber of passengers has notably deteriorated. Back [in the regulated-fare period], well-heeled passengers wore ties and had their shoes shined properly. What we get on board now may be ill-mannered street people whose dress and behavior can be pretty obnoxious...' *Unfriendly Skies*, p. 120. On January 10, 1993, in an unprecedented two-page spread, Continental Airlines pictured its quintessential white male business-class passenger, enjoying more leg room, better food and wine, and hooked into 5 different 'electronic' systems, only one of which — the personal colour TV — is geared toward entertainment. Specially designed reclining seats promoted a suspiciously cradle-like appeal in the forward cabins, and British Airways, in its 1996 advertising campaign, literally pictured this traveller as a happy infant securely cradled in the arms of a female flight attendant dressed like a middle-class woman of the 1940s or 1950s.

36 Airline attendants discovered that on long-distance flights, business types were barricading themselves in the bathroom while they charged the batteries of their portable computers. Upper-echelon types can avoid all such inconveniences by taking the corporate jet.

37 See, for example, Robert E. Calem, 'Look, No Wires! But the Pages Fly', *New York Times*, November 8, 1992; Anthony Ramirez, 'A Telephone Visionary Who Is Cutting the Cords for Consumers', *New York Times*, November 15, 1992; and Peter H. Lewis, 'Next: Wireless Widgets', *New York Times*, November 24, 1992.

38 The new Denver airport, long in completion and vastly over cost, may well have been a costly mistake but could hardly be criticised, since the mayor who promoted it, Federico Pena, had become the US Secretary of Transportation.

39 Aircraft traffic bound for commercial, general, and military airports criss-cross over large cities. The dangerous airspace around Los Angeles is called Indian Country because of the (racist) names of small private craft clogging it.

40 Captain 'X' and Dodson, *Unfriendly Skies*, p. 117. The captain did not offer a solution, but can we envision the pilot, in the plane as in the flight simulator — and in some military cockpits — in virtual-reality helmet and gloves?

41 The onset of Reaganism forestalled the minimal protections proposed for small airlines and unprofitable routes. In the 1980s, these policies fostered an industry dominated by a very small number of airlines, or 'carriers', run by aggressive corporate raiders spawned by these policies. Monopolistic practices were condoned or even encouraged in this industry as in all others, practices that formerly would have been forbidden by prewar anti-trust laws. These new companies were highly 'leveraged' — that is, created through the incursion of gigantic amounts of debt — and hostile to the interests of employees.

A number of these raiders immediately sought bankruptcy protection under liberalised rules, which allowed them to abrogate union contracts and wring wage concessions from their employees. Competitive practices were touted as allowing customers to achieve lower fares on small airlines; instead, increasingly monopolistic control over pricing, scheduling, and routing led to higher fares, far fewer airlines, and a reduced schedule.

The US market, dominated by a few carriers, is an unstable oligopoly. Thanks to deregulation, margins of both profit and safety have been reduced. The breaking of the PATCO strike in 1981 meant that 11,500 air-traffic controllers with every degree of seniority and experience were fired, and managers and new hires were put on the job. One may speculate on the significance of the Reagan administration's high-profile breaking of this particular professional association of government employees and the permanent banning of its striking members. Aside from signalling the end of the 'historic compromise' between big capital and big labour that had characterised the post-war economy, no doubt it also made plain the government's intention to back the airline industry in labour disputes to come. Clearly, the airline (and airplane) industry is a leading one, and the mechanisms for its operation were being realigned in favour of the most aggressive companies. In its first few days in office in 1993, the Democratic Clinton adminstration stated its willingness to consider rehiring some of the PATCO strikers fired and banned a dozen years before, and the process of repairing at least that part of the system was begun.

Yet the hostility of the pilots and other employees to the manoeuverings of the corporate raiders has guaranteed work stoppages and service disruptions for a long time to come — particularly on the part of pilots, who are the only employees in a position to shut down the system entirely, since 'replacement workers' cannot be put in place. The 1980s restructuring of the airline industry, like many other industries, led to the creation of a dual wage structure in many companies, in which newly hired workers entered at significant disadvantage. In these companies, in every non-executive airline position, including mechanical maintenance, ticketing, flight services, and piloting, there are now two tiers of employees, 'A' and 'B'; the 'A' are decently compensated and have job protections and pension and health benefits. Working alongside them are the 'B' employees — including 'B' pilots — un-unionised, with low salaries and few protections, less training, and less experience. They also have been shown to suffer greater stress. New 'start-up' airlines with highly questionable safety records often have been operating with what in older companies would be people working with 'B' employment conditions. The 'shaking out' of the airline industry continues apace, with most of the major airlines in the United States in extreme financial difficulty or just emerging from it. In 1993 the high-flying Robert Crandall, steely head of American Airlines, claimed in a long article in the *Sunday New York Times Magazine* that if he knew then what he knows now, he would have chosen another career and that 'unless the world changes, we [American Airlines] will never buy another airplane. The company simply won't be here any more'.

Soon after, American's flight attendants staged a strike to prevent the company from continuing to hold down compensation. See Stephen D. Solomon, 'The Bully of the Skies Cries Uncle', *New York Times Magazine*, Sep. 5, 1993, pp. 12–15, 29, 34–38. (PS: Crandall doesn't mean it. While employees of various US airlines, some of which have already involved their employees in stock-ownership schemes, have tried (and mostly failed) to buy out their respective bankrupt companies and keep them going, Air France workers in late 1993 paralysed Paris airports in violent actions against the prospective privatisation of the relatively unprofitable airline by the newly installed conservative government. See, for example, 'Strike Disrupts Airports in France', *New York Times*, Oct. 21, 1993, and Roger Cohen, 'Tear Gas and Chaos as Belts Tighten in France', *New York Times*, Oct. 22, 1993.

42 Even more unsettling is a situation such as Air France's two-airport system in Paris, which forces flyers going elsewhere arriving from overseas at one airport, but going elsewhere than Paris, to take a long bus ride in the middle of the night before boarding another flight for their actual destination.

43 This would necessitate changing US law against foreign ownership and abrogating the postwar international air-trade agreements known as the Bermuda treaties.

44 The interior of the plane, however, does little to evoke the female, drawing upon the masculinist realms of the factory and the office.

45 This argument may be more applicable to US airports than to European ones, where state control of the one major airline means a greater identification of the airline and the airport with the state.

46 And, inevitably, ordinary crime; see below.

47 In the perfect space of the terminal, retail is frequently extortionate and eminently partial. A recent visit to London's Heathrow revealed large signs promising that the prices in the airport were no higher than in the high street in town.

48 In US airports, nothing is left uncapitalised, and even using the luggage carts necessary for moving baggage from baggage-claims areas, through customs and out of the terminal costs (US) money.

49 It is intriguing but probably of no moment that John Sculley, until recently the Chief Executive Officer of Apple Computers, was trained as an architect, since in the interim he was a Pepsi Cola executive.

50 The outworn bird metaphor posed by the terminal, with its dual wings, was vulgarly interpreted by airport workers as a woman's brassiere.
At any rate, airplanes and the experience of flying have nothing to do with the flight of birds — any more than road travel reminds one of bunnies running down the road — except insofar as birds pose hazards to planes by virtue of their annoying habit of being sucked into jet engines, causing the planes to crash. At Kennedy, and surely elsewhere, regular though surreptitious bird shoots organised by airport officials make short work of the bird populations that nest in the marshy ground surrounding the airport.

51 'I don't think there's anything wrong in using a building to connote achievement and a certain commercial power. I think that's the way architecture has been used historically. Great statesmen, great emperors, great dictators always built great buildings.' Helmut Jahn quoted in Mark Michael Leonhart, 'Helmut Jahn: The Building of a Legend', *New Art Examiner*, Vol. 15, No. 3 (Nov. 1987), p. 29.

52 William H. Whyte, *City: Rediscovering the Center* (New York: Doubleday, 1988), p. 358, note to p. 121, citing an article by Robert Sommer in the *New York Times* for March 3, 1974.

53 The status of shopping malls in this regard has not been finally resolved.
It may be worth noting that the tranquillity of the mall owner's private property is solicitously guarded, but there is little protection for the unsuspecting person at home accosted by real or robotised hucksters, on television or over the telephone at unlikely hours of the day and night.

54 With regular mall prices, not the usual extortionate air-terminal prices.

55 Michael deCourcy Hinds, 'Airport Offers Flights of Meditation', *New York Times*, October 2, 1992.

56 Suzanne Carmichael, 'Stuck at the Airport? Then Look at the Art', *New York Times*, December 15, 1991. Art as a last resort!

57 Debord, *The Society of the Spectacle*, prop 168. The frustrating sameness of tourist destinations has been described by Jean Baudrillard and such other commentators as the Australian Donald Horne. All these accounts, overstated as they surely are for theoretical effect, point out the homogenisation of culture: the beaten path beats down that which it managed to reach with such difficulty. Erasure of difference always leads to efforts by the coloniser to 'preserve' it, but as a de-politicised, aestheticised set of cultural practices — as a 'destination'.

58 John Rockwell, 'Photo File of World's Wonders', *New York Times*, March 5, 1992. What makes this preservation through image appropriation notable is that it is a project of Unesco, the United Nations Educational, Scientific and Cultural Organisation, under the impetus of its new Spanish director, Federico Mayor. The project is substantially underwritten by grants from the immensely rich La Caixa Foundation, based in Barcelona and supported by its municipal pension funds. Technical services will be donated by Kodak, France Telecom, and the Gamma photo agency. The idea is to make images of endangered treasures before, according to the *New York Times*, 'they are further damaged by war or the environment'. It is important that it is Unesco initiating this project, which can be of interest only to the advanced industrial countries, because under its previous, African director, Unesco was boycotted by these countries because of its challenge to their control of information. (The US withdrew from Unesco in 1984.) Under Mayor, Unesco claims to have turned toward 'universality'. Experience tells us that claims for universality translate into excuses for domination.

59 'Realism' breaks through the implacable denial of the fragilities of flight when the anti-terrorism 'expert', paid to create a frisson in his employers and other listeners, refers to a 747 as 'a tin can full of several hundred hostages at forty thousand feet'.
An amusement item in the *New York Times* (October 23, 1993), 'Bomb Threat on an Airliner? No, He Meant His Bladder', explains that a drunken German tourist, Johann Peter Grzeganek, has been incarcerated for nine months because on a flight home from Florida, a German-speaking flight attendant interpreted a German phrase he used, roughly translatable as 'then the roof flies' — denoting an overly full bladder — as a bomb threat.
In another vein, one cannot photograph in many areas of Heathrow, particularly in areas that look out onto the 'apron', a prohibition enforced by men seated in little booths at frequent intervals along the corridors.

60 At New York City's Kennedy Airport, when a bomber blew up some baggage lockers in the late 1970s, all public lockers anywhere in the entire airport were promptly and permanently removed. Most airports, in fact, do not have baggage lockers.

61 Surveillance, of course, misses the big crimes that are the ordinary accompaniments of big business, ranging from extortion of protection money from freight carriers to the far more significant and successful profiteering at public expense occasioned by the constant building and rebuilding at airports.

62 Remarkably enough, Pascale Blin, 'Aerogares — Le Confort du design', in Air France's in-flight magazine for November 1993, remarks that 'comfy' chairs have had to be removed from Paris' Charles De Gaulle airport because of 'a desire on the part of the airport authorities to avoid attracting too many homeless people' (p. 76; the French text, on the same page, reads: 'Les banquettes de Joseph Motte, ayant seduit un grand nombre de sans domicile fixe, ont d'ailleurs ete detruites l'hiver dernier et remplaces par un style rigide.') This article, in touting a new departure from sheer engineer-driven functionality to architected and designed pleasurable airport spaces, nevertheless refers to these spaces as modules and units and explains that 'new security measures require complete separation of flows of arriving and outgoing passengers'. (p. 76)

63 Computerised flight information and reservations in the United States are listed in four nationwide systems, two of which, owned by two major airlines, control 70 percent of the market. These systems were forced by the federal government to include information about rival flight schedules, but their operators still charge high fees to competitors even to list their flights, and travel agents must sign exclusive long-term contracts. The resulting cost to travellers of the limited and distorted information has been estimated to be as much as $1 billion a year. See Franklin M. Fisher, *Architectural Bias in CRS (Computer Reservation Systems): The Loss in Consumer Welfare* (Washington, D.C.: Public Citizen Litigation Group, 1992).

64 John Cushman, Jr., 'Progress Is Slow in New Effort to Find Bombs', *New York Times*, November 15, 1992.

65 The use of drug-courier 'profiles' by law-enforcement agencies has led to well-documented charges of racism. The US Customs service is obsessed with 'swallowers', who have special profiles. The extreme concentration on drugs at Kennedy has caused Customs' interest in undeclared dutiable items to wane dramatically.

66 Preferred, that is, by management, which always would rather see the blame placed at the door of fallible individual workers than on itself, its machinery, or its mandated maintenance procedures.

67 Other still unsolved crashes in which sabotage is suspected include the crash of an Air India jet out of Canada, the crash of a US military charter flight over Gander, Newfoundland, in 1985. Each of these crashes has led to the expenditure of millions of dollars in investigative costs and damage payments.

68 On the question of airport noise, see, for example, Eric Weiner, 'Rising Clamor by Airport Neighbors Brings Gains in Fight Against Noise', *New York Times*, April 17, 1990; 'You Have to Shout to Get Quieter Airplanes' (a group of readers' letters), *New York Times*, May 5, 1990; and James Bennet, 'Plane Noise Faces Limits from F.A.A.' *New York Times*, Nov. 21, 1992.

69 Land values near some airports but not in the flight path are sometimes increased, as in the case of the Greater Pittsburgh International Airport, discussed above. Corporate, commercial, and residential complexes of significant scale are being developed nearby right along with the airport's billion-dollar expansion.

70 In 1978, in San Diego (where the airport is actually right in town, a fact growing out of San Diego's character as a city wholly formed by and for the military), an in-coming Pacific Southwest Airlines (PSA) plane with 144 aboard clipped a small plane also approaching this very dangerous airport. Both planes fell, setting ablaze a long swath of small houses in the immediate neighborhood. In Amsterdam's suburban Bijlmermeer district in 1992, an unknown number of poor immigrants of colour — originally estimated as over 100 — many from such former Dutch colonies as Surinam and Aruba, were killed when an El-Al cargo plane taking off from Schiphol crashed into a pair of high-rises situated in the flight path, at the undesirable outskirts of town.

71 Henri Lefebvre, *The Production of Space*, p. 287. The continued subordination of time to space is not my subject here, although everyone can attest to it — particularly women. But as I write this at a European airport in the temporal space left as a necessary blank by the enforced wait between my arrival at the gate for an international flight and the flight's departure, I note once again the inexplicable scarcity of clocks at airports. Time drags on and is extended and abridged in air travel whether one is at rest or in motion, whether walking or transported, in the air, on the ground, on the way to and from the airport, or within its precincts.

72 Trains, especially the high-speed ones designed for those who might otherwise fly business class, are made more like planes. In particular, the seats are more plane-like. Suggesting a cross between a school desk and a dentist's chair, these rather cramped 'modular moderne' units (to coin a phrase), are conducive to working or to self-isolation, disaccommodating those who wish to socialise.

73 Plans are afoot to convert the main Manhattan post office, of the same style and provenance as the razed Penn Station across the street, into a new-old Penn Station. Many people, I have discovered, share a fantasy I never previously confessed to: that Penn Station could somehow miraculously be rebuilt, like the Russian and Polish buildings razed by the Nazis in the Second World War. See David W. Dunlap, 'Amtrak Unveils Its Design to Transform Post Office', *New York Times*, May 2, 1993, p. 47.

74 An important brief in the case was written by David Bonderman, a former civil-rights lawyer who is now considered a 'takeover artist' and who tried, with Air Canada, to take control of the bankrupt Continental Airlines, America's fifth-largest carrier. See Adam Bryant, 'Deal Maker Takes Aim at Skies', *New York Times*, November 11, 1992, Business Section, pp1.
In 1989 the tremendous lighted Kodak 'Colorama' sign, a unitary image of Americana in place for 40 years, was removed as not in keeping with the terminal's plan. But in 1993 plans to install a gigantic high-definition television set were announced.
See Lisa W. Foderaro, 'Plans for a TV Screen at Grand Central Draws Criticism', *New York Times*, November 5, 1993.

75 Gertrude Stein, *Picasso* (1938, reprinted New York: Dover, 1969).

Jeremy
Millar 110/117
1997

Metaleph

is METALEPH. Everywhere is here. I've been walking around the terminal for a while now, killing time (think of it as a pre-emptive strike). Past wide, white walls, walkways, past the illuminated signs which hang from the ceiling, blocks of bright yellow with bilingual text, one black, one white, both incomprehensible. I've never been here. This is my first time in this place, wherever this place is, wherever it is that I am.

But I am finding it hard to convince myself of this. Not so much that it reminds me of other places, other places that I've been, but that it reminds me so much of *this* place, wherever this place is, wherever it is that I am. I've stopped noticing that the planters are the same (although of course they are, brushed stainless steel rings), or that the clustered arrangements are the same (although of course they are, in a progression of threes) but am becoming convinced, instead, that the plants are the same (although of course…) Every few minutes, I come across a wall on the left, each one with the same three doors, each with its own pictogram. I almost expect to see someone enter one and re-emerge from another further down, just as I reach it. These areas are not really mirror images but holographic, each part containing everything else. Trying to understand what is happening here is like watching an old science fiction film, or the news now, where from the part of some being, it is possible to clone the whole. Looking at each window, each passageway, each wall, I'm becoming convinced that if METALEPH was in some way destroyed, it would be possible to take any of these elements and reconstruct it in its entirety.

I'm told that there is a man who has been stranded here since just after it opened, unable to enter because he doesn't have the correct documentation, unable to leave because he doesn't have the correct documentation. He's state-less, and it's not a great state to be in, not a great state for any of us to be in. Astronauts on the moon experienced this dislocation and look what happened to them, drunks or recluses, suicides or angels. We can all try it now. We often think of communication technologies allowing us the luxury, the poverty, of being in two places at once, but we don't need their help here. I am here, in this place, METALEPH, but METALEPH is also in this country (whichever one it is) and I am not. I'm in METALEPH, but I'm not in the country that METALEPH's in. I've never been here. I won't be entering this country, whichever one it is.

I've been to a few airports in my time and every time, time appears different. For a place which is so closely controlled, where each action is allocated its own specific period, airports are curiously time-free zones. Times of the day seem to disappear, with people arriving from different places, from different days. That doesn't mean that time isn't important here; in fact it becomes more important, like everything else which has been taken away. I'm not sure how long I've been here now (I have no watch). I know the time of the flight I took yesterday, and I know the time of the flight I will take later today, but it is this time in between, between places and between times, which seems to lack any sense of definition, of certainty or of understanding. Time is like the architecture here, forever replicating itself, each moment containing the accumulation of all the other moments, moving forward or looping back again.

I'm approaching a large clock which I think I've passed before. Above it are the words, this time intelligible, YOUR GLOCAL TIME IS… followed by the time and date. Then it becomes unintelligible again. I am sitting in an airport, thousands of miles from home, looking at a clock which is telling me that it is now the same time on the same date as when I put my keys in the ignition and looked at the dash on my dash to the airport. I've been in two places at the same time. I've had an extra day, a day extra, and it's been spent on a plane or here. Is this the deal, that you can only have an extra day if you are in a place where you don't notice it? What did I do with it? Slept a little, drank a lot, read a book. I need to take my mind off this. I join some other suits in a shop looking at money magazines. *Capital*. *Forum*. *Foreign Exchange*. *Penthouse*. *High-Interest*. *Gilt-Edged*.

Flights are called above our heads, in languages which seem to correspond with neither the destination nor any possible stopover. Whole groups of people seem to respond in any case (I must wait a little longer). The whole world is here. Here

there are people, many people. They have come from all over the world, for all the reasons in the world, for all the reasons under the sun (some people must only decide why when they are already on their way). They come to meet people, to meet old people, new people, to meet different people. Perhaps the person which these people want to meet most of all is themselves, their new identity, the version of themselves which this new situation creates, or allows, or demands. Of course, you need the correct documentation, the right papers (you already have to be free in order to liberate yourself, to be able to prove who you are before you can become someone else). It is the privilege of those people with an identity to be able to lose it. Those without have to find one first.

I move towards the Lounge, its opaque glass doors sliding open almost in anticipation of my finding the access card amongst the others in my bag. Once inside, the space, the light, is quite unlike the rest of the terminal. The thick rust chairs certainly operate to an altogether different criterion of efficiency than the laser-cut benches elsewhere in the building. The walls are not patterned, indeed are for the most part empty, yet their surfaces appear to possess a certain amount of depth (one can imagine the designer looking, once more, at the Rothko postcard floating on the wall to the left of his desk). A row of telecommunications devices on the table on the right open on to yet another space. The light is thicker — it seems to be evening here — although a dial on my watch advises otherwise. I take a table near the centre of the room, albeit displaced slightly towards the window, my back to the view. A steward arrives at the table just as I look up and, after confirming how I take my coffee, he brings the small hand-painted cup to me. There is one other woman in the room, about my age, her skin like caramel cashmere, her hair as glossy as the pages she disinterestedly flicks. Her shoes match her bag. Her husband is asleep. I decide not to smile. Further down the room, towards the bar, a TV screen is for the most part black; rows of codes, abbreviations and numbers, roll by in candy columns: flight details or currency rates, the fluctuating combinations of global exchanges. A young man, much younger, emerges from a doorway by the side of the bar. Dressed in immaculate Friday casuals, he approaches his table — I can now see his leather satchel on the floor — and sits facing the window. He reaches down with his left hand towards the satchel (already unbuckled) and removes a paperback. They are probably about the same age. Leaning forward, the book cradled in his hand, he begins to read the large black type on the back cover. Of the spine which faces me, only the letters THE VOY are visible above his thumb nail, and further down, in blue, E-GR. A rich sweet smell floats from the open toffee pages, like marsh-mallows, like wood, like toffee. I flick passed the title pages and read the first line. *It was as if no-one had heard*.

I notice an older woman at the table to my right looking at my hands. Her eyes shift when she notices I've noticed. I decide not to smile. I close my eyes tight, open them wide, hoping to fix the words onto the page below them. I left the city early this morning, although you can never be early enough to beat the 24-hour traffic jams. Perhaps I should have left yesterday, or the day before (but you can never leave early enough to beat the 24-hour traffic jams). The journey to the station was long, although I didn't mind that (I love coming here). In fact, I found it reassuring, as if the city were saying, 'We read your paper and you were right. And to prove it…' I sat in the cab, concrete ribbons swerving around us and through the city faster than anything upon them. There were two more Expressways (love that) running above, weaving almost in parallel with us, and another below, with two walkways running across us, between them (they'd be perpendicular if there were any straight lines). I could barely see the ground from there. In that paper I mentioned earlier, I describe these Expressways as the most important buildings in the city, 'the perfect symbol of a hypertrophied capitalism, where everything is in circulation and nothing can circulate.' I'm supposed to be presenting it again tomorrow, and I think I might drop this journey in somewhere, as evidence. Now, if it had made me miss my flight… On the west coast they love this city, they can't get enough of it (and they have quite a bit already). There

I welcome the transience, alienation and discontinuities, and its unashamed response to the pressures of speed, disposability and the instant impulse. Here, under the flight paths of Heathrow, everything is designed for the next five minutes. Its temple, and for me the most inspiring building in England today, is Michael Manser's superb Heathrow Hilton, near Terminal 4. Its vast atrium resembles a planetarium in the way that it salutes the vast skies above its roof.

By comparison with London Airport, London itself seems hopelessly antiquated. Its hundreds of miles of gentrified stucco are an aching hangover from the 19th century that should have been bulldozed decades ago. London may well be the only world capital — with the possible exception of Moscow — that has gone from the 19th century to the 21st without experiencing all the possibilities and excitements of the 20th in any meaningful way. Visiting London, I always have the sense of a city devised as an instrument of political control, like the class system that preserves England from revolution. The labyrinth of districts and boroughs, the endless columned porticoes that once guarded the modest terraced cottages of Victorian clerks, together make clear that London is a place where everyone knows their place.

By contrast, at an airport like Heathrow the individual is defined not by the tangible ground mortgaged into his soul for the next 40 years, but by the indeterminate flicker of flight numbers trembling on an annunciator screen. We are no longer citizens with civic obligations and band-rated identities, but passengers for whom all destinations are theoretically open, our lightness of baggage mandated by the system.

Airports have become a new kind of discontinuous city, whose vast populations, measured by annual passenger through-puts, are entirely transient, purposeful and, for the most part, happy. An easy camaraderie rules the departure lounges, along with the virtual abolition of nationality — whether we are Scots or Japanese is far less important than where we are going. I've long suspected that people are only truly happy and aware of a real purpose to their lives when they hand over their tickets at the check-in.

Above all, airports are places of good news. I miss the days when celebrities were photographed as they stepped through airliner doors. The headiest ozone of glamour and optimism crossed the Atlantic in the Constellations and Stratocruisers as Hollywood stars, Presidents and tycoons waved from the steps, bringing their confidence and likeability to this northern European corner of the depressed world.

I suspect that the airport will be the true city of the 21st century. The great airports of the planet are already the suburbs of an invisible world capital, a virtual metropolis whose faubourgs are named Heathrow, Kennedy, Charles de Gaulle, Nagoya, a centripetal city whose population forever circles its notional centre, and will never need to gain access to its dark heart.

A mastery of the discontinuities of metropolitan life has always been essential to the successful urban dweller — we live in a street where we know none of our neighbours, and our close friends live equally isolated lives within 50 square miles around us. We work in a district five miles away, shop in another and see films and plays in a third. A failure to master these discontinuities, whether social or genetic in origin, leaves some ethnic groups at a disadvantage, forced into enclaves that seem to reconstitute ancestral village mental maps.

But the modern airport defuses these tensions, and offers its passengers the pleasures and social reassurance of the boarding lounge, an instantly summoned village whose life span is long enough to claim us, and short enough not to be a burden.

The terminal concourses are the ramblas and agoras of the future city, time-free zones where all the clocks of the world are displayed, an atlas of arrivals and destinations forever updating itself, where briefly we become true world-citizens. Air travel may well be the most important civic duty that we discharge today, erasing class and national distinctions and subsuming them within the unitary global culture of the departure lounge.

In addition to the airport itself, I value the benevolent social and architectural influence that a huge transit facility like Heathrow casts on the urban landscape around it. I have learned to like the intricate network of perimeter roads, the car rental offices, air freight depots and travel clinics, the light industrial and motel architecture that unvaryingly surrounds every major airport in the world. Together they constitute the reality of our lives, rather than some mythical domain of village greens, cathedral closes and manorial vistas. Much as I admire, say, Syon House, now home to a huge garden centre and venue for business entertaining, I feel more at home driving through an office park like the New Square complex at Bedford, its high-tech corporate hangars only a javelin's throw from the Heathrow perimeter road, and surely influenced by the proximity of all those 747 tailplanes that cruise the tarmac like the fins of amiable sharks.

Even the old terminal buildings, 1, 2 and 3, have a certain period charm. Together, they and the main control tower represent the last survival of the Festival of Britain. I look forward to their replacement in due course, and to the new terminal 5, and beyond that to terminals 6 and 7, and the transformation of Britain into the ultimate departure lounge. After all, we have every reason to leave.

Towards the Development of an Air Terminal Site

122/
129

Robert Smithson 1967

Towards the Development of an Air Terminal Site

Robert Smithson
First published Artforum, June 1967

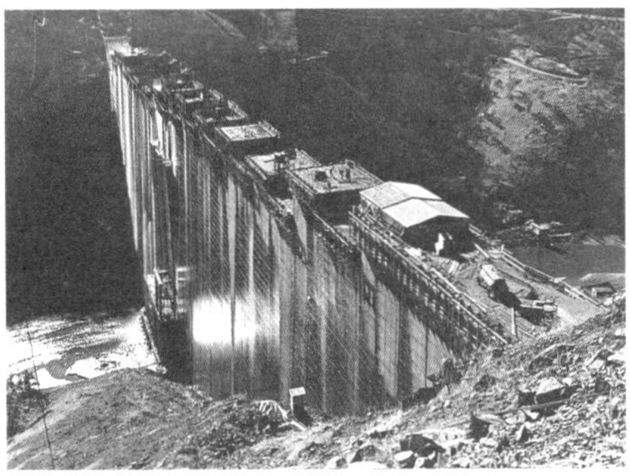
8.01

If it resembles something, it would no longer be the whole. — Paul Valéry

Since July 1966, I've been rendering consultation and advice as an 'artist consultant' to Tippetts-Abbett-McCarthy-Stratton (Engineers and Architects). The project concerns the development of an air terminal between Fort Worth and Dallas. From time to time, after studying various maps, surveys, reports, specifications, and construction models, I meet with Walther Prokosch, John Gardner and Ernest Schwiebert in order to discuss the overall plan. I have engaged in these discussion not as an architect or engineer, but simply as an artist. The discussions do not operate on any presupposed notion of art, engineering or architecture. The problems disclose themselves, as we encounter them. The actual meaning follows an exploratory path.

The actual meaning of an air terminal and how it relates to aircraft is one such problem. As the aircraft ascends to higher and higher altitudes and flies at faster speeds, its meaning as an object changes — one could say even reverses. The streamlined design of our earlier aircraft becomes increasingly more truncated and angular. Our whole notion of airflight is casting off the old meaning of speed through space, and developing a new meaning based on instantaneous time. The aircraft no longer 'represents' a bird or animal (the flying tigers) in an organic way, because the movement of air around the craft is no longer visible. The meaning of airflight has for the most part been conditioned by a rationalism that supposes truths — such as nature, progress, and speed. Such meanings are merely 'categorical' and have no basis in actual fact. The same condition exists in art, if one sees the art through the rational categories of 'painting, sculpture and architecture'. The rationalist sees only the details and never the whole. The categories that proceed from rational logic inflate a linguistic detail into a dated system of meaning, so that we cannot see the aircraft through the 'speed'. Language problems are often at the bottom of most rationalistic 'objectivity'. One must be conscious of the changes in language, before one attempts to discover the form of an object or fact.

Let us now try to delimit some new meanings in terms of actual facts of today's new aircraft. By extracting aesthetic morphologies from existing aircraft, the same way an artist extracts meanings from a given 'art object', we should find a whole new set of values.

If an aircraft discloses itself on an instant network of time, the result is an immobilisation of space. This immobilisation of space becomes more apparent if we consider the high altitude satellite. The fartherout an object goes in space, the less it represents the old rational idea of visible speed. The streamlines of space are replaced by the crystalline structure of time. An example of this is the SECOR surveying satellite fabricated by the Cubic Corporation. This 45-pound object enables surveyors to tie together land masses separated by more than 2000 miles of land or water, roughly the distance between the US mainland and Hawaii. It increases the capability of the geodetic surveying program.

This kind of 'aerosurveying' derives from a more elementary type of land surveying. The instrument that the surveyor uses on the ground level is a telescope mounted on a tripod and fitted with cross hairs and a level. This enables the surveyor to find the points of identical elevation. The surveyor locates the boundaries of land tracts by measuring various sites within a network of lines and angles. This he does with the aid of the 'surveyor's measure':

7.92 inches = 1 link
100 links = 1 chain or 66 feet
80 chains = 1 mile
625 square links = 1 square pole
16 square poles = 1 square chain
10 square chains = 1 acre
640 acres = 1 section, or 1 square mile
36 sections = 1 township

The maps that surveyors develop from coordinating land and air masses resemble crystalline grid network. Mapping the Earth, the Moon, or other planets is similar to the mapping of crystals. Because the world is round, grid coordinates are shown to be spherical, rather than rectangular. Yet, the rectangular grid fits within the spherical grid. Latitude and longitude lines are a terrestrial system much like our city system of avenues and streets. In short, all air and land is locked into a vast lattice. This lattice may take the shape of any of the six Crystal Systems. '... I saw all the mirrors in the planet and none reflected me ...' (Borges).

Alexander Graham Bell (1847–1922), known to most people as the inventor of the telephone, was also interested in the problems of aerodynamics, aeronautics, shipbuilding engineering science, medicine, electrical engineering, and surveying. In Konrad Wachsmann's book *The Turning Point of Building*, we learn something of Bell's concern with 'airborne structures' and how they relate to mass production. Bell designed kites based on tetragonal units, that on an aesthetic level resemble the satellites such as the SECOR. His units were prefabricated, standardised and crystalline, not unlike Buckminster Fuller's inventions.

He also built a pyramid-shaped outdoor observation station that reminds one of the art of Robert Morris. (Unlike Bell, Morris would not want to 'live' in his art.) From inside his solid tetrahedron Bell surveyed his 'flight' projects — the tetragonal lattice-kites. A grid connection was established by him between ground and air through this crystalline system. The solid mirrored the lattice. The site was joined to the sky in a structural equation. Bell's awareness of the physical properties of language, by way of the telephone, kept him from misunder-standing language and object relationships. Language was transformed by Bell into linguistic objects.

In this way he avoided the rational categories of art. The impact of 'telephone language' on physical structure remains to be studied. A visual language of modules seems to have emerged from Bell's investigations. Points, lines, areas, or volumes establish the syntax of sites.

All language becomes an alphabet of sites, or it becomes what we will call the air terminal between Fort Worth and Dallas. The entire project shall rest on an elevation of about 550 feet to 620 feet. The area is well drained and practically free of trees and natural obstructions. The subsurface site of the project contains sediments from the Cretaceous Age. This underground site was penetrated by 'auger borings' and 'core borings'. All the soil samples encountered in the borings were visually classified and tested. These samples ranged from clay to shale rock. The 'boring' if seen as a discrete step in the development of the whole site has an aesthetic value. It is an 'invisible hole', and could be defined by Carl Andre's motto — 'A thing is a hole in a thing it is not'. The 'boring' like other 'earth works', is becoming more and more important to artists. Pavements, holes, trenches, mounds, heaps, paths, ditches, roads, terraces, etc., all have an aesthetic potential.

8.01 Pine Flat Dam, Sacramento, California. This dam is seen as a functionless wall. When it functions as a dam, it will cease being a work of art and become a 'utility'. (Site selection made by Robert Smithson.)

8.02 Dam foundation site, somewhere in Texas. If viewed as a 'discreet stage' it becomes an abstract work of art that vanishes as it develops. (Site selection made by Robert Smithson.)

8.03 Dallas Fort Worth Regional Airport Layout Plan (Tippetts, Abbett, McCarthy & Stratton)

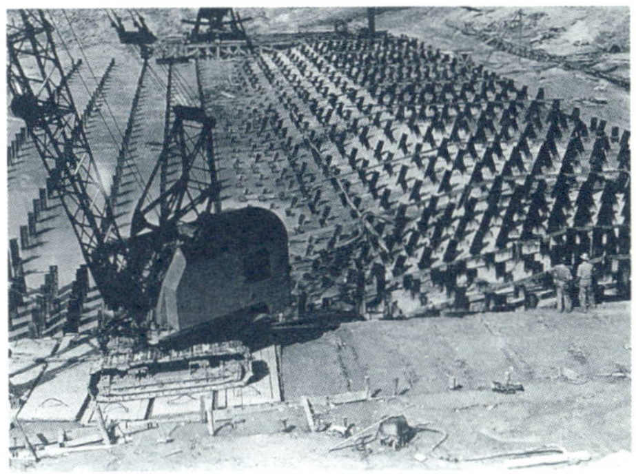

8.02

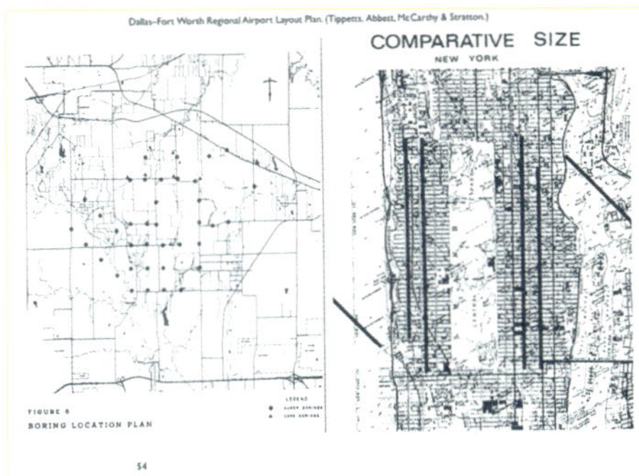

8.03

Remote places such as the Pine Barrens of New Jersey and the frozen wastes of the North and South Poles could be coordinated by art forms that would use the actual land as a medium. Television could transmit such activity all over the world. Instead of using a paintbrush to make his art, Robert Morris would like to use a bulldozer. Consider a 'City of Ice' in the Arctic, that would contain frigid labyrinths, glacial pyramids, and towers of snow, all built according to strict abstract systems. Or an amorphous 'City of Sand' that would be nothing but artificial dunes, and shallow sand pits.

The air terminal — also known as the Universe — rests on a firmament of statistics. Here statistics are the abysmal archetypes that engender the entire complex of buildings. This terminal area of approximately 600 acres is enclosed by a two-way taxi system approximately 9,000 feet in length by 3,000 feet in width. This inscrutable terminal exceeds and rejects all termination. The following 'spaces' have been engendered by the individual airlines:

Terminal Buildings

Airline	Square Feet
American	1,400
Braniff	100,300
Central	14,500
Continental	34,400
Delta	70,700
Eastern	13,700
Mexicana	3,400
Trans-Texas	17,700
Western	13,800
Total	329,900

The process behind the air terminal endlessly plans and replans its concessions, agencies, and facilities from masses of information. Here unit terminals are not conceived as trip terminus points. Here no gate position has a unique location. The distribution of car traffic is maintained by a central axis of roadways that develops according to statistical probability. Extra terminal space may crystallise off this central linear axis. Framing this central complex of terminal units are the runways and taxiways.

Width of Land strip 500ft.
Width of Runway (R/W) 150ft.
Width of Taxiway (T/W) 75ft.
Distance between R/W Centreline and T/W Centreline 500ft.
Distance between Parallel T/W's 300ft.
Distance between Centreline T/W and Aircraft Parking 300ft.
Distance between Centreline and Obstacle 250ft.
Distance between Centreline and Building Line 750ft.
Maximum Runway Effective Gradient 0.25%
Maximum R/W and T/W Longitudinal Grade 1.00%
Maximum R/W and T/W Transverse Grade 1.50%

It is most probable that we will someday see upon these runways, aircraft that will be more crystalline in shape. The shapes suggested by Alexander Graham Bell and the Cubic Corporation show evidence of such a direction. Already certain passenger aircraft resemble pyramidal slabs, and flying obelisks. Perhaps aircraft will someday be named after crystals. As it is now, many are still named after animals, such as DHC 2 Beavers; Vampire T.; Chipmunk T. Mk. 20; Dove 8s; Hawker Furies; Turkey; etc. At any rate, here are some names for possible crystalline aircraft: Rhombohedral T.2; Orthorhombic 60; Tetragonal Terror; hexagonal Star Dust 49; etc.

The enormous scale of the runways will isolate such aircraft into 'buildings' for short spaces of time, then these 'buildings' will disappear. The principal runways will extend from 11,000 feet to 14,000 feet, or about the length of Central Park. Consider an aircraft in the shape of an enormous 'slab' hovering over such an expanse.

Tippetts-Abbett-McCarthy-Stratton have developed other sites that have limits similar to the air terminal project. They include port and harbour facilities like the Navy pier in Chicago, a port in Anchorage and San Nicholas Harbour in Aruba. Such sites rest on wide expanses of water, and are generated by ship voyages and cargo movements. Bulk storage systems are contained by mazes of transfer pipelines that include hydrant refuelling pump houses and gas dispensers. The process behind the making of a storage facility may be viewed in stages, thus constituting a whole 'series' of works of art from the ground up. Land surveying and preliminary building, if isolated into discrete stages, may be viewed as an array of artworks that vanish as they develop.

Water resources that involve flood control, irrigation, and hydroelectric power provide one with an entirely new way to order the terrain. This is a kind of radical construction that takes into account large land masses and bodies of water. The making of artificial lakes, with the help of dams, brings into view a vast 'garden'. For instance, the Peligre Dam in the Republic of Haiti consists of 250-foot high concrete buttresses. This massive structure, with its artificial cascades and symmetrical layout, stands like an immobile facade. It conveys an immense scale and power. By investigating the physical forms of such projects one may gain unexpected aesthetic information. I am not concerned here with the original 'functions' of such massive projects, but rather what they suggest or evoke.

It is important to mentally experience these projects as something distinctive and intelligible. By extracting from a site certain associations that have remained invisible within the old framework of rational language, by dealing directly with the appearance of what Roland Barthes calls 'The simulacrum of the object', the aim is to construct a new type of 'building' into a whole that engenders new meanings. From the linguistic point of view, one establishes rules of structure based on change in the semantics of building. Tony Smith seems conscious of this 'simulacrum' when he speaks of an 'abandoned airstrip' as an 'artificial landscape'. He speaks of an absence of 'function' and 'tradition'.

What is needed is an aesthetic method that brings together anthropology and linguistics in terms of 'buildings'. This would put an end to 'art history' as sole criterion. Art at the present is confined by a dated notion, namely 'art as a criticism of earlier art'. The myth of the Renaissance still conditions and infects much criticism with a mushy humanistic content. Re-birth myths should not be applied as 'meanings' to art. Criticism exists as language and nothing more. Usage precedes meaning. The 'meanings' derived from the word Renaissance, such as 'truth', 'beauty', and 'classic', are diseased words and outmoded criteria. As one becomes aware of discrete usages, the syntax of aesthetic communications discloses the relevant features of both 'building' and 'language'. Both are the raw materials of communication and are based on chance — not historical preconceptions. Linguistic sense-data, not rational categories, are what we are investigating. Carl Andre has made it clear that without linguistic awareness there is no physical awareness.

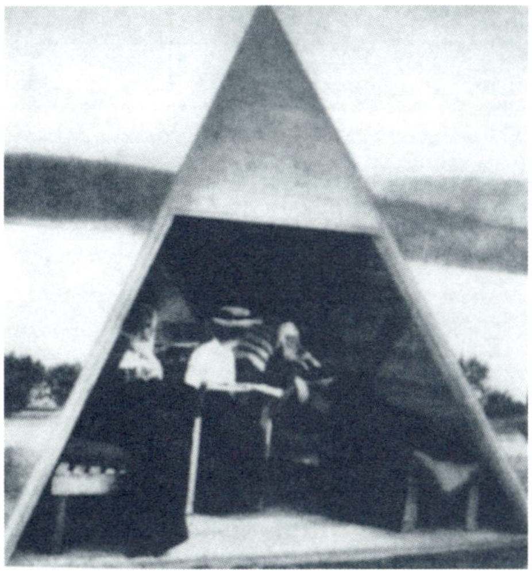

8.04

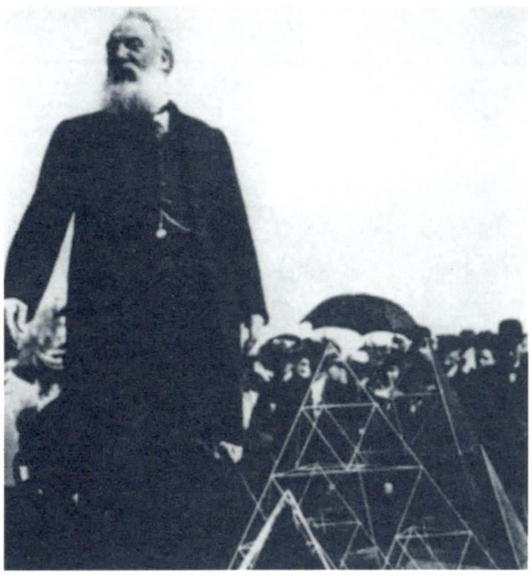

8.05

8.04 Alexander Graham Bell in his outdoor observation station

8.05 Alexander Graham Bell with his tetragonal lattice kites

Tony Smith writes about 'a dark pavement' that is 'punctuated by stacks, towers, fumes and colored lights'. (*Artforum*, December 1966.) The key word is 'punctuated'. In a sense, the 'dark pavement' could be considered a 'vast sentence', and the things perceived along it, 'punctuation marks'. '…tower…' = the exclamation mark (!). '…stacks…' = the dash (—). '…fumes…' = the question mark (?). '…colored lights…' = the colon (:). Of course, I form these equations on the basis of sense-data and not rational-data. Punctuation refers to interruptions in 'printed matter'. It is used to emphasise and clarify the meaning of specific segments of usage. Sentences like 'skylines' are made of separate 'things' that constitute a whole syntax. Tony Smith also refers to his art as 'interruptions' in a 'space-grid'.

The impressionistic world-view imitates that architectural detail — the window. The rational category of 'painting' was derived from the visual meaning of the word 'window' and then extended to mean 'wall'. The transparency of the window or wall as a clear 'surface' becomes diseased when the artist defines his art by the word 'painting' alone. Perhaps that is what Tony Smith is getting at when he says that his works are 'probably malignant'. 'Painting' is not an end, but a means, therefore it is linguistically an out-of-date category. The linguistic meaning of a 'wall' or 'window', when emptied of rational content, becomes surfaces, and lines.

The most common type of window in the modern city is composed of a simple grid system that holds panes of clear glass. The 'glass wall' is a part of many standard stores and office buildings. By emphasising the transparent glass we arrive at a total crystalline consciousness of structure, and avoid the clotted patchy naturalistic details of 'painting'. The organic shapes that painters put on the 'canvas-pane' are eliminated and replaced by a consciousness that develops a new set of linguistic meanings and visual results.

'Sculpture', when not figurative, also is conditioned by architectural details. Floors, walls, windows, and ceilings delimit the bounds of interior sculpture. many new works of sculpture gain scale by being installed in a vast room. The Jewish Museum and the Whitney Museum have such interiors. The rooms of these museums tend away from the intimate values of connoisseurship, towards a more public value. The walls of modern museums need not exist as walls, with diseased details near or on them. Instead, the artist could define the interior as a total network of surfaces and lines. What's interesting about Dan Flavin's art is not only the 'lights' themselves, but what they do to the phenomenon of the 'barren room'.

'Site Selection Study' in terms of art is just beginning. The investigation of a specific site is a matter of extracting concepts out of existing sense-data through direct perceptions. Perception is prior to conception, when it comes to site selection or definition. One does not impose, but rather exposes the site — be it interior or exterior. Interiors may be treated as exteriors or vice versa. The unknown areas of sites can be best explored by artists.

Note

Impressionism is a popular theory derived from 'symbolist theory'. It has nothing to do with individual artists. I use the word 'impressionism' according to its recent linguistic mutation. The original meaning of the word is less important than its recent usage. We are not concerned with what 'impressionism' was but rather what it is today. But it should be remembered that symbolist theory is prior to impressionist theory.

8.06 SECOR Surveying Satellite. (Cubic Corporation, San Diego, California)

8.07 Robert Smithson, *Plunge*, 1966. Painted steel, 10 units, square surfaces, 14.5 to 19 inches (0.5 inch increments.

8.08 Robert Morris, model and cross-section for *Project in Earth and Sod*, 1966. Plaster, 1x20x24 inches.

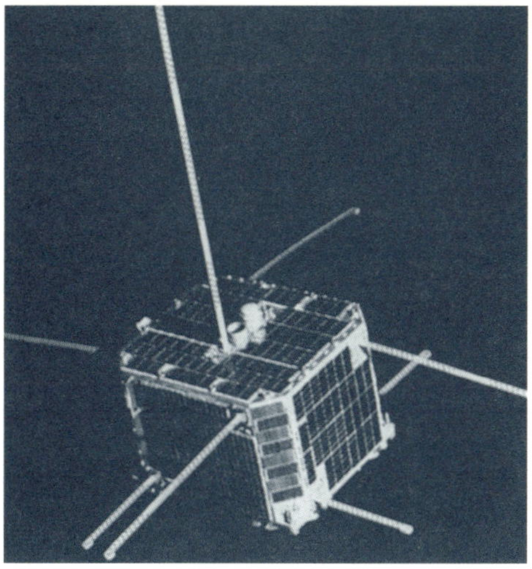
8.06

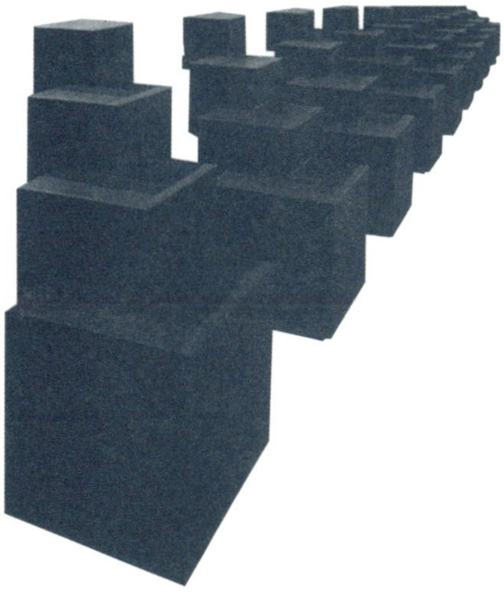
8.07

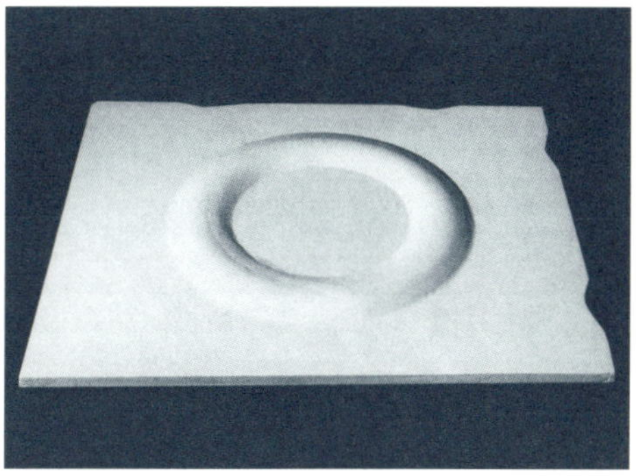
8.08

Steven
Bode
Planespotting

1997

130/133

In the transit lounge she looks up at the monitor, watching for news of her connecting flight. She notes the names of the cities (Frankfurt, Delhi, Nairobi, San Francisco) — blasted out of geography, ordered on the whim of the airlines' schedules. Making the most of her time, she wires her lap-top to her cellphone and hooks into the Internet. The search-engines fly in countless directions (Minneapolis, Cape Town, Paris, Tokyo) in pursuit of a name or a word. Then the interminable delay for the file to download. The speed of connection only exacerbating the frustration and indignity of waiting.

This time, arriving for his flight at Heathrow, he is vividly reminded of his stay at the hospital. Crossing from the rain-damp concourse, through the silently-revolving door, he experiences the same sensation of entering a regulated, antiseptic space. Giving up his bags at check-in, he leaves with the few possessions he is permitted to take with him. He mutely confirms his identity, presents himself at the X-ray machine, raises his arms for the routine body examination, and is made to wait in a vast, anonymous hall. When he is called, he rides the silver walk-way, imagining himself carried aloft on an ingeniously lightweight mechanical stretcher.
The plane awaits at the end of a long corridor; like the operating theatre, kept hidden till the last possible moment, until suddenly, in a glare of artificial light, he is aboard. The stewardess smiling down at him; the disembodied voice of the pilot, checking his instruments. The cool swirl of air; the first steady drip of alcohol to deaden the pain...
At take-off he forces himself to concentrate, thinking he will be able to hold back the moment, but, as always, in an instant, he is gone...
He comes to, on landing, at Orly — blurry-headed, slowly stretching away the discomfort. This side, every extra minute kept waiting is an eternity.
He grabs his bags off the carousel and gets out as fast as possible.

In his lyrical study of the contemporary zeitgeist, *Angels: A Modern Myth*, the French philosopher and historian Michel Serres grounds many of his speculative lines-of-enquiry within the symbolic space of a modern airport. *Angels* is many things: a metaphysical narrative about our fin-de-siecle fascination with the transmission and deciphering of messages; an elaborate photo-roman splicing Classical and Renaissance paintings with scientific and news photographs; a vivid exploration of the emerging global information networks that are shaping and transforming the modern world. Underlying them all is his use of the airport as metaphor — as a place where many of these new signifying networks intersect. At one point in the book, Serres breathlessly describes today's airports as direct descendents of the medieval cathedral — an analogy that regular habitués of Heathrow, Frankfurt or Newark might find rather hard to bear. But Serres insists that the buildings on the ground are only the *foundation* — for a vast virtual architecture (of radio signals, electronic relays, encoded information) enveloping the thousands of passengers and aircrew who are aloft at any moment in time; frescoed angels in the invisible cathedral's vaulted spire.

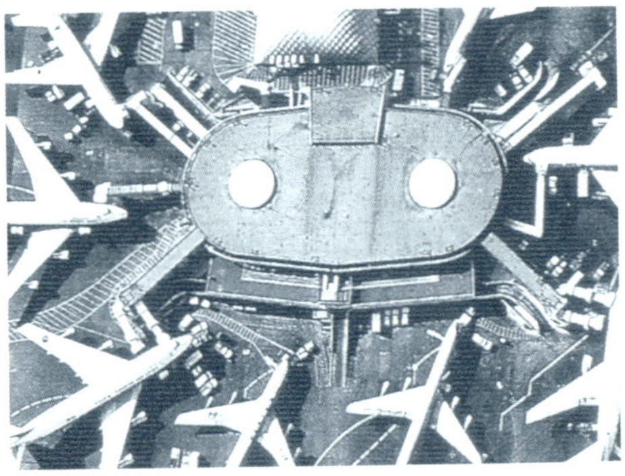

9.01

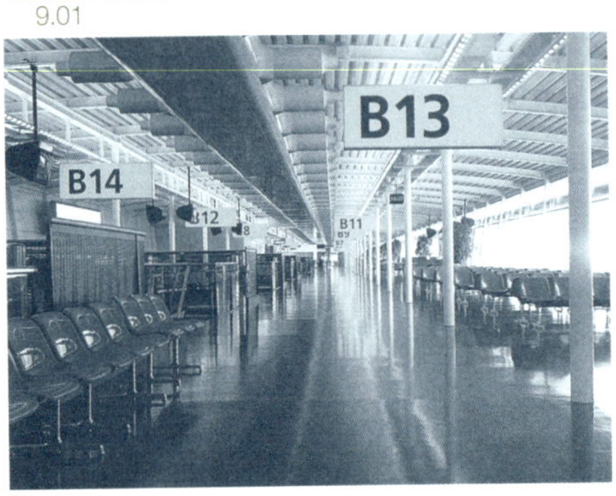

9.02

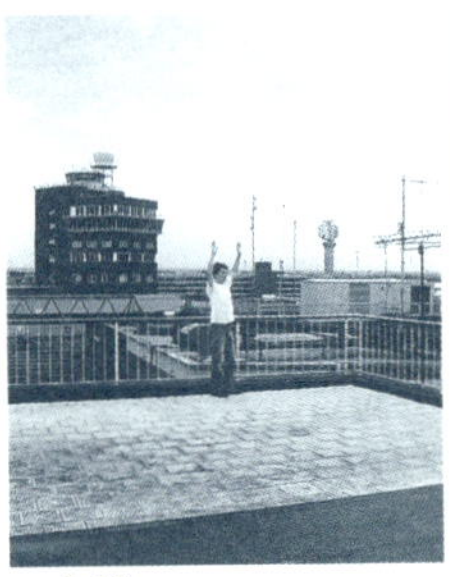

9.03

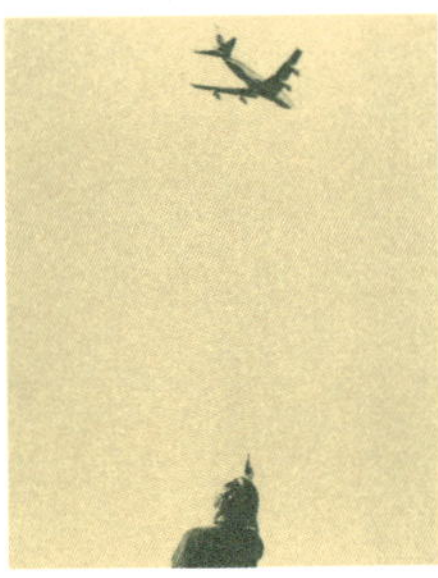

9.04

The history of terrorist attacks on international airports has legitimated a panoptical regime of surveillance, now so familiar as to be almost invisible. As the Air Traffic Control radar sweeps through the ether, keeping the planes circling until ready for clearance, a parallel network of round-the-clock cameras, X-ray scans and computer-aided searches restlessly patrols the shuffling crocodile of passengers, killing time until they, too, are called.

For many people, by far the most stressful and troublesome aspect of air travel is the trip to the airport. Finally making it to the check-in desk, after fretting in a tailback on the airport approach road, or having endured the queues and crushes of the underground, is an almost blissful moment. You are here. You have kept your part of the bargain. The rest is up to the airline — and, by extension, to Fate. Disburdening yourself of the luggage that slowed you and encumbered you on your journey is like casting off your worldly cares; inducing a feeling of a light-headedness that intensifies as you move Airside. In this state, the swish, smart store fronts that greet you are not so much a temporary distraction as a consumer phantasmagoria, brimming with items you never knew you wanted until now. Duty-free shopping is responsibility-free shopping — somewhere deep in our subconscious we are making the calculation: this cheque may never be cashed because the plane I am travelling on may never arrive.

9.01 Aerial view of aircraft at an international air terminal

9.02 Amsterdam Airport, Schiphol, courtesy of Bentham Crouwel, architects

9.03 Graham Gussin, *Surrendering (For The Third Time)*, 1994, courtesy of the artist

9.04 Chris Burden, *from Chris Burden's Deluxe Photo Book, 1971–73,* courtesy of London Projects.

Evening, London City Airport. For the city-dweller, aircraft are distant thunder, a necessary evil whose noisy, dirty activities only used to be tolerated outside the city walls. Now, as thousands leave the run-down inner city for a new-build in the suburbs, for the multiplexes, malls and techno-parks around Stansted, Gatwick or Heathrow, the city is forced to convert its blighted, empty spaces to welcome in the planes. In America, they call the airlines carriers — movers of people or agents of contamination? In a few years, this airport colony will have spread, putting down delivery stations, feeder-buildings, transport terminii; a bridgehead from which to deliver up even more of the city to the encircling suburban sprawl.

Futurist Manifesto of Aerial Architecture

FT Marinetti
1934

134/
139

Futurist Manifesto of Aerial Architecture

FT Marinetti – Angiolo Mazzoni – Mino Somenzi from Sant'Elia, February 1 1934

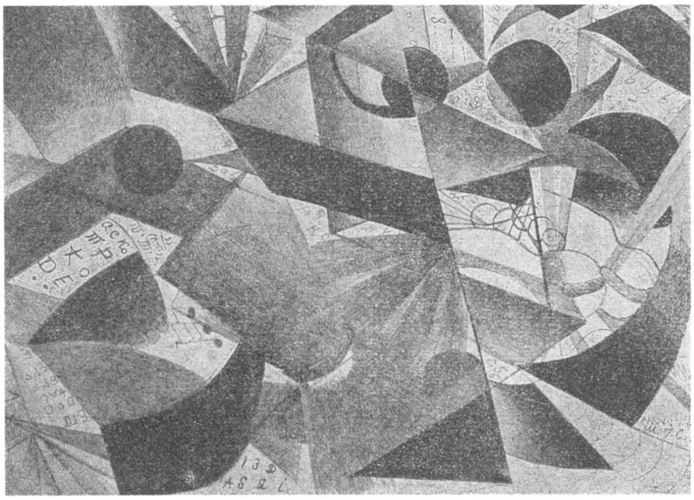

10.01
Kasimir Malevich, *Pilot*, reproduced in *Troe*, c.1913

Today the genius of the Futurist Architect Antonio Sant'Elia, the creator of a new world architecture, imposes everywhere the geometric, lyrical splendour of new buildings materials.

The Fiat Lingotto was the first Futurist invention in building. In 1924 in Monza Fortunato Depero created for a Publishing House an Advertising Pavilion based on typographical characters. In 1928 Enrico Prampolini designed the Futurist Pavilion at the National Exhibition of Decorative Arts. The first exhibition of Futurist architecture was organised by Fillia with Mussolini as its high patron.

In Paris in 1931 the Colonial Pavilion of the Futurist Architect Guido Fiorini was a triumph, the interior enriched with mural plastic works by Enrico Prampolini. Then in 1932 Fiorini invented Tensistructure, the first mechanical architecture in iron without reinforced concrete, which supports its sides by means of a central steel mast with tie bars and which allows passage under its almost entirely suspended base. The Futurist Architect Angiolo Mazzoni constructed the first large Futurist public buildings in Italy (Post and Telegraph Building and Station in Littoria, Colonia Marina di Calambrone).

The genius of Sant'Elia lighted on the buildings of the Milan Triennale: there Enrico Prampolini's 'Civil Airport' shone out for the perfect harmony of interior with exterior.

To the glorious and indispensable *Manifesto dell'Architetto Futurista Antonio Sant'Elia* launched by the Italian Futurist Movement in 1914 and on which all innovatory architects have based themselves, is added today a new factor of importance: Aviation.

This, civilly and militarily, is changing the world, putting new artistic, social, political, industrial, commercial problems on the agenda and hence a new spiritual atmosphere gives birth to this single manifesto which enlarges the wingspread of the first. Thus the urban planning of Sant'Elia, taking nourishment from speeded-up ruralism, aeropoetry, aeropainting, aerosculpture, gives birth to the single City with continuous lines to admire in flight.

Almost all the beautiful cities praised by motorists, having been built by men who knew nothing or cared little for flying, have, when seen from above, a poverty-stricken and mediocre look.

To people flying, in fact, they look like scrapheaps, piles of masonry, scatterings of bricks or open sores.

Neither colour, nor character, nor geometry, nor rhythm, the cities most alive appear wrapped in reeking grey fumes, the old cities reveal a petrifaction of bigots in mourning and black monks prostrate in a circle under a mute bell-tower.

If we land in their smell of petrol mould cooking incense tobacco and washing, we feel the livid whitewash of the walls burning with a desire for green fresh flight, like us incapable of living in that place: tormented fragments of sky!

The new or renovated cities commit the mistake of copying, making monstrous and ugly, the wrinkled huddles of houses from the past.

If we enter one of these dwellings we are anguished by the squashing together of individuals, all of them uneasy, all of them crushed, not enlivened by the humanity of others.

The absurd madness of boxing people in like this, anti-spiritual, anti-hygienic, anti-practical. Old new or renovated these cities are all defenseless and destroyable by an enemy squadron.

They are all anti-sporting because they oddly squash a man into the sedentary mass of spectators of the sport instead of quickening his individual sporting qualities.

We Futurist poets, architects and journalists have conceived the large single City with continuous lines to admire in flight, parallel thrust of Aeroways and Aerocanals fifty metres wide, separated from one another by slender habitation/suppliers (spiritual and material) which will feed into all the different and distinct never intersecting speeds. The Aeroways and the Aerocanals (which will link the rivers straightened in harmony with the air lines) will change the shape of plains hills and mountains.

For aesthetic reasons and to harmonise ever more pathetically the life on the earth with life in the sky, ports and seaplane stops will no longer have rooted cliffs, but mobile steel jetties to offer an embrace in every sense to seaplanes and organise plastically the long ranks of waves cut by the white flights of gulls, the iridescent aureolas of the foam of take-offs and the cascades of diamonds which deck the moorings on the intense green of the depths of the sea.

Consequently the winding roads of dust or mud will be abolished; irrigation covered; fields freed from their four walls of trees, thus aiding any long landing.

The Aeroways, by day visible at a distance because of their bright colour and at night lit up by ground level lights and floods, will be provided every fifty miles with habitation/suppliers which will stretch on till they meet, at all points touching the lonely pure hygienic countryside hence offering at all points escape and shelter in case of aerial bombardment.

The underground aerostations and armoured seaplane ports will open into the edges of the Aeroways and the aerocanals. The Aeroways will run the length of the peninsula, they will slant down from the Appennines to the sea, they will become, on hills and passes, from peak to peak, immense easy mountain landing-strips with numerous panoramic terraces.

Each inhabitation/supplier will have its own characteristic, autonomous features.

The single city with continuous lines will display to the sky its parallelism of turquoise gold orange, shining Aerocanals and long habitation / suppliers with moving surfaces, which will communicate with the highest aeroplanes in a literary plastic daily way, through polymaterial harmonies of metals glass marbles waters immobile rough or cascading expulsion of coloured smokes.

Every habitation/supplier will have its own original geometric form and distinctive rhythm.

Neither laws of verticality nor laws of horizontality. The buildings in the shape of the sphere, cone, pyramid, straight triangular prism, oblique square prism, scalene triangle, isosceles triangle, polyhedron, lozenge, will have an aesthetic and practical individuality, but will be subject to the dominant theme of the habitation/supplier. To people flying over this will appear as an arrow, a ring, a propeller, a crucible, a brilliant, a matrix. It will look funnel-shaped, fibroradiated, radicellular, split-levelled, arborized, scaliform and blown. Special curves will encourage the floating of yellow silk reflections under the sun's rays.

The dominant theme of the habitation/supplier will follow or act as complement to the landscape and the climate harmonising, for example, a supplied and blue habitation with the orange desert, cylindrical habitation/supplier with triangles of rocks in the sea, flat horizons with the verticality of clusters of lifts for helicopters. Below ground conduits of seawater, mountain air, post, etc.

The interior of the house altogether mechanical plastic luminous transparent, always variable with spherical furniture and automatic double and triple walls, will make even silence and intimacy possible. No bedroom, dining or reception room but as much shaping as you like of all the imaginable spaces. A polymaterial chromatic slope in the floors and ceilings.

The habitation/supplier will have a perfect balance between the different parts devoted to dwellings, education, art, military life, political life, industry, commerce, agriculture, sport, etc. Like vast coloured and dynamic sculptures rich in hanging gardens and orchards on staircases and spiral ramps, the habitation/suppliers will aesthetically incorporate rivers, lakes, hills, peaks, glaciers in their unity.

Each building however will completely express, in its mobile polymaterial variety and its gardening, the soul of its owner who will appear and perfume rose acacia violet vanilla, etc. A forest crossed or a mountain passed or a special inhabited supplier will constitute the people's homage to a great man or a glorious event.

We shall abolish the night with enormous floodlights or flying or fixed suns, to obtain the continuity of the day and the scientific distribution of sleep. On the highest terraces, electromagnetic electrical radiations will thin out clouds and fogs or shape and colour them elegantly.
The Aeroways with the habitation/suppliers with iron glass reinforced concrete frames, faced in marble, stone, glass, metal, terracotta, electricity, luminous gasses, ceramics, porcelain, linoleum, stoneglazed materials, gardens in flower, mirrors and waterfalls, will also abolish all regionalism local patriotism ruralism and will give to Italy a single city with continuous lines of speed health pleasure in life, truly worthy of Fascist Aviation and its Chief Benito Mussolini.

The Aeroways will mostly be painted in an eye-catching optimistic and imperial gold, so that, flying they will seem the very wakes of the sun in the ocean mixed with blue air and soft earth green.

Flying at night with the suns turned off, we shall have them beneath us like shining milky ways starred by the quiet explosion of effulgent letters of this strand, stretching from the Alps to Mogadesh: Italy.

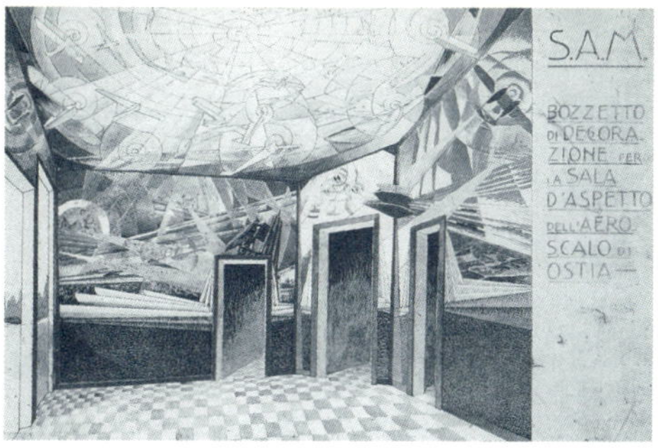

10.02
Gerardo Dottori, *Design for the decoration of the seaplane station at Ostia*, c.1928

Notes on Contributors

Paul Andreu
is the director of Architecture and Engineering at Aéroports des Paris. He was recently described in *Metropolis* magazine as 'the master of airport design'.

Amsterdam Airport Schiphol
has commissioned work by international artists for installation in and around its terminal buildings. These artists include Sol LeWitt, Dennis Adams and Niek Kemps.

Artspace
is the exhibition programme at Arlanda airport, Stockholm and is organised by Thomas Adlercreutz Gallery. In creating movable displays and making temporary interventions in the working of the airport, the programme develops works which can appear where they are least expected.

Marc Augé
is the Director of Studies at the Ecole des hautes études en sciences sociales in Paris. His books include *La traversee du Luxemborg*, *Un ethnoloue dans le metro* and *Domaines et chateaux*.

The BAA Art Programme
was first established in 1994, both as a commitment to enhancing the airport environment for passengers and staff and to create an internationally recognised art collection. High profile commissions from internationally acclaimed artists are balanced with work from recently established artists. As gateways to Britain, BAA's airports are in a unique position to reflect the diversity of contemporary visual culture.

JG Ballard
is one of the most influential writers of our times. He has published over twenty books, including *Crash*, *The Atrocity Exhibtion* and *Empire of the Sun*, which was shortlisted for the Booker Prize. A collection of essays and reviews, *A User's Guide to the Millenium*, was published in 1996.

Steven Bode
is director of Film and Video Umbrella and co-curator of the touring exhibition, *Airport*.

Douglas Coupland
is a writer of both fiction and non-fiction. His books include *Generation X*, *Shampoo Planet*, *Life After God*, *Microserfs*, and most recently, *Postcards from the Dead*, as well as numerous pieces for *Wired* and other magazines.

Karen Eslea's
work has been included in *The Institute of Cultural Anxiety*, ICA, London in 1994 and *Trust*, Tramway, Glasgow in 1995 as well as in solo exhibitions at Viewpoint Gallery, Salford in 1994 and at Rum in Malmö in 1995.

Peter Fischli + David Weiss
have worked in collaboration for over twenty years, in many different media including sculpture, photograpy, video and installation. They represented Switzerland in the 1995 Venice Biennale and have had many solo exhibitions, including one the Serpentine Gallery, London in 1996.

Stephen Gill
has exhibited photographs in *The Institute of Cultural Anxiety*, ICA, London in 1994 and *Soccerscape* at Middlesbrough Art Gallery in 1996. His work has also been published in *Creative Camera* and *Blueprint*.

Andreas Gursky's
photographs have been exhibited widely. In Britain, his group exhibitions include *The Epic and Everyday* at the Hayward Gallery, London 1994 and *Never Walk Alone* at The Photographers' Gallery, London 1996. Gursky also had a solo exhibition at the Tate Liverpool in 1995.

FT Marinetti
was born in 1876 in Milan and became a poet and publisher of a radical literary journal. On 20 February 1909, he published the first *Futurist Manifesto*, in *Le Figaro*, which, amongst other things, called for the glorification of war. Although his politics veered towards Italian Fascism, his work has influenced much art of the twentieth-century.

Jeremy Millar
is an artist and Programme Organiser at The Photographers' Gallery, London.

Julian Opie's
constructions and drawings have been frequently exhibited since his first solo exhibition in 1983. In 1993 he had a major solo exhibition at the Hayward Gallery, London and will this year represent Britain in the Indian Triennale, Delhi.

Martha Rosler
is an artist and writer whose work has offered a critical analysis of society politics and the media. Her work has been widely exhibited and has recently been shown in *Inside the Visible* at the Whitechapel Gallery, London 1996 and at the San Francisco Museum of Modern Art in 1995.

Frits Rotgans
was born in Amsterdam in 1912 and began working as a professional photographer around 1950. Well-known for developing his own large-format camera, he photographed Amsterdam's Schiphol airport from the early 1960s until his death in 1978.

Gabriella Sancisi's
portraits of different workers have been widely exhibited in Britain and in Italy. Her work has recently been shown at the RPS, Bath, and at Viewpoint Gallery, Salford. Viewpoint have also published a catalogue of her work, *Residual Resemblances*.

Robert Smithson
was born in Passaic, New Jersey in 1938 and, through his writings, earthworks and *Non-Sites* exhibitions, became one of the most influential artists of his age. He was tragically killed in a plane crash in 1973.

John Thackara
became the first director of the Netherlands Design Institute, Amsterdam in 1993. He has written and lectured widely on the social importance of design issues.